Nineteenth-Century Major Lives and Letters

Series Editor: Marilyn Gaull

This series presents original biographical, critical, and scholarly studies of literary works and public figures in Great Britain, North America, and continental Europe during the nineteenth century. The volumes in *Nineteenth-Century Major Lives and Letters* evoke the energies, achievements, contributions, cultural traditions, and individuals who reflected and generated them during the Romantic and Victorian periods. The topics: critical, textual, and historical scholarship, literary and book history, biography, cultural and comparative studies, critical theory, art, architecture, science, politics, religion, music, language, philosophy, aesthetics, law, publication, translation, domestic and public life, popular culture, and anything that influenced, impinges upon, expresses, or contributes to an understanding of the authors, works, and events of the nineteenth century. The authors consist of political figures, artists, scientists, and cultural icons including William Blake, Thomas Hardy, Charles Darwin, William Wordsworth, William Butler Yeats, Samuel Taylor, and their contemporaries.

The series editor is Marilyn Gaull, PhD (Indiana University), FEA. She has taught at William and Mary, Temple University, New York University, and is Research Professor at the Editorial Institute at Boston University. She is the founder and editor of *The Wordsworth Circle* and the author *of English Romanticism: The Human Context*, and editions, essays, and reviews in journals. She lectures internationally on British Romanticism, folklore, and narrative theory, intellectual history, publishing procedures, and history of science.

PUBLISHED BY PALGRAVE MACMILLAN:

Shelley's German Afterlives, by Susanne Schmid
Coleridge, the Bible, and Religion, by Jeffrey W. Barbeau
Romantic Literature, Race, and Colonial Encounter, by Peter J. Kitson
Byron, edited by Cheryl A. Wilson
Romantic Migrations, by Michael Wiley
The Long and Winding Road from Blake to the Beatles, by Matthew Schneider
British Periodicals and Romantic Identity, by Mark Schoenfield
Women Writers and Nineteenth-Century Medievalism, by Clare Broome Saunders
British Victorian Women's Periodicals, by Kathryn Ledbetter
Romantic Diasporas, by Toby R. Benis
Romantic Literary Families, by Scott Krawczyk
Victorian Christmas in Print, by Tara Moore
Culinary Aesthetics and Practices in Nineteenth-Century American Literature, edited by Monika Elbert and Marie Drews
Reading Popular Culture in Victorian Print, by Alberto Gabriele
Romanticism and the Object, edited by Larry H. Peer
Poetics en passant, by Anne Jamison
From Song to Print, by Terence Allan Hoagwood
Gothic Romanticism, by Tom Duggett
Victorian Medicine and Social Reform, by Louise Penner
Populism, Gender, and Sympathy in the Romantic Novel, by James P. Carson
Byron and the Rhetoric of Italian Nationalism, by Arnold Anthony Schmidt
Poetry and Public Discourse in Nineteenth-Century America, by Shira Wolosky
The Discourses of Food in Nineteenth-Century British Fiction, by Annette Cozzi
Romanticism and Pleasure, edited by Thomas H. Schmid and Michelle Faubert

Royal Romances, by Kristin Flieger Samuelian
Trauma, Transcendence, and Trust, by Thomas J. Brennan, S.J.
The Business of Literary Circles in Nineteenth-Century America, by David Dowling
Popular Medievalism in Romantic-Era Britain, by Clare A. Simmons
Beyond Romantic Ecocriticism, by Ashton Nichols
The Poetry of Mary Robinson, by Daniel Robinson
Romanticism and the City, edited by Larry H. Peer
Coleridge and the Daemonic Imagination, by Gregory Leadbetter
Dante and Italy in British Romanticism, edited by Frederick Burwick and Paul Douglass
Jewish Representation in British Literature 1780–1840, by Michael Scrivener
Romantic Dharma, by Mark S. Lussier
Robert Southey, by Stuart Andrews
Playing to the Crowd, by Frederick Burwick
The Regions of Sara Coleridge's Thought, by Peter Swaab
John Thelwall in the Wordsworth Circle, by Judith Thompson
Wordsworth and Coleridge, by Peter Larkin
Turning Points in Natural Theology from Bacon to Darwin, by Stuart Peterfreund
Sublime Coleridge, by Murray J. Evans
Longing to Belong, by Sarah Juliette Sasson
British Literary Salons of the Late Eighteenth and Early Nineteenth Centuries, by Susanne Schmid
Coleridge's Experimental Poetics, by J. C. C. Mays
Emily Dickinson's Rich Conversation, by Richard E. Brantley
Sara Coleridge, by Jeffrey W. Barbeau
Staging Romantic Chameleons and Imposters, by William D. Brewer

FORTHCOMING TITLES:

John Thelwall, edited by Judith Thompson
Louisa Stuart Costello, edited by Clare Broome Saunders
Other British Voices, by Timothy Whelan

Staging Romantic Chameleons and Imposters

William D. Brewer

palgrave
macmillan

STAGING ROMANTIC CHAMELEONS AND IMPOSTERS

First published in 2015 by
PALGRAVE MACMILLAN®
in the United States—a division of St. Martin's Press LLC,
175 Fifth Avenue, New York, NY 10010.

Where this book is distributed in the UK, Europe and the rest of the world, this is by Palgrave Macmillan, a division of Macmillan Publishers Limited, registered in England, company number 785998, of Houndmills, Basingstoke, Hampshire RG21 6XS.

Palgrave Macmillan is the global academic imprint of the above companies and has companies and representatives throughout the world.

Palgrave® and Macmillan® are registered trademarks in the United States, the United Kingdom, Europe and other countries.

ISBN: 978–1–137–38921–3

Library of Congress Cataloging-in-Publication Data

Brewer, William D. (William Dean) author.
Staging Romantic Chameleons and Imposters / William D. Brewer.
pages cm.—(Nineteenth-Century Major Lives and Letters)
Includes bibliographical references and index.
ISBN 978–1–137–38921–3
1. Romanticism—England. 2. Impostors and imposture in literature. 3. English literature—18th century—History and criticism. 4. English literature—19th century—History and criticism. I. Title.

PR447.B744 2015
820.9′145—dc23 2014028836

A catalogue record of the book is available from the British Library.

Design by Newgen Knowledge Works (P) Ltd., Chennai, India.

First edition: January 2015

10 9 8 7 6 5 4 3 2 1

Previous Publications

The Shelley-Byron Conversation (1994)
The Mental Anatomies of William Godwin and Mary Shelley (2001)
St. Leon, by William Godwin, ed. (2006)
The Works of Mary Robinson, gen. ed. (2009–2010)
Walsingham; or, The Pupil of Nature, by Mary Robinson, ed. (2010)
Miscellaneous Prose and Dramas, by Mary Robinson, co-edited with Sharon Setzer (2010)

For Tracy, and in memory of Max Clifton Brewer,
1924–2012

Contents

Illustrations

Acknowledgments

Special thanks are due to Marilyn Gaull, who has encouraged my work for many years. Dean Anthony Calamai, Interim Chair Jim Fogelquist, and the Department of English at Appalachian State University granted me a sabbatical to write this book. Early drafts of two chapters received helpful feedback from the members of my faculty learning community at Appalachian. I presented portions of *Staging Romantic Chameleons and Imposters* at conferences sponsored by the North American Society for the Study of Romanticism and the International Conference on Romanticism and benefited from the comments of Fred Burwick, Ashley Cross, Regina Hewitt, Wendy Neilsen, and Anne Mellor. At Palgrave, Brigitte Shull and Ryan Jenkins (an Appalachian alumnus) have been helpful and supportive. The staff at Belk Library and Information Commons at Appalachian State responded quickly and efficiently to interlibrary loan requests, and the Huntington Library provided me with a microfilm reproduction of the Larpent manuscript of Hannah Cowley's comedy *The World as It Goes; or a Party at Montpelier* (1781).

I thank Larry Peer for permitting me to reproduce my essay "Subverting Individuality: Mary Robinson and Polygraphs," originally published in *Inventing the Individual: Romanticism and the Idea of Individualism* (International Conference on Romanticism, 2002). A modified version of my article, "Copies, Protean Role-Players, and Sappho's Shattered Form in Mary Robinson's *The False Friend*" (*European Romantic Review* 22.6 [2011]) is reprinted with permission from Taylor & Francis. The illustration "John Bannister as Echo in 'The World'" is reproduced courtesy of the Rare Book & Manuscript Library of the University of Illinois at Urbana-Champaign. Dennis Sears of the Rare Book & Manuscript Library kindly provided a high-resolution copy of the image. I am grateful to the Social Law Library in Boston, Massachusetts, for giving me permission to reproduce the frontispiece portraits of Charles Price (aka the Social Monster) in his usual dress and in disguise from *The Fourth Edition Much Improved: Being a More Minute and Particular Account of that Arch Imposter, Charles Price* (1786).

ACKNOWLEDGMENTS

Introduction

The Chameleon Metaphor

Staging Romantic Chameleons and Imposters examines cultural attitudes toward imposture and theatrical and literary representations of chameleonic identities in the late eighteenth and early nineteenth centuries in England. During this period, chameleonism evoked both anxieties about depersonalization and social instability and fantasies regarding empowerment and self-fashioning. Human chameleons blurred boundaries between human and reptile, upper and lower class, master and servant, female and male, domestic and foreign, natural and imitative, and authentic and theatrical. Imposters such as the Social Monster, the Northern Imposter, the pretended Duke of Ormond, John Hatfield, the Witch of Leeds, and Princess Caraboo scandalized, mystified, and captivated the British public.[1] Late Georgian dramatists created self-consciously theatrical characters who used performance to reinvent themselves or manipulate their dupes. The actress, celebrity, and author Mary "Perdita" Robinson both enacted and critiqued chameleonism, constantly refashioning her public image and portraying deracinated and predatory chameleons in her works. Although Proteus is a shape-shifting Greek sea-god rather than a color-mutating lizard, the terms Proteus and chameleon were employed synonymously.[2]

In *The English Expositor* (1616), John Bullokar explains that the "*Chamelion*...changeth himself quickly into any Colour that he sitteth upon, except White and Red; wherefore Men that are inconstant and fickle, are sometime called *Chamelions*" (n. pag.). For Bullokar, the label "Chamelion" was pejorative and suggested instability and disloyalty. Eighteenth-century and Romantic-era writers regarded the chameleon as both an exotic lizard and an evocative metaphor for imitative, simulated, and serial identities. Thomas Boreman's children's reader, *A Description of Three Hundred Animals,*

Viz. Beasts, Birds, Fishes, Serpents, and Insects (1730), summarizes the chameleon's reputed attributes:

> A CAMELEON is very rare to be seen. It is firmly asserted by some Naturalists, that it lives on Air. Tho' others have asserted, from their own Experience, as they assure us, that, upon the Dissection of this Animal, Flies have been found in its Belly; from whence it seems reasonable to conclude, that, however it may live some Time by sucking in the Air, yet that is not its only Nourishment. It is said frequently to change its Colour, very often three or four Times in Half an Hour, which commonly is grey. The Colour it mostly changes to, is a very fine green, spotted with yellow. Its Skin is very thin, and almost transparent. Its Tongue is as long as its whole Body. It is said to be so timorous, that, when it descends from any Height, it moves very cautiously, and curls its Tail, by which it can hold fast about some Thing or other in its Way, lest it should slip. This Creature is like a Lizard. (30)

In *An History of the Earth, and Animated Nature* (1774), Oliver Goldsmith reports that the chameleon can alter its shape and its color: "the thickness of the body is different at different times;...for it can blow itself up, and contract itself, at pleasure" (7.151–152). "[W]hen the animal is removed into the sun," Goldsmith continues, "then comes the wonderful part of its history. At first it appears to suffer no change of colour, its grayish spots still continuing the same: but the whole surface soon seems to imbibe the rays of light; and the simple colouring of the body changes into a variety of beautiful hues" (7.153). Besides being a color-changer and shape-shifter, the chameleon reputedly could live on air, and this myth prompted comparisons between the lizard and people who received nourishment from incorporeal sources. Thus Goldsmith writes in *An Enquiry into the Present State of Polite Learning in Europe* (1759) that "the light cameleon has been supposed to exist on air; a sparer diet even than this, will satisfy the man of true genius, for he makes a luxurious banquet upon empty applause" (92). Similarly, in "An Exhortation" (1820), Percy Bysshe Shelley compares chameleons who "feed on light and air" to poets whose "food is love and fame" (1–2).[3]

In *Staging Romantic Chameleons and Imposters*, I contend that the fascination with chameleonism during the Romantic era reflected uncertainties, anxieties, and fantasies regarding personal identity during a period of profound economic, social, and political transformation. The factors that contributed to the late-eighteenth-century identity crisis include the monetization of identity, the erosion of class distinctions, the American Revolution, the proliferation of secondhand clothes, and the popularity of masquerade and theatrical transvestitism. As J. G. A. Pocock has observed, the burgeoning credit economy of the eighteenth century made identities seem contingent and relational: "Once property was seen to have a symbolic value, expressed in coin or credit, the foundations of personality themselves appeared imaginary or at best consensual: the individual could exist, even in his own sight, only at the fluctuating value imposed upon him by his fellows" (464). In a study of Romantic "conceptions of the self that do not involve a notion of depth," Andrea K. Henderson "argue[s] that the continuing extension of market relations, the rapid early development of industrialization, the weakening of larger patriarchal family ties, and the attack on aristocratic privilege precipitated [a] major shift in the conception of identity in the late eighteenth century" (2, 39). According to Dror Wahrman, the late-eighteenth-century anxiety regarding "the potential inadequacy and unreliability of identities" was instigated by the American Revolution, which raised "questions of whether the colonists were brethren or enemies; whether American identity had evolved far enough to make this a foreign rather than a civil war; whether one could put forth *any* reliable category of identity to clarify who was against whom in this conflict and why; [and] whether identity categories could now be trusted at all" (261). Because of the thriving trade in secondhand clothes, apparel was no longer a dependable indicator of class identity (Lemire 1–24); Mary Robinson reports in her essay on the *Present State of the Manners, Society, &c. &c. of the Metropolis of England* (1800) that in London, "The duchess, and her *femme de chambre*, are dressed exactly alike" (198). Moreover, the stability of gender identities was challenged by transvestitism in masquerades, the proliferation of cross-dressing roles on the Georgian stage, and well-publicized accounts of transgendering soldiers such as Hannah Snell and the Chevalier D'Eon (Wahrman 22–33, 160).[4]

Whereas Wahrman argues that by the 1780s the modern understanding of the self as "personal, interiorized, essential, [and] innate" superseded "the *ancien régime*" conception of identity as relational, performative, and malleable (276, xiii), *Staging Romantic Chameleons and Imposters* maintains that the earlier notion of identity retained its currency during the Romantic period.[5] According to Wahrman, masquerades went suddenly out of fashion in the late eighteenth century because disguises, transgendering, and fluid identities conflicted with the new regime of selfhood.[6] But while masquerades lost their cultural prominence, the cultural fascination with chameleonism continued. Numerous tales about criminal chameleons appeared in the periodical press, and hastily written biographies, and dramatists, essayists, and novelists assessed the morality, benefits, and drawbacks of imposture and self-reinvention. Whereas the masquerade was "a metonym for society writ large" (Wahrman 167) for much of the eighteenth century, the paradigmatic cultural institution during the Romantic period was the theater.[7] Betsy Bolton explains that "[l]ate eighteenth-century theatrical reception increased the emotional, sexual, and political frisson associated with public performers by blurring the boundaries between stage and life" (5). And as Judith Pascoe has shown, "an attraction to and appropriation of performative modes of self-representation" was an integral "facet of late eighteenth- and early nineteenth-century British culture" (3). In the early 1800s, the most popular dramatic genre in London was the pantomime, which "dramatised the city as an unstable, contingent, spectacular world, as a place of metamorphosis, innovation and relentless self-fashioning" (Moody, *Illegitimate Theatre* 218).

I will argue that Romantic-era readers and spectators evaluated the performances as well as the ethics of chameleonic humans. In many cases they condemned the mendacity and criminality of imposters while praising the culprits' acting skills, apparel, handsomeness, charm, and gentility. Courtrooms, prison cells, and scaffolds became stages on which protean swindlers performed before appreciative onlookers. When imposters were played on stage by popular comic actors like John Palmer (1744–1798), John Bannister (1760–1836), and William Thomas Lewis (*c.* 1746–1811), who directly engaged their audiences with confessional soliloquies and conspiratorial asides, theatergoers and reviewers were charmed and amused by them. Comedy and theatrical charisma deflected moral judgment.

During the Romantic period, criminal imposters and theatrical and political chameleons elicited a wide range of moral, intellectual, cultural, and emotional responses. Biographical and literary portrayals of them explored the advantages and disadvantages of labile identities and the value of authenticity. Social commentators disagreed about whether imposture was anomalous or pervasive. While some writers depicted chameleons as antipathetic monsters, others represented them as lovable rogues. The behaviors of the chameleons portrayed in eighteenth-century and Romantic-era texts range from evil to comical, from pathological to normative, from Jacobin to apolitical, and from puppetlike to creative. To demonstrate the behavioral and moral diversity of Georgian chameleons, I will provide examples of some of their most culturally significant variants: transgressive, imitative, urbane, intellectual, sentimental, transgendering, and poetic.

Transgressive Chameleons

For Georgian readers, the archetypal predatory chameleon was Lovelace, the libertine rapist in Samuel Richardson's *Clarissa, or, The History of a Young Lady* (1747–48). Delighting in his ability to manipulate others, Lovelace boasts that "Ovid was not a greater master of metamorphoses than [him]" (2.13). Clarissa describes his inconsistent behavior to her female correspondent: "I am strangely at a loss what to think of this man. He is a perfect Proteus. I can but write according to the shape he assumes at the time. Don't think *me* the changeable person, I beseech you, if in one letter I contradict what I wrote in another; nay, if I seem to contradict what I said in the same letter; for he is a perfect chameleon; or rather more variable than the chameleon; for that, it is said, cannot assume the *red* and the *white*; but this man *can*. And though *black* seems to be his natural colour, yet he has taken great pains to make me think him nothing but *white*" (2.82). Through Lovelace, Richardson links chameleonism to libertinism, deceit, and performativity. He contrasts Lovelace's "Protean flux" to Clarissa's Christian "fixity" (Harris 328). But despite Lovelace's villainy, many eighteenth-readers were attracted by his charisma. William Godwin notes in *The Enquirer. Reflections on Education, Manners, and Literature* (1797) that Richardson "has drawn in Lovelace and [Sir Charles] Grandison models of a debauched and of an elevated character. Neither of them is eminently calculated to produce imitation; but it would not perhaps be adventurous to affirm that more readers have wished to resemble Lovelace, than have wished to resemble Grandison" (138). Among Lovelace's literary descendants is Mr. Treville, the clerical villain of Robinson's epistolary novel *The False Friend: A Domestic Story* (1799). The surreptitious libertinism of this "Proteus [who] change[s] his conduct with every circumstance that favour[s] his design" (2.190) makes the novel's heroine suspect that "the character of Lovelace" is not "out of nature" (2.172).

The transgressive chameleons in William Beckford's *Vathek* (1786), Matthew Lewis's *The Monk* (1796), and James Hogg's *The Private Memoirs and Confessions of a Justified Sinner* (1824) are diabolical tempters. In *Vathek*, the title-character's depraved mother transforms herself through language: "Carathis,...like a cameleon, could assume all possible colours. Her cursed eloquence had often driven [the vizier Morakanabad] to his last shifts" (50). She encourages her son to blaspheme and "obtain favour with the powers of darkness" (51). *The Monk* features the protean Matilda, who induces the Monk

Ambrosio to fornicate, murder, and rape. Fashioned, according to Lucifer, from "a subordinate but crafty spirit" (440), Matilda initially poses as a male novice named Rosario but subsequently alters both her gender and her personality. In *The Private Memoirs and Confessions of a Justified Sinner*, the demonic Gil-Martin has "the cameleon art of changing [his] appearance" (137) and may be either Robert Wringhim's psychological double or the devil. Under Gil-Martin's influence, Robert becomes a murderer.

The figure of the villainous chameleon took on a political significance during the French Revolution. Literary and polemical allusions to conspiratorial chameleons provoked fears of Jacobin subversion and social anarchy. In *The False Friend*, Mrs. Ferret pretends to be a chauvinistic English counterintelligence agent but is actually a French operative. An anti-Jacobin exposé of a Scottish-born imposter titled *The History of the Swindling and Amorous Adventures of James George Semple, &c. &c.* (1795?) alleges that Semple "was an emissary to Robespierre." It provides testimony from "an unfortunate woman of distinction" who depicts Semple as a chameleonic "monster":

> This perfect cameleon, like his ferocious dictator Robespierre, must have sprung from the race of a Damien[s],[8] and chosen this distracted soil to quench his thirst after innocent blood, and to extinguish every idea of moral virtue. He possesses a perpetual enthusiasm, but fluctuating in its objects, and without any fixed principle, except a propensity for blood and rapine. He changes suddenly from apparent mildness to unrelenting cruelty, when it is to accelerate his own interest, or when he is excited by other wicked spirits towards the objects of their vengeance. He is at the same time ferocious and cowardly, haughty and submissive, and flies from one extreme to another. In the same instant he changes his affected countenance of affability and goodness, to that of rage and fury; and when he is expressing the most violent love in his eyes, either the poniard of the assassin is in his hand, or a warrant from the executioner's axe is in his pocket. (134)

The History...of James George Semple suggests that the "unfortunate woman of distinction" who provided this account was one of Semple's victims and represents him as a Robespierrist bogeyman: evil, fanatical, sadistic, opportunistic, and duplicitous. According to the *Secret History of the French Revolution* (1797), Betrand Barère, a member of the notorious Committee of Public Safety and ally of Robespierre, prided himself on his chameleonism: "this Proteus, this political cameleon, boasted of having passed through all the factions; he has been seen (his opinions varying with his dress) alternately

Feuillant, Jacobin, aristocrat, royalist, moderé, exalté" (Pagès 175). Barère's unprincipled malleability helped him evade the guillotine and become one of Napoleon's secret agents. In the novel *Ormond; or The Secret Witness* (1799) by Godwin's American disciple Charles Brockden Brown, the title-character is associated with an Illuminati-like organization consisting of "schemers and reasoners, who aimed at the new-modelling of the world, and the subversion of all that has hitherto been conceived elementary and fundamental, in the constitution of man and of government" (193). Ormond is a ventriloquist and a master of disguises who "exchange[s] his complexion and habiliments for those of a negro and a chimney-sweep" (100). He is also, like Lovelace, a sexual predator.[9]

The arch-conservative writer Robert Bisset alleged that John Thelwall, Thomas Holcroft, Charlotte Smith, Mary Robinson, and other English Jacobins adopted chameleonism to further their nefarious plots:

> One prominent feature often mentioned in Jacobinism is its versatility; totally unrestrained by any principle of morality or religion, it scruples not to assume any form which may promote its general purpose of involving every country in anarchy, to facilitate schemes of plunder and desolation. The Jacobin is at one time a pamphleteer, pouring out his inculcations in grave and serious absurdity and nonsense. We have him (or her) next as a novel-monger, trying by extravagant fictions, to prove that all persons rising to the rank of gentlemen are wicked and profligate; that existing institutions are inimical to wisdom and virtue...Next, the Jacobin tries his hand at play-writing, and labours to show that all rich men are wicked, and that a poor man becoming a villain may plead retaliation as his defence. The Jacobin now changes himself into the form of a lecturer...As he has no moral or religious principles of his own, he will pretend to assume those of persons whom he conceives likely to prove easy dupes and useful instruments...he is a Socinian, a Methodist, a Seceder, a Presbyterian, a Roman Catholic, or a Mahometan; he has projected to be a Hindoo[.] (2.241–243)

In Bisset's opinion, Jacobin chameleons are amoral, predatory, and insidious. Their fluid identities enable them to confuse and manipulate their naive victims, and they are capable of "assum[ing] any form which may promote [their] general purpose of involving every country in anarchy, to facilitate schemes of plunder and desolation." During the 1790s, antirevolutionary polemicists like the author of *The History...of James George Semple* and Bisset terrified and inflamed their fellow citizens with paranoid visions of politically subversive chameleonism.

IMITATIVE CHAMELEONS

Whereas transgressive chameleons possess immoral agency, imitative chameleons compulsively mimic others. Matthew Prior's poem "The Chameleon" (1718) features a callow rural squire who imitates his London acquaintances:

> As the Chameleon, who is known
> To have no Colours of his own;
> But borrows from his Neighbour's Hue
> His White or Black, his Green or Blew;...
> So the young 'Squire, when first he comes
> From Country School to WILL's or TOM's;[10]
> And equally, in Truth, is fit
> To be a Statesman, or a Wit;
> Without one Notion of his own,
> He Saunters wildly up and down;
> 'Till some Acquaintance, good or bad,
> Takes notice of a staring Lad;
> Admits Him in among the Gang:
> They jest, reply, dispute, harangue:
> He acts and talks, as They befriend Him,
> Smear'd with the Colors, which They lend Him.
> Thus merely, as his Fortune chances,
> His Merit, or his Vice advances. (1–4, 9–22)

Prior suggests that the migration from country to city has erased the chameleon's nascent identity. The young squire lacks an innate moral sense and is thus a tabula rasa shaped, for better or worse, by his urban associates. Depending on whom he meets, he could become a somber statesmen or a frivolous wit.

In Sarah Fielding's *Familiar Letters between the Principal Characters in David Simple* (1747), imitative chameleonism is clearly maladaptive. One of Fielding's letter writers depicts a chameleonic husband whose inconsistent behavior tortures his long-suffering wife:

> Her Husband has no Characteristic, and yet there are very few Characters, which may not be said at different times to belong to him. As the Cameleon assumes the Colour of every Object to which he approaches nighest, so *Filius* varies his Sentiments, and changes his Disposition by every new Acquaintance he meets with...His first

> Friend, after he was married, was of a sour severe morose Disposition: *Filius* immediately turned from the tender Lover, into the imperious Husband; and poor *Cloe* must suffer all the Torments of such a dreadful Change...In short, in the little time I have known him, he has assumed such a Multitude of Characters, as in the Repetition would appear almost incredible. He is good or bad, estimable and contemptible, silly and sensible, all by turns, just as Accident throws those various Characters in his way[.] (21–22)

Filius's constantly shifting identity causes domestic misery. Obsessed with role-playing, he is incapable of understanding or empathizing with his wife: "he is resolved to act the Tamer of the Shrew, and only forgets, that it is necessary, in order to top the Part, to have a Shrew to tame; for that *Cloe* is one of the meekest and most submissive temper'd Women in the World, is a Circumstance that never once enters into his Thoughts" (22–23).

Charlotte Smith's novel *Ethelinde, or the Recluse of the Lake* (1789) and Elizabeth Inchbald's novel *Nature and Art* (1796) associate imitative chameleonism with the decadent upper class. In *Ethelinde*, a wealthy young squire named Tom Davenant is corrupted by London society:

> Davenant had a mind which, resembling the imaginary qualities of the cameleon, received its predominant colour from the object which was most immediately near it. Deficient in that strength of intellect which gives determinate character, he was
>
> "Every thing by turns, and nothing long."[11]
>
> At Oxford, he drank, without loving wine; and kept hunters, without loving violent exercise. In town, he sauntered about all the morning, without pleasure or pursuit; and went to a gaming table at night, though he always lost his money—an operation to which he had a very great aversion.
>
> He was the mere creature of the day: his dress, his expences, his pleasures, his sentiments, being regulated by the opinion of others, rather than by his own inclinations. (12–13)

Davenant becomes "the copyist...of numberless debauched and dissipated young men...and commit[s] folly with no other hope, and to no other end, than to obtain the suffrage of fools" (13). He imitates Lord Danesforte, "a modern Lovelace" (152) who encourages him to pursue the novel's title-heroine. Spurned by Ethelinde, Davenant attempts to rape her, but she is rescued by his servants. He subsequently becomes a bloated alcoholic. Smith indicates that if Davenant "had fallen into good company only," his "facility of temper" might have "rendered [him] a useful, if not a brilliant member of society" (13). In *Nature and Art*, Lord Bendham is "wholly made up of observance, of obedience, or dependence, and of imitation—a borrowed character—a character formed by reflection" (41). Environment determines his wife's metamorphoses: she "took her hue, like the chameleon, from surrounding objects; her manners were not governed by her mind, but were solely directed by external circumstances. At court, humble, resigned, patient, attentive—At balls, masquerades, gambling-tables, and routs, gay, sprightly, and flippant—At her country seat, reserved, austere, arrogant, and gloomy" (41–42). While in the country, the childless Lady Bendham turns puritanical and relentlessly persecutes unchaste women: "the young woman who lost her virtue in the village of Anfield, had better have lost her life" (42). Her behavior is either mindlessly conformist or spiteful.

James Kenney's play *The World! A Comedy* (1808) features an imitative chameleon who, unlike Davenant and the Bendhams, develops a moral compass. When Jack Echo arrives in London, he is "incapable of any fixed character whatever": "his habits, opinions, . . . his very manners, change with the hour; and his last acquaintance, however unworthy of his imitation, generally serves him for an example" (I.i.5). Eventually, however, Echo's love for the virtuous Eleanor Barclay inspires him to repudiate his mercenary and fashionable mentors and regain "the independence of [his] mind" (V.iii.79). He ceases to be a copyist when he listens to the "voice" of "Nature . . . within [his] bosom" rather than "the world" (I.ii.12, V.iii.72). If he had not, however, been reformed by "good company," he might have remained "the ape and bye-word of inferior beings" (V.iii.79). Imitative chameleons derive their virtues and vices from their role models and environments. Whereas transgressive chameleons flout social and moral norms, imitative chameleons aspire to conformity.

Urbane and Intellectual Chameleons

In his influential *Letters Written by the Late Right Honourable Philip Dormer Stanhope, Earl of Chesterfield, to His Son* (1774), the Earl of Chesterfield endorses urbane chameleonism. He explains to his son that a man of the world must constantly change personae: "I need not (I believe) advise you to adapt your conversation to the people you are conversing with: for I suppose you would not, without this caution, have talked upon the same subject, and in the same manner, to a Minister of State, a Bishop, a Philosopher, a Captain, and a Woman. A man of the world must, like the Cameleon, be able to take every different hue; which is by no means a criminal or abject, but a necessary complaisance, for it relates only to Manners, and not to Morals" (2.91). In contrast to Prior's rustic chameleon and the gaffe-prone Echo, Chesterfield's man of the world is an adept social performer who calibrates his speech and behavior to suit different audiences. Because Chesterfield's letters privilege urbanity over authenticity and recommend dissimulation, they were denigrated by eighteenth-century moralists. According to Samuel Johnson, "they teach the morals of a whore, and the manners of a dancing master" (Boswell 1.266). In Hannah Cowley's comedy *The World as It Goes; or, A Party at Montpelier* (performed 1781), a scheming valet de chambre is convinced that Chesterfield's letters will teach him how to impersonate his master and seduce Frenchwomen: "I'll up to my Garret, read Chesterfield's Letters, and then Monsieurs, take Care of your Wives" (III.iii.54).

Godwin, unlike Chesterfield, was a staunch proponent of sincerity.[12] In *The Enquirer*, he links chameleonism with intellectual development rather than dissimulation. He maintains that when he examines "a well-written book...His mind becomes ductile, susceptible to every impression": "When I read Thomson, I become Thomson; when I read Milton, I become Milton. I find myself a sort of intellectual camelion, assuming the colour of the substances on which I rest" (96). William Hazlitt makes a similar point in his essay "On Personal Identity" (1828). Although he has no desire to become "Shakespear in reality," he claims that while reading "Milton, Pope, Dryden, and a thousand more [writers],...we have in our possession, enjoy, and *are*...their thoughts." Thus the mind is an amazingly impressionable "microcosm": "What a Proteus is the human mind! All that we know, think of, or can admire, in a manner becomes ourselves" (274). In Godwin's view, chameleonism is ubiquitous and prevents humans from falling into ignorance and savagery: "Man in society is variously influenced by the characters of his fellow men; he is an imitative animal, and, like the camelion, owes the colour he assumes, to the colour of the surrounding objects...Man taken by himself is nothing. In the first portion of his life, he is more ignorant and worthless than the beasts...Why are men not always savages? Because they build upon one another's structures" (234). Given Godwin's advocacy of political and social reform, it is not surprising that he was more comfortable with fluid identities than were his conservative and anti-Jacobin contemporaries. He celebrated the human mind's chameleonism, its ability to absorb intellectual influences and build on them.

SENTIMENTAL AND TRANSGENDERING CHAMELEONS

In Georgian comedies, sentimental chameleons metamorphose themselves to overcome romantic obstacles and gratify those they adore. They tend to be sympathetic figures, particularly when their stratagems foil oppressive parents or guardians. Colonel Fainwell, the protagonist of Susanna Centlivre's comedy *A Bold Stroke for a Wife* (1718), is one of the most versatile sentimental chameleons in eighteenth-century drama.[13] Fainwell cannot marry Ann Lovely unless her four mutually antagonistic guardians agree to their union. To obtain their signatures on marriage consent contracts, Fainwell poses as a French fop, a virtuoso, a Dutch merchant, a steward, and a devout Quaker. Confident of success, he dubs himself "Mr. *Proteus*": "From changing Shape and imitating Jove, / I draw the happy Omens of my Love. / I'm not the first young Brother of the Blade / Who made his fortune in a Masquerade" (IV.ii.42). After informing the guardians that they have unwittingly authorized him to marry the heiress, Fainwell declares that he is an honorable soldier who detests fashionable "Dress and Breeding." In his opinion, "Love and Religion ne'er admit Restraint" (V.i.68), and Lovely's cruel entrapment justifies his duplicity. Chameleonism is linked to sentimental devotion in Kenney's *Debtor and Creditor* (1814). The spendthrift Arthur Rushfort tells his beloved Barbara that she has reformed him and offers to reinvent himself for her: "For thee I could be every thing! a prisoner, a pilgrim, a hero, a monk, or a martyr."[14] Convinced of his sincerity, she urges him to escape from "a gentleman of the law" (IV.i.62–63) who is in hot pursuit by changing coats and identities with a boxer named Sampson.

During the late eighteenth century, comedies that featured transgendering female chameleons were in vogue. For instance, in David Garrick's popular farce *The Irish Widow* (1772), Widow Brady changes her personality, accent, and gender to escape being forced into marriage with a wealthy 65-year-old named Whittle. Whittle's nephew and she are in love, but when Whittle becomes infatuated with her, he and Widow Brady's father decide "to make her [Whittle's] wife directly" (I.i.2). To repel her elderly fiancé, Widow Brady pretends to have a thick Irish brogue, uncouth manners, and a frivolous personality. She is hesitant about assuming "a character contrary to [her] disposition" (I.ii.13), but she concludes that her imposture is "an act of despair to punish folly, and reward merit: 'tis the last effort of pure honourable love" (I.ii.16). The widow also poses as her brother, Lieutenant O'Neale, and challenges Whittle to a duel. She, like Fainwell, regards chameleonism as a legitimate response to arbitrary patriarchal oppression.

Victoria, a dedicated wife in Hannah Cowley's *A Bold Stroke for a Husband* (1783), is another female chameleon who switches gender in a "last effort of pure honourable love." After her besotted spouse signs over Victoria's fortune to Laura, his mistress, Victoria poses as a gallant cavalier to captivate and circumvent her romantic rival. She reveals to a female friend that she has resorted to transvestitism out of desperation:

> *Victoria.* You, who know me, can judge how I suffered in prosecuting my plan. I have thrown off the delicacy of sex; I have worn the mask of love to the destroyer of my peace—but the object is too great to be abandoned—nothing less than to save my husband from ruin, and to restore him, again a lover, to my faithful bosom. (II.ii.22)

As Florio, Victoria tricks Laura into falling in love with her and rejecting her husband, and with the aid of a servant masquerading as a wealthy old lecher, she regains her family's estate. Her reluctant chameleonism has allowed her to fulfill her "duties as wife and mother" (V.ii.32). The fluid identities of Fainwell, Rushfort, Widow Brady, and Victoria benefit their loved ones as well as themselves. Within the context of comic drama, imposture in the service of "honorable love" is always pardonable and often commendable. The popularity of transgendering "breeches" roles such as Widow Brady and Victoria waned, however, during the 1790s (Wahrman 49–54).[15]

Chameleon Poets

In *Two Dissertations Concerning Sense and the Imagination. With an Essay on Consciousness* (1728), Zachary Mayne asserts that "the *Imagination* [is] like the Cameleon, of which Creature it is reported, that it changes its Hue according to the Colour of the Place where it happens to be" (74).[16] During the late 1780s, the chameleonic imaginations of the Della Cruscan poets inspired them to create numerous poetic personae. Robert Merry, Bertie Greatheed,

William Parsons, and Hester Lynch Piozzi inaugurated the Della Cruscan movement with the publication of *The Florence Miscellany* (1785), a motley collection of poems, "imitations," and translations written by themselves and unnamed Italian poets. After returning to England in 1787, Merry published "The Adieu and Recall to Love" in the *World* under the pseudonym Della Crusca.[17] Writing as "Anna Matilda," Hannah Cowley responded with "The Pen," and their ensuing verse dialogue inspired numerous imitators to adopt pseudonyms, address amatory poems to each other, and create impassioned and histrionic personae. The most protean Della Cruscan was Mary Robinson, whose pennames included Laura, Laura Maria, Lesbia, Oberon, Sappho, Julia, Tabitha Bramble, Horace Juvenal, T. B., M. R., Titania, Portia, and Bridget. As Pascoe points out, Robinson "used these pseudonyms to proliferate herself, the numerous guises facilitating poetic experimentation. Although the poems [she] published under each pseudonym are not uniform in style, the individual names...represent distinctive voices." For example, her Tabitha Bramble persona "enabled her to write sharply critical poetry utterly unlike the softer effusions of Laura Maria or Oberon" (Pascoe 174).[18] In a series of satirical letters entitled *The Sylphid* (1799–1800) that appeared in *The Morning Post*, Robinson adopts the persona of a protean, mobile, and insect-like creature that observes and comments on various facets of London society. The Sylphid lists her abilities in her opening letter: "I am allowed the power of changing my form, as suits the observation of the moment. I can assume the minute exterior of the smallest insect, or *personate*, if I may be allowed the expression, the most inanimate objects...Sometimes I steal into the garret of a poet; and, by skimming with light wings over his busy brain, impregnate his mind with all the fantastic forms which, at times, I am permitted to exhibit." Her mobile polymorphism allows her to "penetrate...the most obscure recesses of political as well as amorous intrigue" (165), expose society's "dissipated folly" (171), and stimulate the poetic imagination with "fantastic forms." She composes occasional verses: an "impromptu" satirizing a grand tourist and his tutor and "short admonitory Stanzas" addressed to a hypocritical female moralist (180, 192). Anticipating John Keats's chameleon poet, Robinson's Sylphid is vigilant, curious, impressionable, and identityless.[19]

Michael G. Cooke has argued that Lord Byron is the "consummate chameleon poet, changing themes and schemes quicker than the mind, let alone the eye, can follow" (226).[20] In her *Conversations of*

Lord Byron (1834), Lady Marguerite Blessington portrays the poet as both an imitative and theatrical chameleon:

> Byron is a perfect chameleon, possessing the fabulous qualities attributed to that animal, of taking the colour of whatever touches him. He is conscious of this, and says it is owing to the extreme *mobilité* of his nature, which yields to present impressions... [T]he chameleon-like character or manner of Byron renders it difficult to portray him; and the pleasure he seems to take in misleading his associates in their estimate of him increases the difficulty of the task. This extraordinary fancy of his has so often struck me, that I expect to see all the persons who have lived with him giving portraits, each unlike the other, and yet all bearing a resemblance to the original at some one time. Like the pictures given of some celebrated actor in his different characters, each likeness is affected by the dress and the part he has to fill. The portrait of John Kemble in Cato resembles not Macbeth nor Hamlet, and yet each is an accurate likeness of that admirable actor in those characters; so Byron, changing every day, and fond of misleading those whom he suspects might be inclined to paint him, will always appear different from the hand of each limner. (71–72)

Lady Blessington's description of Byron's mobility is contradictory. Initially, she claims that it is passively imitative: because of "the extreme *mobilité* of his nature" he takes "the colour of whatever touches him" and "yields to present impressions." But she subsequently represents his chameleonism as a volitional and theatrical stratagem intended to frustrate those who would attempt to paint a definitive portrait of him. Byron continually misrepresents himself and jokes that his "favourite *rôle*" is that of "a sort of sublime misanthrope, with moments of kind feeling" (220). According to Blessington, his mobility is simultaneously natural and artificial, genuine and deceitful, involuntary and deliberate.[21] It is also morally ambiguous: she quotes from a conversation in which he describes himself as extremely "changeable" and "a strange *mélange* of good and evil" (220). Her declaration that "Byron is a perfect chameleon" recalls Clarissa's characterization of Lovelace and thus links Byronic mobility to aristocratic libertinism. Byron's claim that he has "no character at all" reminds one of Keats's declaration that "the camelion poet... has no character" (*Letters* 1.387), but Byron stipulates that "[t]here are... two sentiments to which [he is] constant.—a strong love of liberty, and a detestation of cant" (*Conversations* 220). Somewhat paradoxically, the perfect chameleon loathes insincere speech. In a note to Canto XVI of *Don Juan* (1824),

Byron offers an ambivalent assessment of mobility: "It may be defined as an excessive susceptibility of immediate impressions—at the same time without *losing* the past; and is, though sometimes apparently useful to the possessor, a most painful and unhappy attribute" (*Works* V.769). He does not specify how mobility may be "useful to the possessor" but insists that this condition causes suffering, perhaps because the chameleon's memories are in constant and agonizing conflict with her or his present impressions and mutations. In *Don Juan*, however, Byron defends mobility's "vivacious versatility" and claims that it engenders "actors, artists, and romancers, / . . . speakers, bards, diplomatists, and dancers" (*Don Juan* XVI, 818, 825, 827).

As I have already noted, Shelley compares chameleons to poets in "An Exhortation":

> Poets are on this cold earth
> As Chameleons might be,
> Hidden from their early birth
> In a cave beneath the sea;
> Where light is, chameleons change:
> Where love is not, Poets do:
> Fame is love disguised: if few
> Find either, never think it strange
> That Poets range. (10–18)

In a letter, Shelley describes the poem as "a kind of excuse for Wordsworth" (*Letters* II. 195), with whom he was disillusioned, and his poem warns the reader not to "stain" the chameleon "Poet's free and heavenly mind / . . . with wealth or power" (19–20). Shelley's Dedication to his poetic satire *Peter Bell the Third* (1819) describes the title-character, who is a parodic representation of Wordsworth, as "a polyhedric Peter, or Peter with many sides": "He changes colours like a chameleon, and his coat like a snake. He is a Proteus of a Peter. He was at first sublime, pathetic, impressive, profound; then dull; then prosy and dull; and now dull—o so dull! it is an ultra-legitimate dulness" (*Shelley's Poetry and Prose* 340). The chameleon poet's impressionability is thus a double-edged sword: it can be either inspirational or debasing. In a July 13, 1821 letter to John and Maria Gisborne, Shelley declares that "[p]oets, the best of them—are a very camæleonic [*sic*] race: they take the colour not only of what they feed on, but of the very leaves under which they pass" (*Letters* II.308). Like Godwin's intellectual chameleon, Shelley's "best" poets are mentally enriched and transformed by what they read.

Keats's famous epistolary meditation on the chameleon poet stresses the poet's deracinated impressionability:

> As to the poetical Character...it is not itself—it has no self—it is every thing and nothing—It has no character—it enjoys light and shade; it lives in gusto, be it foul or fair, high or low, rich or poor, mean or elevated—It has as much delight in conceiving an Iago as an Imogen. What shocks the virtuous philosop[h]er, delights the camelion Poet...A Poet is the most unpoetical of any thing in existence; because he has no Identity—he is continually in for—and filling some other Body—The Sun, the Moon, the Sea and Men and Women who are creatures of impulse are poetical and have about them an unchangeable attribute—the poet has none; no identity—he is certainly the most unpoetical of all God's Creatures...It is a wretched thing to confess; but is a very fact that not one word I ever utter can be taken for granted as an opinion growing out of my identical nature—how can it, when I have no nature? When I am in a room with People if I ever am free from speculating on creations of my own brain, then not myself goes home to myself: but the identity of every one in the room begins [so] to press upon me that, I am in a very little time an[n]ihilated—not only among Men; it would be the same in a Nursery of children[.] (October 27, 1818, *Letters* 1.386–387)

Whereas Shelley aligns Wordsworth with chameleon poets who have been stained by wealth or power, Keats dissociates the poetical character "from the wordsworthian or egotistical sublime; which is a thing per se and stands alone" (*Letters* 1.387). He suggests that the fixed identity and self-absorption of the unchameleonic Wordsworth constrict his imagination and prevent him from "filling some other Body." However, like Byron's mobility, Keats's chameleonism seems to be an equivocal condition.[22] While Keats "delights" in his empathetic flights, he must wretchedly confess that since he has "no nature" none of his words and opinions can be reliably ascribed to his "identical nature," and when he is in the company of others their identities overwhelm and annihilate him. The shapeshifting title-character of his poem *Lamia* (1820) is similarly vulnerable: she cannot withstand the pressure exerted by Apollonius's identity. Keats's chameleonism not only frees him from selfhood and expands his imaginative vision but also renders him derivative, antisocial, and passively imitative. As he writes his letter he cannot be sure whether he is "speaking from [him]self" or "from some character in whose soul [he] now live[s]" (1.388). For Keats, Robinson, and Byron, chameleonism is both creatively liberating and vertiginously depersonalizing. It enables the poet to ventriloquize, experiment with personae, explore other consciousnesses, and role-play. But as Shelley and Keats indicate, the hyper-receptivity of chameleon poets makes them extremely susceptible to oppressive influences.

John Clare may have been the most conflicted chameleon poet of the Romantic period. In a draft letter to one of his benefactors, he writes that he wants to assume multiple identities and genders: "I am growing out of myself into many existences & wish to become more entertaining in other genders for that little personal pronoun 'I' is such a presumption ambitious [*sic*] swaggering little fellow that he thinks himself qualified for all company all places & all employments" (*Letters* 504).[23] Ventriloquizing Byron in "Don Juan A Poem" (composed 1841), Clare fantasizes about becoming his "two wives":

> I have two wives and I should like to see them
> Both by my side before another hour
> If both are honest I should like to be them
> For both are fair and bonny as a flower (286–290)

Yet in his autobiographical writings Clare stresses the importance of maintaining one's self-identity: "A very good common place counsel is *Self Identity* to bid our own hearts not to forget our own selves and always to keep self in the first place lest all the world who always keeps us behind it should forget us all together—forget not thyself and the world will not forget thee—forget thyself and the world will willingly forget thee till thou art nothing but a living-dead man dwelling among shadows and falshood [*sic*]" (*John Clare by Himself* 271). Tragically, Clare succumbed to mental illness and forgot himself. In his poem "An Invite to Eternity," written in the Northampton General Lunatic Asylum, he mourns his "sad non-identity" (14).

The Chameleon Debate

For eighteenth- and early nineteenth-century writers, "chameleon" was a slippery and versatile metaphor. Human chameleons could be transgressive or slavishly conformist, fanatically Jacobin or apolitical, manipulative or imitative, rakish or sentimental, free or shackled, histrionic or passively impressionable, creative or derivative. Like Rorschach inkblots, they could be variously interpreted, and often the interpretations revealed more about the interpreters than the chameleons. The phenomenon of human chameleonism prompted numerous questions: is dissimulative behavior anomalous or normative in commercial transactions, fashionable society, and politics? What are the benefits, disadvantages, and moral ramifications of possessing a fluid identity? If imposture is ubiquitous and advantageous, why not practice it? If a plebeian can convincingly pass as a patrician, does that mean that they are inherently equal? Or does it mean that social rank is founded on imposture? Do imposters pose a significant threat to social stability and public confidence in the integrity of economic transactions? Are dress, names, and manners key determinants of identity and, if so, should they be? Commentators often wondered why brilliant criminal imposters, particularly those who ended up on the scaffold, did not use their ingenuity and acting talents to achieve legitimate success. In an age in which private theatricals flourished, theatricality pervaded both the public and domestic spheres.

The commonly held belief that chameleonism was incompatible with authenticity was challenged by Jean-Jacques Rousseau and Byron. Rousseau, the great apostle of sincerity and the unique and unitary self, reveals in *The Confessions* (1782–1789) that he experimented with role-playing.[24] While traveling to Montpellier in a carriage, he masquerades as an English Jacobite named Mr. Dudding, despite the fact that he does not know a word of English. As Dudding, he is seduced by a fellow passenger, Madame de Larnage, and their liaison empowers him: "She had given me that confidence, the lack of which almost always prevents me from being master of myself. For once I was myself. Never have my eyes and my senses, my heart and my mouth, spoken so eloquently" (239).[25] Paradoxically, Rousseau's chameleonism allows him to be more completely himself. As Leo Damrosch observes, "Rousseau's originality was to grasp that both of his roles, the timorous Jean-Jacques and also the passionate Dudding, reflected a deeper unity that he needed to understand... concealed behind the mask of Dudding, he could submit to the advances of a woman who knew exactly what she wanted" (138–139). Performance provides a way for Rousseau to unshackle a repressed aspect of his personality and behave more rather than less authentically.

As I have noted, Byron believed that for excessively impressionable individuals, chameleonism is intrinsic and compulsive. In *Don Juan*, he suggests that Lady Adeline Amundeville's mobility is authentic:

Juan, when he cast a glance
At Adeline while playing her grand role,
Which she went through as though it were a dance,
(Betraying only now and then her soul
By a look scarce perceptibly askance

Of weariness or scorn) began to feel
Some doubt how much of Adeline was *real*;
So well she acted, all and every part
By turns—with that vivacious versatility,
Which many people take for want of heart.
They err—'tis merely what is called mobility,
A thing of temperament and not of art,
Though seeming so, from its supposed facility;
And false—though true; for surely they're sincerest,
Who are strongly acted on by what is nearest. (XVI, 810–824)

Although Lady Adeline is a consummate actress, her role-playing is "A thing of temperament and not of art"—it stems from her constitutional chameleonism. Her mobility is simultaneously false and true, a series of improvisational performances that reflect her "fidelity to the immediate" (Soderholm 154).[26] In Adeline's case, a performative adaptivity to social situations is sincere, whereas for someone with a fixed and unitary identity it would be hypocritical. Unlike Chesterfield's urbane chameleon, she becomes the roles she plays. Her "look scarce perceptibly askance / Of weariness or scorn" hints, however, at a fleeting double consciousness, a soul that disdains her "dance" and emerges "now and then."

Staging Romantic Chameleons and Imposters explores the ways in which chameleonic figures portrayed in the periodical press, on stage, and in literature reflected conceptions of and attitudes toward authenticity, sincerity, performance, uniqueness, autonomy, and identity during the Romantic period. Chapter 1 analyzes the careers of swindlers who scandalized and fascinated the British public, focusing on the genteel, flamboyant, and American-born James Molesworth Hobart (or Hub[b]ard) (1765?–1793). Hobart became known as the Duke of Ormond after using that alias to swindle a London banker. To the journalists who reported on him and the public that marveled at his ingenuity, Hobart was a problematic and enigmatic figure. Despite his manifest criminality, he became a minor celebrity and elicited sympathy from those who visited him in prison, witnessed his trials, and attended his execution. His acting talents and sangfroid were widely admired, and he inspired a novelistic biography by the politically liberal hatter, tailor, and logician John Collard (1769–1810) that evaluates the advantages and drawbacks of a malleable identity. The *soi-disant* Duke of Ormond may have inspired Cowley to invent Tippy, an aristocrat impersonator in her comedy *The Town before You* (1794).

Chapters 2, 3, 4, and 6 focus on Romantic-era comedies that reflect the playwrights' complicated and often conflicted attitudes toward characters with mobile identities. Comedies were enormously popular during the late eighteenth and early nineteenth centuries—*The School for Scandal* (1777), *The Belle's Stratagem* (1780 premiere), and *Raising the Wind, A Farce* (1803) enjoyed long runs and numerous revivals—and addressed contentious social issues such as master-servant relations, cross-class passing, racial and ethnic stereotyping and prejudice, the performativity of gender roles, aristocratic decadence, and wealth's corrupting influence. John Larpent, the Examiner of Plays, recognized the social and political influence of satirical comedies and frequently censored passages in them that he deemed radical. The comedies I will focus on consider the moral, mental, and social ramifications of transgressive, dysfunctionally imitative, or reformative chameleonism. Their reception depended on numerous factors, including the spectators' political and moral prejudices, the reputation of the author, and the public image and comedic talent of the actor playing the chameleonic role. Two of the comedies discussed, Cowley's *The World as It Goes; or a Party at Montpelier* and Holcroft's *Knave, or Not?* (1798), were "damned" by obstreperous theatergoers; the social subversiveness and bawdiness of *The World as It Goes* outraged spectators, and both audiences and reviewers objected to the perceived Jacobinism of *Knave, or Not?*[27] Audiences were, however, captivated by the duplicitous rogues in Richard Cumberland's *The Box-Lobby Challenge, a Comedy* (1794), Cowley's *The Town before You*, and Kenney's *Raising the Wind*. Acting is an inherently chameleonic profession, and, as Wahrman points out, eighteenth-century performance theorists disagreed about whether a great actor like David Garrick lost himself in his role or possessed two identities while on stage: his actual self and the character he was representing (171–174). In contrast, "Plausible Jack" Palmer, who played the imposter Harry Singleton/Lord Janus in Cumberland's *The Imposters* (1789) and Monrose in *Knave, or Not?*, did not attempt to immerse himself in his roles.[28] According to a retrospective appraisal of his acting style, "He was remarkable in *comedy* for the easiness of his deportment, and the freedom and propriety of his action; he made no effort to *appear* the character he represented, but if we could have forgotten his *identity*, we might easily have believed him to *be* so" ("Characteristics of Authors and Players" 110). Whereas Garrick became his roles, theatergoers never forgot that Palmer was acting. In the comedies I will examine, metatheatrical devices, allusions, and scenes underscore the self-conscious performativity of the actors playing chameleonic characters.

As Pascoe and many other scholars have noted, Mary Robinson was perhaps the most chameleonic celebrity of the Romantic period. According to Bolton, "Robinson's writing, relying in part on her celebrity status, blurred the boundaries between literature and performance, just as dramatic romance blurred the boundaries between the stage and the nation, fantasy and reality" (108). In Chapter 5, I will discuss Robinson's depictions of malleable and imitative identities in her musical farce *The Lucky Escape* (1778 premiere), her newspaper essays, and her novels *Walsingham; or The Pupil of Nature* (1797) and *The False Friend: A Domestic Story* (1799). For Robinson, as for many of her contemporaries, English society was inherently dissimulative and implicitly encouraged opportunistic chameleonism. Her attitude toward mobile identities was conflicted. In a letter written near the end of her life to her friend Godwin, she speculates that if she had "been an artificial creature" she "might have been in wealth and vulgar estimation, a creature to be envied!" ("Letters" 316–317). But her novels portray chameleons who are predatory and inwardly empty and whose lives end tragically. A female character's lifelong transvestitism in *Walsingham* enables her to enjoy the financial and social prerogatives of a male baronet. She views herself, however, as "[a] monster of dissimulation" (155), and she is so devastated by her inability to reveal her gender and sexual orientation to the man she loves that she attempts suicide. An astute student of chameleonism, Robinson considers its social and financial benefits and its moral and psychological consequences in her works.

Most of the historical and imaginary chameleons discussed in this book are transgressive, opportunistic, and acquisitive commoners. They metamorphose themselves to improve their financial and social positions, either temporarily or permanently, and include forgers, swindlers who pose as wealthy patricians to hoodwink bankers or merchants, ambitious manservants in dramatic comedies who "dress up" to impersonate their masters, and impecunious rogues who misrepresent themselves to marry advantageously. To pass for elite members of society, they adopt aliases, wear fashionable clothes, and speak and behave genteelly. In many cases, facial recognition dooms their schemes. These upwardly mobile chameleons flout class boundaries, undermine the reliability of identity markers, and embody both patriarchal fears of social destabilization and plebeian fantasies of self-reinvention. Their primary resources—wit, impudence, and acting ability—are as intangible as the air on which reptilian chameleons purportedly lived.

CHAPTER 1

THE CASE OF THE PRETENDED DUKE OF ORMOND

PROLOGUE: THE PRETENDED DUKE'S PREDECESSORS

On June 4, 1663, Mary Carleton, nicknamed "the German Princess" by a fascinated public, and also known as Maria von Wolway from Cologne, Mary Modders from Canterbury, and Mary Steadman, stood trial for bigamy in the Justice Hall of the Old Bailey. Her husband, John Carleton, and his family maintained that she was the daughter of a Canterbury fiddler, had been previously married, and had tricked them into believing that she was a foreign noblewoman. In court, Mary Carleton's performance as Maria von Wolway confounded prosecution witnesses, charmed spectators, and resulted in her acquittal (Kietzman 61–63). Soon after the trial, however, she published a short autobiography in which she conceded that she may have posed as a German aristocrat. In *The Case of Madam Mary Carleton* (1663), she claims that her imposture was justifiable: "What harme [*sic*]," she asks, "have I done in pretending to great Titles?" (36).[1] According to her, it was not "unjust" for her "to contrive [her] own advancement by such illustrious pretences as they say [she] made use of, to grant the Question, that [she is] not so honourably descended as [she] insinuated to the Catch-dolt [her] Father in Law" (36–37).[2] She explains that her performance was intended to "counterplot" those who had a "design" to take advantage of her and argues that "*to deceive the deceiver, is no deceit*" (38). Carleton's story was dramatized in a play titled *A Witty Combat: Or, the Female Victor* (1663) in which she played the role of "Mary Moders" and recited the epilogue:

> You think me a bold Cheat, put case 'twere so,
> Which of you are not? now you'd swear I know;
> But do not least [lest] that you deserve to be
> Censur'd worse than you yet can censure me.
> The Worlds a Cheat, and we that move in it
> In our degrees do exercise our Wit:
> And better 'tis to get a glorious Name
> However got; then live by common Fame. (Porter n. pag.)[3]

For Carleton, the world is a masquerade in which everyone plays a role. She misrepresented herself to thwart deceivers and was rewarded with the "glorious Name" of German Princess. Her acquittal at the bigamy trial was, however, a fleeting triumph. She became a professional thief and was sentenced to transportation to Barbados as an indentured servant. After violating the conditions of her sentence by returning to England, she resumed her criminal career under various aliases, including the German Princess, and on January 22, 1673 she was executed at Tyburn for stealing "a silver cup and spoon" (Kietzman 225, 209).

As Mary Jo Kietzman has demonstrated, Carleton's bravura performance as the German Princess "appealed to London's non-elite populace because it democratized self-fashioning for both men and women of the lower classes" (6).[4] Imposters like Carleton were viewed as skillful participants in the "universal masquerade."[5] According to Dror Wahrman, imposture developed a "bad reputation" (259) in the late eighteenth century as the modern conception of the stable and internalized self became normative. In certain cases, however, Romantic-era responses to imposters and disguises were ambivalent or even sympathetic. In 1817, for example, another counterfeit princess appeared in England: a servant named Mary Baker convincingly masqueraded as "Caraboo, the princess of an island called Javasu" (Russett 115).[6] Unlike the German Princess, Princess Caraboo refrained from bigamy and larceny. As Margaret Russett has shown, after Baker's fraud was discovered, "her 'talents' evoked ambivalent admiration" (114), and a contemporary observer wondered at "the imposter's inventive genius" and her "consummate art" (Gutch 5n, 54).[7] The unmasked Baker sailed for America, returned to England in 1824, and "died in late 1864 or early 1865, after a long and comparatively prosperous life during which she married and raised a daughter" (Russett 135).

This chapter focuses on a Romantic-era male imposter who posed as several English aristocrats and elicited respect and sympathy as well as condemnation from his contemporaries: the American-born James Molesworth Hobart (or Hub[b]ard) (1765?–1793), whose aliases included the Duke of Ormond, Lord Massey, and the Duke of Manchester.[8] Like Carleton, Hobart was an eloquent speaker and astute performer who won acquittal in a highly publicized trial and whose criminal career ended on the scaffold. Moreover, both Carleton and Hobart became celebrities and inspired literary characters. Daniel Defoe modeled the protagonist of his novel *Roxana* (1724) partly on the German Princess, and a review from the *Morning Chronicle* asserts that Tippy, a charming rogue in Hannah Cowley's comedy *The Town before You*, "is obviously drawn from the Duke of Ormond, whose feats, as the counterfeit of different men of rank, are on record" (December 8, 1794).[9] I will argue that the public responses to Hobart's impostures reflect a widespread fascination with criminal chameleonism and an uncertainty about how to understand and evaluate the phenomenon. The case of the *soi-disant* Duke could be used to support either the egalitarian notion that the nobility are indistinguishable from genteel and well-dressed commoners or the conservative fear that imposters who pose as aristocrats and assume their prerogatives threaten social order. While contemporaneous accounts deplored Hobart's illicit actions, they often praised his acting ability, charm, attractive appearance, sangfroid, and excellent manners. In a culture that prized theatrical spectacle, his flawless impersonations of aristocrats and charisma in the courtroom and on the scaffold inspired wonder and admiration. *The Life and Extraordinary Adventures of James Molesworth Hobart, Alias Henry Griffin, Alias Lord Massey, the Newmarket Duke of Ormond, &c.* (1794) asserts that "he possessed many excellent qualities, both natural and acquired" and attributes his corruption to his lack of "moral discipline," immoral mentors, and "little circumstances which gradually debase the mind" (Dralloc 247, iii).

Among Hobart's chameleonic precursors were two notorious eighteenth-century serial imposters, Charles Price (1730?–1786), nicknamed "The Social Monster" (Figure 1.1), and James George Semple (1759–1815), dubbed "The Northern Imposter," whose life stories were recounted in popular 1786 biographies. In *Memoirs of a Social Monster; or, The History of Charles Price*, Price is demonized as the "twin-brother" (ix) of Lucifer, and the work's author declares that "with a thousand bad qualities, those who knew him most intimately cannot recollect, that he had even one good one" (38). A talented

Figure 1.1 "Charles Price in his usual Dress. Charles Price in Disguise."
"CHAs. PRICE in his usual Dress. CHAs. PRICE in Disguise as described in the Public Papers vide Page 13 of these Memoirs." Frontispiece to *The Fourth Edition Much Improved: Being a More Minute and Particular Account of that Arch Imposter, Charles Price* (1786). Reproduced courtesy of the Social Law Library in Boston, Massachusetts.

polymorph, Price assumed innumerable aliases, frequently wore disguises, and posed as a Methodist minister to rob "an old methodistical lady…of near 3000 pounds" (89). As his biography points out, "he, who knew so well how to *become all things to all men*, could as easily become a Methodist preacher, as any other profession he had before" (87–88, italics in original). *Memoirs of a Social Monster* explains that Price's upbringing as the son of a tailor and clothes salesman informed his criminal career: "the idea of disguising himself, which he has practised for so many years past, was suggested to him by the circumstance of having been brought up where he had opportunities to shift his cloaths as he pleased" (32). In 1780, Price masqueraded as

Mr. Brank, the elderly and infirm guardian of a "young nobleman of great fortune" (208), and hired a naive youth named Samuel to pass counterfeit banknotes. His unwitting accomplice

> saw an apparent old man affecting the foreigner, seemingly very gouty, wrapped up with five or six yards of flannel about his legs, a camblet [*sic*] surtout buttoned up over his chin, close to his mouth, a large patch over his left eye, and every part of his face so hid, that the young fellow could not see any part of it, except his nose, his right eye, and a small part of that cheek. To carry on the deception still better, Mr. Price thought proper to place the man on his left side, on which eye the patch was, so that the old gentleman could take an askance look at the young man with his right eye, and by that means discover only a small portion of his face. He appeared, by this disguise, to be between sixty and seventy years of age; and... not much under six feet high, owing to boots or shoes, with heels very little less than three inches high... Mr. Price affected great age, much bodily infirmity, and a faint hectic cough, with a disability of almost getting out of the coach. (207–208)

After the unfortunate Samuel "obtained cash, and other valid securities, to the amount of fourteen hundred pounds, on [Price's] forged notes" (215), he was arrested and spent 11 months in prison. The Social Monster's elaborate disguise prevented him from being identified, and he absconded with the money. He was, however, arrested in early 1786, identified as a forger, and averted execution by hanging himself. According to *The Complete Newgate Calendar*, "The depredations of this villain amounted in the whole to upwards of one hundred thousand pounds" (Crook 164), making Price the most successful swindler of his era.[10]

Although Price's biographer admires his subject's ingenuity, he condemns him as an inhuman "monster" whose suicide indicated "that his cowardice was as great as his cunning" (*Memoirs of a Social Monster* 343). The biographer worries, however, that the reader might be more amused than outraged by the forger's impersonation of a pious philanthropist: "What we are most afraid of is, that the narrative will be read with a smile, and a warmth of imagination, when it ought to throw the human frame into an ague fit" (263). If the scoundrel's impostures are sufficiently entertaining, there is a danger that he will be perceived as a comic rather than a vicious character. Unlike Hobart, who flaunted his good looks, youth, and polished manners, Price masked his appearance, pretended to be old and diseased, and seems to have been bereft of gentility. Whereas

The Life and Extraordinary Adventures of James Molesworth Hobart insists that Hobart possessed "many excellent qualities," *Memoirs of a Social Monster* declares that Price's "road from his *cradle* to his *grave*, was the road of vice and dishonesty, of fraud, rapine, and plunder, of dissimulation and hypocrisy" (304). These biographical accounts, published eight years apart, offer very different portraits of criminal chameleons: Hobart's charisma and urbanity contrast sharply with Price's effrontery and grotesque masquerades. What seems to separate the humanlike from the monstrous chameleon is the ability to deliver a sympathetic and gentlemanly performance. While *The Life and Extraordinary Adventures* characterizes Hobart as a promising and well-bred youth corrupted by intemperance and circumstances, Price's biography portrays its subject as a lifelong rogue whose appearance frequently changed but whose duplicity and ruthlessness were innate and immutable.

Hobart more closely resembled Semple, who possessed "an elegant figure, a person exceeding[ly] well made, and a genteel deportment [that] gave him a pre-eminency in point of attraction" (19) and frequently claimed to be related to or associated with the highborn and powerful. The "compiler" of *The Northern Imposter; Being a Faithful Narrative of the Adventures, and Deceptions, of James George Semple* (1786) proclaims that "the GREAT CHARLES PRICE" and Semple were the leading figures in an unprecedented upsurge of swindlers: "a very few years have eclipsed the transactions of ages, and . . . England can boast of more renowned exploits in that short period of time, than ever were signalized throughout all Europe during the last century" (13–14). According to the compiler, this crime wave was caused by inadequate legislation: "whilst the absurdity of our penal statutes have opened doors of invitation to ingenious chicanery, the scandalous and contemptible artifices of dirty pettifogging attornies [*sic*], and Old Bailey bar-orators, have given a loose and encouragement to every species of fraud and imposition" (14). Sponsored by Semple's alleged victims, *The Northern Imposter* presents him as a mock-heroic reprobate claiming descent from the Lisles, "a noble family in Scotland" (28). In his autobiography, *The Life of Major J. G. Semple Lisle* (1799), Semple protests against the "anonymous libels" (vii) published in earlier accounts of his life, but while *The Northern Imposter* is clearly biased against its subject, the information it presents is corroborated by contemporary news stories, and Semple's memoir is vindicatory and frequently improbable.

The Northern Imposter informs the reader that Semple was born and educated in Scotland, where "he was soon made conversant in

Latin and Greek" and developed "an understanding capable of every improvement, and an affability of temper, so consonant to *the things that be*, that he was a most engaging companion, wherever he could introduce himself" (19, italics in original). Semple's autobiography contends that his vicissitudes resulted from his privileged upbringing: "Born of an antient and noble race, but not possessed of riches equal to their rank, I naturally imbibed ideas of a too lofty kind; flattered in my youth by my rich and powerful friends, I formed to myself plans of future grandeur; plans, which my impetuosity of disposition prevented me from realizing" (363). His autobiography also claims that Semple's "military *debût* was made in America, in the year 1775, at the age of sixteen" (3) and that after being captured and wounded in the conflict, he returned to England in 1777. According to this account, Semple, like Hobart, was a veteran of the American Revolution who turned to crime after leaving the military. As J. M. Beattie points out, demobilization "brought back to England large numbers of disreputable men who had spent several years being further brutalized by service in the armed forces, without any provision being made for their re-entry into the work force" (226). Both Semple and Hobart employed military aliases: Semple posed as Major Harrold, Major Maxwell, Major Grant, Major Cunningham, Colonel Crawford, and Major Winter, and Hobart pretended to be "an officer in the Coldstream regiment to the Duke of York" (*Authentic Memoirs* 13), Captain Blundell, and Captain Monson of the Dragoons. Another factor in the rising crime rate during the eighteenth century was urbanization (Gladfelder 159–161), and *The Northern Imposter* attributes Semple's corruption to his residence in London: "It was to [the] inadvertent step in the elder Semple, of intrusting his son as his own master in a town, where the utmost resolution and fortitude are too often ineffectual security against vice and debauchery, that the younger Semple owes his ruin. It was more highly criminal in him, as he knew the natural bent of his son's inclinations. Let us pity, therefore, whilst we condemn" (24). Although this life of Semple denounces his crimes and argues that swindling should be made a capital offence (96), it portrays him as a rogue corrupted by metropolitan temptations rather than as a social monster like Price.

The compiler of *The Northern Imposter* explains the swindler's modus operandi:

> Wherever Mr. Semple attempted to obtain, or was successful in obtaining either money or goods, the imposition was founded on his real or pretended knowledge of some respectable character who he knew was

> acquainted with, or was a customer to, the person he applied to, either to borrow cash, or take up goods upon credit.—This artifice was seconded by the deception of his own personal appearance, which, added to the natural plausibility of his language, was as specious and as alluring as the Grand Deceiver's... This will, once and for all, account for his success in that line of Swindling, at which he was so complete an adept[.] (43)

The Northern Imposter provides numerous instances of Semple's name-dropping and fraudulent networking. While in Cologne, Semple allegedly befriended a German baron: "He stiled himself a Major in his Britannic Majesty's service, described himself of a noble family in Scotland, and boasted his great intimacy with the first of the English nobility" (28). He then falsely claimed that he was in exile from England after killing two gentlemen in separate duels and in dire financial straits. Moved by this gentlemanly performance, the baron invited Semple to live "on [his] bounty as a man of consequence and fashion" (30). *The Northern Imposter* testifies that on another occasion Semple was brought before a magistrate for absconding without paying a fare to a post-chaise driver. Unabashed, the culprit "ran through his lineage and history, even from the year 1547, when the title of Lord Viscount Lisle became extinct,... harangued on his importance to government[,]... declared himself the bosom friend of Mr. Pitt; [and] said he was on his Majesty's service with the expresses of the most important and serious nature to this kingdom" (76). The magistrate was so impressed that he paid Semple's fare and supplied him with cash.

Along with William Pitt (then Chancellor of the Exchequer), Semple pretended to have connections with Lord Salisbury, the Earl of Kerry, Lord Verney, and "the noble family of Lord Semple, of Scotland" (73). In 1786, the *General Evening Post* reported that among other swindles, Semple "assumed the character of an Ambassador to the Court of Russia, and nearly ruined an unfortunate taylor, who prepared for him a wardrobe of 400l. a considerable part of which was delivered" (July 8–11, 1786). Semple denied this allegation in a letter to the *Morning Chronicle* (July 17, 1786) and also disputed "a story... about [his] personating a certain noble Marquis, and swindling two maiden sisters out of their whole fortune, 1500l." (*The Northern Imposter* 61). In contrast to Hobart, Semple preferred to claim associations with rather than impersonate aristocrats, and he appears to have been a mediocre courtroom performer. *The Northern Imposter* states that Semple's defense during his 1786 trial for stealing a post chaise "was not uttered in a manner that did much honour either to his education, his acknowledged abilities, or his appearance" (113–114). But Semple, unlike Hobart, managed to elude the hangman's noose. He was sentenced to seven years' transportation for the post-chaise theft, but after languishing "a considerable while" in Newgate Prison, he was transferred to Woolwich and "received his Majesty's pardon, on condition of going abroad" (*Life of Major J. G. Semple Lisle* 75).

Semple emigrated to France and claims that while there he "formed a strict intimacy with General Beruyer, Commandant of the interior" and witnessed the execution of Louis XVI (*Life* 76, 94). In the paranoid political climate of the 1790s, his French sojourn aroused suspicion. An anonymous and propagandistic attack against Semple titled *The History of the Swindling and Amorous Adventures of James George Semple, &c. &c.* (1795?) alleged that he was a Jacobin agent: "This perfidious monster, in the shape of an aristocrat, but actually a spy and emissary of Robespierre's and the Jacobins, hurried numerous credulous victims into misery, by revealing their family secrets to that dreadful wolf, his patron. Thus this despicable excrescence of the human race, assumed Proteus like, every shape that could enable him to gratify his beastly lusts and passions" (102). The nefarious British chameleon described in *The History* is an anti-Jacobin's nightmare: his aristocratic appearance masks his revolutionary allegiances and allows him to gain the trust of loyalists, whom he then betrays. Among other far-fetched allegations, *The History* asserts that Semple devised a plan for a French invasion of England. Semple does not appear, however, to have had strong political convictions of any sort. After returning to England, he was arrested for swindling several tradesmen, convicted of fraud, and transported in 1797. His autobiography, which reads like a picaresque novel, recounts his experiences on a convict ship bound for Australia and his adventures in Brazil. An incorrigible recidivist, he died suddenly in 1815 en route to Morocco, "to which he had engaged to transport himself, on the Prince Regent's remitting the sentence passed on him at his last conviction for defrauding a cheesemonger of bacon and eggs" (*The Ipswich Journal*, December 16, 1815).

The Criminal Chameleon
James Molesworth Hobart

Like Price, Hobart was a forger, and like Semple, he was a habitual name-dropper. In March 1791, he assumed the alias Lord Massey and committed the crime for which he was eventually executed. The

Morning Post and Daily Advertiser provided a detailed account of the swindle:

> Last Tuesday, a genteel man went to the shop of Mess. Willerton and Green...; he looked at several articles of jewellery, and saying, that he was recommended by his friend, the Marquis of Salisbury, who actually deals at that shop, he ordered a pair of diamond ear-rings, a diamond necklace and a gold watch, set round with brilliants, to be sent to Lord Massey at half past four, in St. James's Place. Mr. Green carried the articles which in value amounted to upwards of seven hundred pounds: the pretended Lord Massey agreed to take them, and presented in payment a draught for 1400l. purporting to be drawn by Lord Tankerville on Messrs. Cout's and Co. Bankers. The balance, Mr. Green said, he had not about him, and Lord Massey observed, that it was of no consequence, as he must have proper cases for the jewels before he could present them to the lady, he therefore begged Mr. Green to bring such cases, and the difference of the bill as soon as convenient, saying, he might leave the jewels. When Mr. Green went from St. James's Place, it was too late to go to Couts's, but as he had no doubts of the bill, he went home, prepared the cases immediately...and hasted to settle with his Lordship. On his arrival in St. James's Place, he was informed that Lord Massey had just gone out;—he called again, and was informed that he had not returned, when, concluding that his Lordship had gone to dinner, he declined calling again that evening. On Wednesday morning he called again, but still no Lord Massey was to be found! Mr. Green then began to entertain some fears, and went to the House of Messrs. Couts, where he was informed that Lord Tankerville kept no money, and that the Bill might be presumed to be a forgery. He then went to Lord Tankerville who assured him that it was a forgery. Mr. Green caused the servant of the pretended Lord Massey to be apprehended and examined at the Public Office in Bow-street, where the poor fellow's innocence was perfectly clear: He said that he was engaged on that very Tuesday morning, from having advertised in a Newspaper, and that his master only entered on the lodgings the same day. (March 22, 1791)

Hobart also "passed himself upon a watch-maker in Holborn, as the Duke of Manchester, and ordered two valuable watches to be sent to his lodgings...; but, the watch-maker having discovered that his grace was abroad, instead of watches, sent him two officers from Bow Street. Hobart happened at the time to be near his own lodging, and on seeing the myrmidons, whom he well knew, hastily decamped" (Dralloc 181–182).

The swindler's ability to impersonate aristocrats was probably facilitated by the ready availability of high-quality secondhand clothes, many of them discarded by patricians, and the contemporary vogue for different social classes to dress alike. As Beverly Lemire has demonstrated, during the eighteenth century the flourishing trade in secondhand clothes "enabled untold thousands to wear clothes above their rank and beyond their means had the garments been new," and thus "Fashion became more generally uniform across the nation and the classes of society" (4–5). Even though the spendthrift Hobart was frequently "reduced to extreme necessity" (Dralloc 181), he would not have needed much cash or credit to outfit himself as a peer.

In October 1791, the counterfeit Duke of Ormond began to attract the attention of the periodical press. The *London Chronicle* reported that "Mr. Hammond, the Banker of Newmarket, was defrauded of two hundred pounds, on Friday evening, by a man, who called himself the Duke of Ormond, and gave a forged draft upon a Banker in London" (October 8–11, 1791). Given Hobart's need for a credible alias, his selection of the Duke of Ormond is puzzling, since the last Duke of Ormond had died in 1745. Perhaps he regarded this controversial duke as a kindred spirit. Impeached by the House of Commons for high treason, the second Duke of Ormond (1665–1745) was a Jacobite conspirator who, like Hobart, became a deracinated figure, exiled from his native country. A story in the *Evening Mail* mentioned the fake Duke of Ormond's gentlemanly demeanor and described how he further established his credibility by knocking at the Duke of Queensbury's door where the banker could see him:

> On Friday evening, a man, who had much the appearance of a gentleman, went to the house of Mr. Hammond, a banker of this place. He said, he was the Duke of Ormond, and told Mr. Hammond he wanted 200l. for which he offered a draft upon a London Banker: Mr. H. without hesitation advanced the sum, and received the draft in return. The *Duke* then double-knocked at the Duke of Queensbury's door, which is within sight of Mr. Hammond's, and enquired if the Duke was at home: being answered in the negative, he left the name of *Ormond*, and went away, and very soon after his *Grace* left the town. The next morning, Mr. Hammond, upon enquiry, found that the other securities he had for his two hundred pounds were—a false title, and a forged draft. (October 10–12, 1791, italics in original)

The *Public Advertiser* emphasized the swindler's aplomb: "The man who defrauded Mr. Hammond of Newmarket, of two hundred pounds, did it with much coolness. He even desired Mr. H. to accompany him to Mr. Vernon, or the Duke of Queensbury, that his person might be identified, as Duke of Ormond. Both those persons had, however, left the town for the race ground" (October 13, 1791). The culprit's aristocratic alias, his refined and poised appearance and behavior, and his attempt to link himself to the nobility recalled the earlier fraud by the fake Lord Massey. On October 22, 1791 the *World (1787)* reported that "It is said...the *Duke* of *Ormond*, who lately *did* the Country Banker for two hundred pounds, is the very identical *Lord Massey*, who some time ago *did* the London Jeweller."

Soon after the theft of £200, the *soi-disant* Duke of Ormond made a fatal mistake: he eloped with Miss Spooner, the daughter of a Leicester innkeeper. According to John Collard, Hobart's biographer, although his behavior was gentlemanly, Hobart's "taste" in women was "so truly vulgar, that he was more captivated with the smiles of a beautiful plebeian, than even with the favors of nobility itself" (Dralloc 126). After his two high-profile swindles, his decision to run away with Miss Spooner to Birmingham and then to nearby Vauxhall was incredibly reckless. He must have known that her enraged father would pursue them and that they would therefore attract attention—the Newmarket banker had publicized his description and one of his recent aliases, Henry Griffin (Dralloc 193). But Hobart seems to have been a contradictory and self-thwarting figure, both a poised, calculating swindler and a rashly impulsive lover. A news story in the *St. James's Chronicle or the British Evening Post* described the bogus Duke of Ormond's arrest:

> Yesterday a very genteel well-made man, about seven and twenty, was apprehended at Vauxhall, near this town, on suspicion of being the pretended Duke of Ormond who lately swindled Mr. Hammond, the Newmarket Banker, out of 200l. He arrived at the hotel in this place, on Sunday last, accompanyed [*sic*] by a young lady whom he called his sister. On Monday he removed with the same female to Vauxhall, as Capt. Monson, of the 4th dragoons. Yesterday evening, however, the father of the young woman, who is the master of the Bell Inn, in Leicester, reached this place in pursuit of his daughter; and applied to Mr. Wallace, one of our constables, who, accompanyed by his eldest son, went to apprehend the Captain. (His real name is said to be *Griffin*, and that he is the son of a tailor at Hagley, in this neighbourhood). They had no sooner entered his room, than he fired at young Wallace; the ball struck his front teeth, and knocking out several of them, lodged in a part of his cheek. With a second pistol he attempted to shoot the elder Mr. Wallace, but it missed fire; and he was then knocked down and secured by one of the assistants, who has beaten him very much indeed. He has a servant with him, who seems much attached to him. Hundreds have been to see him in the

> dungeon; and he certainly answers the description of the swindler in Mr. Hammond's advertisement. He has been before the Magistrates this morning; but refuses to answer the question, whether or not he was the person who took Mr. Hammond in. He complains much of the treatment and blows he received after he was secured;—says he resisted upon the lady's account, who wished not to go back to her father; and that he meant to marry her.—The father, however, has carried her back to Leicester. (November 3–5, 1791)

The *Evening Mail* reiterated the tale that the pretended Duke was actually "one Griffin, of Hagley, about twelve miles from Birmingham, a taylor by trade" (November 4–7, 1791). Perhaps recalling that the serial imposter Charles Price was the son of a tailor and old clothes salesman, journalists were prepared to accept that a village tailor or a tailor's son could have convincingly posed as Lord Massey and the Duke of Ormond.

Hobart may have adopted the pseudonym Henry Griffin to dissociate himself from the Duke of Ormond and his other aristocratic aliases. According to his biographer, Hobart endorsed the bills he swindled from the Newmarket banker "in the name of Henry Griffin" (Dralloc 193), and he signed his letters from Warwick prison by that name. Collard asserts, however, that Hobart later regretted the use of this plebeian alias: "There happened to be a Henry Griffin, of Hagley, about ten miles from Birmingham, a taylor by trade, whose conduct had been a little irregular, and it was generally believed that this was the same Henry Griffin; Hobart, notwithstanding his unhappy condition, felt himself much injured by this report, and took every means in his power to rectify the mistake; for, degraded as he was, he still considered himself by no means reduced to the level of a taylor" (195–196). Even though Collard was "a hatter and tailor" (Langford 118), he does not object to Hobart's snobbery. The claim that Hobart "took every means in his power to rectify the mistake" is undermined by the reproduction of a letter written by Hobart from Newgate in which he reverts to his Henry Griffin alias, after previously signing a letter from Bury with "his real name" (Dralloc 222), J. M. Hobart. Reporting on the swindler's final trial, the *London Recorder or Sunday Gazette* identified him as Henry Griffin and listed Hubbard as an alias: "Henry Griffin, alias George [*sic*] Hubbard, alias Lord Massey, alias the Duke of Ormond, was tried for capital offence, in forging an order for payment of money, purporting to be signed by the Earl of Tankerville, and directed to Messrs. Coutts and Co. banker. Guilty—DEATH" (December 16,

1792).[11] Much to his chagrin, the gentlemanly Hobart found himself portrayed in newspapers as an artful village tailor.

Charged with shooting the constable's son, John Wallis (or Wallace) the younger, Hobart displayed excellent manners during his initial courtroom appearance, despite his serious injuries: "Griffin was taken before the Magistrates at Birmingham—he was so roughly treated with the bludgeon the day before, that he was obliged to be assisted in ascending the stairs leading to the Public Office. On being interrogated, he said very genteelly, that he wished not to appear contemptuous, but begged leave to decline answering any interrogatories then" (*Evening Mail*, November 4–7, 1791). When Hobart's trial at Warwick began on August 21, 1792, his arrival in court inspired both admiration and pity: "the Prisoner, neatly dressed, entered the Court; his deportment was exceedingly graceful and genteel; and his appearance drew from the numerous Spectators pity for the perilous situation in which they saw him, as well as their condemnation of the imprudencies which had placed him in it" (*The Trial* 3). Collard notes that the women in the audience were especially moved by Hobart's plight: "On being arraigned, his perilous situation excited the pity of the numerous spectators; and the display of the handkerchiefs in the gallery, sufficiently discovered the sensibility of many of the ladies" (Dralloc 204).

During his trial, Hobart/Griffin garnered public sympathy by portraying himself as the gentlemanly victim of a brutal beating and newspaper "calumnies" (*The Trial* 15) who had chivalrously attempted to protect the woman he loved. His speech in his own defense, recorded in shorthand by "a gentleman" (*The Trial* 2) and reproduced in *The Trial of Henry Griffin, Alias George Hubbard, (The Pretended Duke of Ormond)* (1792) and *Authentic Memoirs of the Life and Adventures of James Molesworth Hobart* (1793), was a tour de force that appears to have mesmerized both the courtroom audience and the jury. According to the trial's transcriptionist, the prisoner "delivered, with the most fascinating and expressive action, [his] address; in the course of which he displayed considerable oratorical abilities" (*The Trial* 14). Hobart praised the judge's "impartiality and justice" and the jury's "good sense and integrity," reminded them to disregard the press reports libeling him, protested against his "illegally prolonged imprisonment," and emphasized his impetuous knight-errantry: "You will not deem the act of firing to be an act of premeditated murder—the act of a bad heart—but rather the act of a moment, produced by the critical and peculiar situation in which I then stood—an act of intemperance—and that intemperance, My

Lord, under the imprest [*sic*] idea of sheltering the most amiable of the female sex; who had claimed from me protection; whom I had vowed to protect with my life—whose lovely image was nearest to my heart" (*The Trial* 15). Although Hobart presents his narrative as an "impartial statement of the facts," it reads like a miniscule Gothic romance and features a tyrannical father, "an envious and an enraged [romantic] rival," an abduction, savage beatings and kickings inflicted on him by his persecutors, and "an impenetrable dungeon" (16, 18). He insisted that if he had not fired his pistol he would have been guilty of cowardice: "To see men, without authority, violently enter my apartment, to wrest from me by force, her, without whom my existence was not worth preserving, and not to have repelled such meddling, unjustifiable intruders, would not have been acting the part of a man" (16–17).

In *The Life and Extraordinary Adventures of James Molesworth Hobart*, Hobart's speech is more than double the length of the address printed in *The Trial of Henry Griffin*, and Collard's appraisal of the defendant's oratorical skill is slightly less enthusiastic than the trial transcriptionist's assessment. He observes that "When [Hobart] began the...speech, he seemed to be a little embarrassed, but he soon recovered himself, and spoke in a masterly manner, displaying occasionally great force, action, energy and eloquence" (Dralloc 221). In Collard's version of Hobart's address, Hobart portrays Miss Spooner's father as a brute "who in a paroxysm of passion, aided by intoxication, would...have used her extremely ill," notes that "Wallis was not a peace-officer of any description," points out that the arresting constable acted outside of his jurisdiction, and protests against his assailants' "most daring invasion of the liberty of the subject" (215–217). He offers the jury two possible justifications for the shooting: "the impulse of self-preservation, or...temporary delirium" (216). Responding to the charge that he "maliciously shot at John Wallis," Hobart argues that "malicious" can be defined as either "a cool, deliberate, and premeditated determination to do an essential injury" or "being ill-disposed to another," and argues that neither definition applies to his case. He identifies the contradictions in the testimonies of Wallis the elder and the younger, details the nearly fatal beatings he suffered after his apprehension, indignantly denies newspaper reports that he has "assumed various titles," pathetically declares that "[t]hese are the fair and ingenuous sentiments of a mind enfeebled by the miseries of confinement, and almost wholly depressed by reflecting on its melancholy situation" (220), and asks for the jury's understanding. In his biography of Hobart, Collard seems to have transformed the relatively straightforward defense recorded in the trial transcript into a grandiloquent rhetorical performance befitting the sham Duke of Ormond.

Following Hobart's oration, the judge summed up the evidence and reminded the jury "[t]hat if an officer be killed in endeavouring to enter an apartment to secure an offender, it cannot be deemed murder, except the officer shall have acquainted the offender by what authority, and for what offence, he is about to secure him" (18–19). The jury quickly found Hobart not guilty; it is unclear whether they were more influenced by the defendant's oratory or the judge's instructions. Collard priggishly reports that "A very indecent applause now succeeded this verdict, and it was some minutes before order was restored in court" (Dralloc 221). Hobart's triumph was, however, short-lived: Hammond, the Newmarket banker, came forward to lodge "a detainer again the prisoner, for defrauding him in the name of the Duke of Ormond" (*Authentic Memoirs* 21), and Hobart was transferred to the jail at Bury St. Edmunds. From Bury St. Edmunds he was taken to Newgate prison in London to answer the allegation that under the alias Lord Massey he had used a forged check to defraud the jewelers Willerton and Green. Collard writes that when Hobart was informed of this new charge, his confidence failed him: "he appeared much agitated, and exclaimed, 'Good God! what can this mean? Mr. Green would not swear to me in Birmingham.' From this moment he seems to have been convinced that his fate was inevitable" (Dralloc 223).

While Hobart was able to portray himself as a chivalrous lover and genteel victim of abuse in his trial for shooting Mr. Wallis, his trial for the comparatively unglamorous crime of forgery did not provide him with the opportunity to deploy a Gothic-sentimental narrative that might have elicited sympathy and support. In his speech at the Old Bailey, he was reduced to casting doubt on the testimony of eyewitnesses and arguing that physical appearance was an unreliable marker of identity: "I need not tell you what a wonderful coincidence in manner, size, appearance and voice, there may be between two persons without the smallest connexion, as to the same identical person. We know a man of the brightest genius is likely to err as to identity, and more particularly where the view has been transient, as appears in the present instance" (Dralloc 239).[12] Hobart asked the jury to consider the unlikely possibility that the witnesses had observed his double, a criminal imposter who remained at large. His genteel persona had served him well during the shooting trial, but in the forgery trial it may have undermined his argument by reminding jurors of the newspaper accounts of the dapper Lord Massey. Rather than facial or shapeshifting, his chameleonism was behavioral, sartorial, and pseudonymous, and his recognizability proved fatal. The jury was not persuaded by his coincidence defense and "after a short deliberation returned their verdict[:] GUILTY" (Dralloc 244). Definitively identified as the sham Lord Massey, the man indicted as "*Henry Griffin, otherwise George Hubbard, otherwise Lord Massey*" (Dralloc 225) was sentenced to death by hanging. Hobart appealed for clemency to the Secretary of State, but, not surprisingly, his petition was denied. During the late eighteenth century, forgers were never pardoned, and he had been convicted not only of swindling tradesmen, but also of defrauding the Earl of Tankerville by signing the Earl's name on a bill of exchange.[13]

The pamphlet *Authentic Memoirs of the Life and Adventures of James Molesworth Hobart* contains an anecdote regarding Hobart's final days that Collard omits in his 1794 biography:

> On hearing the late order of the court, for mourning, on the death of the king of France, [Hobart] sent for a taylor who lives opposite to Newgate, to measure him for a suit of mourning. The taylor, thinking his customer's *tricks* at an end, immediately made the cloaths, and carried them to the cells, where Hobart very deliberately put them on, declaring he was never better fitted, and paid many compliments on the neatness of the cut, &c. The taylor perceiving no overtures of payment, reminded his employer of his charge. Hobart turning round, replied, "true, Mr. Taylor, your charge is moderate, and I will put you in a way of being paid. I know (*continued the malefactor*) that you let out your house at sixpence a head at every hanging-bout, now as I am shortly to be hanged, and you know Mr. Taylor, I am no common rascal, I would advise you to raise your price to half-a-crown.—If that wont do, why you may have your cloaths again, but I am determined first to be hanged in them." (*Authentic Memoirs* 27)

Hobart's obsession with apparel and fashion, his manipulative charm, his financial shrewdness, and his self-conscious theatricality were all on display in his negotiations with the tailor. As Frederick Burwick points out, in the eighteenth century "public executions were . . . theatrical events" (*Playing to the Crowd* 143), and as a celebrity criminal Hobart wanted to be well-dressed for his final performance. He could no longer impersonate aristocrats, but he could play the role of an uncommon rascal with panache. Apparently he did not disappoint the onlookers. *Authentic Memoirs* reports that "[t]here have been few instances where eight men reduced to the same dreadful predicament have exhibited so genteel an appearance. The extraordinary character of Hobart attracted an unusual concurrence of spectators. Dressed in a fashionable suit of mourning, covered with a blue surtout, he approached the awful scene of death with firmness and composure; nor did that accommodating address, which distinguished him through life, forsake him even in the hands of the executioner, whom he assisted in loosening his shirt-collar and adjusting the rope" (*Authentic Memoirs* 26). In *The Life and Extraordinary Adventures*, Collard adds that when the hairdresser arrived to prepare Hobart's hair for the execution, his razors were confiscated by the guards. Somewhat pettishly, Hobart told the man that since he could not be shaved, his hair would "not be dressed." "A few seconds before the platform dropped, [Hobart] fixed his regard on a gentleman who accompanied the sheriff, as if he wished to say something," and the brief conversation that followed "seemed to afford him much comfort" (Dralloc 246). One wonders whether this last-second appeal for consolation was a manifestation of inner turmoil, a delaying tactic, or part of Hobart's valedictory performance. If, as Collard asserts, Hobart was born "about the latter end of the year 1765" (Dralloc 1), he would have been 27 when he was executed; other accounts put his age at 25 or 26.[14]

Along with the tailor anecdote, *Authentic Memoirs* reproduces "a specimen of [Hobart's] poetic talents," a "Soliloquy, said to have been found in his Cell after his Execution" (*Authentic Memoirs* 28), which Collard does not include in his biography. Written in heroic couplets, the poem portrays Hobart, the ostensible soliloquist, as a poet of sensibility who mourns his tragic destiny: "Shall he ignobly in a rope expire / Whose hand can wake to extacy the lyre? / Shall he be branded with the mob's harsh curse, / Who oft hath pour'd the sweetly vary'd verse? / Whose manly Muse, indignant of controul [*sic*], / Can wake such notes as harrow up the soul?" (1–6). Although Hobart, or the writer who ventriloquizes him, alludes to his "keen Remorse" (25), he only admits to "erring once amidst the storms of strife" (11). Borrowing a line from the Ghost of Hamlet's father, he implores "Justice" (13) not to condemn him "[w]ith all [his] imperfections on [his] head" (15; *Hamlet* I.v.79). In lieu of execution, he asks to be transported "to earth's extremest verge" (17), presumably Australia, where he can create "A little useful seminary… / And spread the flame of Reformation" to "the offspring of ill-fated hinds [rustics]" (33–35). Despairing of pardon, however, the soliloquist ends his rhapsody with a prayer for God's mercy. Whether or not Hobart wrote this poem, its inclusion in *Authentic Memoirs* is clearly designed to evoke pity, to portray the convicted forger as a sensitive and gifted poet doomed, like Thomas Chatterton, to a tragic early death. The soliloquy could also be read as yet another imposture by an arch-chameleon desperate to have his sentence commuted. It was reprinted in *The New and Complete Newgate Calendar* (1795) (Jackson 126–127) and in a volume published in America, *Voices from Prison: A Selection of Poetry Written within the Cell, by Various Prisoners* (1849). In *Voices from Prison*, the poem was attributed to H. Griffin and entitled "Prisoner's Lament" (Spear 205).[15]

After Hobart's arrest at Vauxhall, biographical sketches of the pretended Duke of Ormond appeared in numerous British and American newspapers. These articles revealed that the imposter was not a tailor or tailor's son from Hagley; rather, he was the well-educated son of his Majesty's Judge Advocate for Virginia and had served as a loyalist officer during the American Revolution. The following story appeared in the New York *Daily Advertiser* and, with some variations, in numerous other periodicals on both sides of the Atlantic:

> DUKE OF ORMOND
>
> AS many erroneous conjectures have appeared in the public prints respecting the real name and family of the unfortunate young man now confined in the prison at Birmingham in the name of Henry Griffin, charged with defrauding the banker at Newmarket in the name of the Duke of Ormond, we are now enabled to lay before our Readers the following particulars, which may be depended upon as authentic.
>
> His real name is James Molesworth Hubard, son of James Hubard, Esq. late his Majesty's Judge Advocate to the province of Virginia, and was born in North-America.
>
> The virtues of the father were a sufficient recommendation to Lord Dunmore, who immediately took the son under his protection, and placed him in the rank of an officer in one of the regiments of Loyalists, in which he was distinguished soon for his personal and mental accomplishments, having added to a genteel and handsome person a very liberal education.
>
> In the above regiment he was also distinguished for his personal courage, and was looked upon as a very promising officer. With this character, he marched with the corps into winter quarters at New-York, where dissipations and extravagance were at their height. Naturally of a gay disposition, caressed by his superior officers, and his vanity flattered by the particular attention of the first and finest women in the place, it is not to be wondered at that he launched inconsiderately into the follies and vices of the town. His income not being equal to his

extravagant way of living, he absconded with some money belonging to the army. He was then forced to sell his commission.

When he came to [England], the money he obtained by the sale of his commission was soon expended, and having run considerably in debt, he was arrested and thrown into the king's bench prison, from which he was liberated by a certain lady of high rank.

The above connection lasted but a short time; he was again distressed and again set his invention to work, to raise his finances: To this end, he wrote to Lord Howard, under the feigned signature of an officer, who was well known to his lordship, and who at that time stood in need of his pecuniary aid; by which means he obtained a sum of money; he was indicted for this offence, but, by an oversight in the solicitor for the prosecution, he was acquitted. After this, he practised the same fraud on various gentlemen, till at length he was detected in writing the name of an officer in the Coldstream regiment, to the Duke of York, and obtaining from his royal highness twelve guineas; for this offence he was tried and convicted; but at the instance of the duke his sentence was a very mild one.

After this, the first account we have of him is from Ireland, where he was tried by the name of Redman, for shop-lifting, and was sentenced to be transported for seven years, but escaped from the prison, by lowering himself from the top by ropes, in which it is reported, he was assisted by the keeper's daughter.

He then went to France, where he again got connected with a woman of some rank, from whom he obtained upwards of 1500l. and here kept his carriage, and was afterwards concerned with a famous English gambler, who has found it convenient to reside in that country for some time back. They kept a Faro Bank, but quarrelling about the profits, separated. He again came to England, and, by a detainer lodged against him at Birmingham, appears to be the person, who, under the borrowed title of Lord Massey, defrauded Messrs. Willerton and Green, of Jewels and trinkets to the amount of 700l. After this, he passed upon a watchmaker in Holborn, as the duke of Manchester, and ordered two watches to be sent to his lodgings in Charles-street, St. James's Square; but, as the watchmaker was informed that his Grace was abroad, instead of watches, he sent him two officers from Bow street. Hubard being of that time near his own lodgings, and seeing the officers, whom he well knew, decamped.

The story of the Duke of Ormond is fresh in the minds of the public; we need not therefore repeat it.

After this, he went to York races, where he met Shaw, who is admitted an evidence against the mail robbers [*sic*], and was by him advised to reform his life, as he had got off so well from Newmarket. He assured Shaw he would, but that there was a girl at Leicester, whom he tenderly

> loved, and that he would obtain her at any rate. The sequel is well known; he was taken in running away with her.
>
> He has for some time kept a servant in livery, has a horse at this time for which he has been offered a hundred and fifty guineas, and lives in the prison in the most sumptuous stile. The elegance of his address gained him admission to the tables of the first gentlemen in the counties through which he has travelled; and he boasts of having evaded the search made after him; at the same time, that he walked publicly about London, disguised only by wearing spectacles, a cocked hat, and cockade.
>
> At Leicester, in the house from whence he took the daughter of the landlord, he gave several public entertainments, at which the most respectable persons of the neighbourhood were present.
>
> Were his whole history laid before the public, it would, perhaps, exhibit a combination of the most extraordinary incidents that ever concentred in any one man of his age, which apparently is not more than five or six and twenty. He has a mother, two sisters, and a brother, now living at Williamsburgh [*sic*], in Virginia, with whom he has never corresponded since he lost the favour of Lords Cornwallis and Dunmore. His mother is a native of America; her maiden name was Morton; she retains very large possessions in the province of Virginia. (February 21, 1792)

As a loyalist officer serving during the American Revolution, Hobart participated directly in the conflict that, in Wahrman's view, catalyzed the shift in Britain from the *ancien régime* of identity to the modern regime of selfhood. Corrupted during his military service by the "dissipations and extravagance" of New York, exiled from his native country, and alienated from his American family, he became a deracinated, cosmopolitan chameleon. Biographical sketches published in newspapers and pamphlets shed light on Hobart's ability to impersonate aristocrats: the Judge Advocate's son was "genteel and handsome," had received "a very liberal education," had been sponsored by "Lords Cornwallis and Dunmore," and had consorted with "his superior officers" in New York. After the war, he "figured in the most polite circles in London, Paris, Tours, Dijon, Bath, Bristol, Brighton, Buxton, Margate, &c. &c." (*The Trial* 20) and thus had numerous opportunities to study and imitate patrician behavior, speech, and dress. In France, he "was introduced to the acquaintance of people of the first rank," "fluttered away in all the elegant gaiety and bustle of high life; was presented to the Marquis de la Fayette—received successive invitations—and participated in daily public, or private entertainments" (*Authentic Memoirs* 4). He attracted and seduced women from all social ranks but may have treated at least one woman honorably. According to *Authentic Memoirs*, while in Bath "he made so deep an impression on the heart of a young lady of family, possessed of a considerable fortune in her own disposal, that though she was well acquainted with his whole history, not excepting even his most dishonourable transactions, she would have willingly have intrusted him with her person and property. This respectable establishment, it seems, he declin'd, from motives which little accorded with his future conduct; for he frequently declared that he could not be guilty of so vile a piece of injustice to one who had heaped so many favours on him, and towards whom his heart acknowledged no affection but gratitude" (7).

A postscript to the shooting trial transcript concludes that Hobart's "faults, doubtless, are many; yet, were his whole history known, perhaps he might be entitled to some commiseration" (*The Trial* 19). Although contemporaneous commentators recognized that Hobart was a swindler and forger, they tended to depict him sympathetically, as an "unfortunate young man" whose reckless elopement with Miss Spooner and failure to disguise his features and physique led to his conviction and execution. They also portrayed him, paradoxically, as a unique chameleon, an "extraordinary character" (rather than extraordinary characters) blessed with ingenuity, "personal courage," charisma, and acting skill. He was both a serial imposter and an anomalous original whose criminal exploits inspired "Authentic" memoirs. Unlike Price, aka the Social Monster, he was not dehumanized. Late-eighteenth-century chroniclers of his exploits regarded him with amazement rather than moral indignation and did not consider him a threat to society or as symptomatic of an alarming upsurge in criminal imposture. His life story was simultaneously a cautionary tale about the dangers of chameleonic hubris and a celebration of theatrical talent and daring. Through his impersonations of aristocrats and performances during his trials, in prison, and on the scaffold, Hobart created a flamboyant persona that captivated the imaginations and aroused the pity of many of his contemporaries.

The Life and Extraordinary Adventures of James Molesworth Hobart

The Life and Extraordinary Adventures of James Molesworth Hobart portrays its subject as a misguided youth who, with proper counseling, could have been saved from ruin. It is a multifaceted work that can be read as a cautionary tale, a celebration of chameleonic ingenuity, a social satire, a poorly constructed Jacobin novel, or a fantasy of empowerment in which a destitute American adventurer impersonates English aristocrats to enrich himself, and, when put on trial for shooting a constable's son, secures acquittal by playing the part of a chivalrous gentleman determined to protect the woman he loves. The author of *The Life and Extraordinary Adventures* was a hatter, tailor, logician, and member of a Birmingham social club "nicknamed 'the Twelve Apostles' and 'the Jacobin Club'" (Dent 212).[16] As a politically liberal member of the middle-class Birmingham intelligentsia, John Collard's identity, like Hobart's, appears to have been fluid and self-fashioned, circumscribed neither by class nor by occupation. He published under a literary alias, Dralloc, his surname spelled backward. After writing two lives of Hobart, *The Life and Extraordinary Adventures of James Molesworth Hobart* and a "Sketch…in a provincial paper" that "Some needy printer" (Dralloc iv) incorporated in *Authentic Memoirs of the Life and Adventures of James Molesworth Hobart*, Collard penned a series of influential volumes that established him as England's preeminent logician: *An Epitome of Logic* (1795), *The Essentials of Logic: Being a Second Edition of Dralloc's Epitome Improved* (1796), and *A Praxis of Logic: For the Use of Schools* (1799).[17]

In the preface of *The Life and Extraordinary Adventures*, Collard argues that the biography has pedagogical value: "on perusing the work, it will be found, that the inevitable evils which follow the gratification of illicit pleasures, are particularly noticed; great care taken to point out the dangerous tendency of the smallest relaxation in moral discipline; and, above all, in those passages where vice seems to have crept forward imperceptibly, an occasional hint is given to those who superintend youth, by which its dreadful consequences may be frequently averted" (iii). Collard's case study of moral and social maladjustment emphasizes the pernicious influence of Hobart's evil counselors, the cynical Thormax, who espouses hypocrisy, Doctor Torquid, "an original in iniquity" (53) who teaches Hobart that dissimulation is necessary for financial success, and the villainous Caddin, a former attorney who informs the young man "of the inexhaustible resources within the reach of men of genius, in spite of the flimsy barriers of the law" (137).

While Collard admits that *The Life and Extraordinary Adventures* "possesses many…advantages" that are "similar" to those found in novels, he insists that it "is not a novel, where the hero, after scenes of intrigue and debauchery, as though to reward him for his crimes, receives the fair hand of his mistress, but a detail of ordinary facts, communicated by Hobart himself, frequently interrupted by short observations" (iii–iv). But although the biography ends with a hanging rather than a wedding, it is much more than a factual "detail of ordinary facts" interspersed with "short observations." It is a heterogeneous book that contains Collard's moral reflections on his subject's behavior, a philosophical debate between two of Hobart's childhood mentors, the life story of the iniquitous Doctor Torquid, salacious and occasionally grotesque accounts of the protagonist's many amorous escapades, the "affecting tale" (153) of young Nicholas Eyrs, Hobart's prison letters, and transcripts from his trials. The picaresque "short sketch of the early part of the life of Doctor Torquid" (64), which runs for 57 pages, is a digression that pads the volume. As Maximillian E. Novak points out, "some criminal lives are deliberate fictions and others approach fictions because of an inadequate sense of historical truth on the part of the writer" (41). Although Collard claims that his work presents the "facts" that Hobart "communicated" to him, it is unlikely that even an extremely garrulous prisoner would recount such a long, self-incriminating, and circumstantial narrative. I am, however, less concerned with the volume's factual accuracy than with its contribution to the late-eighteenth-century debate on imposture. In contrast to previous accounts of the fake Duke of Ormond, Collard's biography dwells on his subject's libertinism and petty crimes, and a contemporary reviewer was repulsed by the "narrative of licentious amours, and of the ingenious contrivance of knavery, to levy contributions upon simple good nature, and unsuspecting honesty" (*The Analytical Review* 276). The rakish, calculating chameleon presented in *The Life and Extraordinary Adventures* was more objectionable than the gallant, imprudent figure featured in the newspapers. Yet Collard's portrait of Hobart is profoundly ambivalent; interspersed with the often sordid instances of libertinism and skullduggery are episodes in which Hobart displays bravery and resourcefulness (his escape from a Dublin prison) or compassion (his sympathetic response to Eyrs's tragic plight). Written by a middle-class member of a reformist social club, the biography is a semi-factual, quasi-novelistic account of an imposter's formation and an exploration of the advantages and disadvantages of a labile identity.[18]

Collard probably met the subject of his biography when Hobart was incarcerated in the Birmingham jail, awaiting trial for shooting John Wallis the younger. He does not explore the possible link between Hobart's chameleonism and his exile from his native country or the young man's relationship with his father, the Judge

Advocate of Virginia, and other family members. Instead, he contends that Hobart's evolution into a criminal chameleon stemmed from his lasciviousness, lack of self-discipline, and the immoral influence of his mentors. In his *Epitome of Logic*, Collard praises "the admirable theory of Mr. Locke" (Dralloc viii) promulgated in *An Essay Concerning Human Understanding* (1690), and *The Life and Extraordinary Adventures* is informed by Locke's notion that to achieve personhood one must be bound by a moral code. Locke stipulates that "person…is a forensic term, appropriating actions and their merit; and so belongs only to intelligent agents, capable of a law, and happiness, and misery. This personality extends itself beyond present existence to what is past, only by consciousness,—whereby it becomes concerned and accountable; owns and imputes to itself past actions, just upon the same ground and for the same reason as it does the present" (1.467). As Charles Taylor explains, "Locke's person is the moral agent who takes responsibility for his acts in the light of future retribution" (173). According to Collard, Hobart is "a licentious young man, restrained by no one moral principle" (Dralloc iii). Inasmuch as he flouts the law, refuses to accept responsibility for his actions, and is generally undeterred by the threat of legal retribution, Hobart is not a "moral agent" and hence never establishes a stable and unitary personal identity.

In *The Life and Extraordinary Adventures*, Hobart begins his life of crime when he is "about eight years of age" (3), pilfering gold coins from his great-aunt, Mrs. Thormax, to buy a pet squirrel from "a negro, belonging to a neighbouring store" and "for future emergencies" (4). Instead of punishing her grand-nephew, Mrs. Thormax has the slave flogged. Afterwards, Hobart listens while his Presbyterian Scottish tutor and his great-uncle Thormax debate the social consequences of "hypocrisy and dissimulation" (7). The moralistic tutor insists that integrity and mutual confidence are "necessary to the unity and good being of society" (6). Quoting from Cicero, he declares that "[h]e who consults his own indulgence, without regarding the property of his neighbour, deserves to be extirpated from society" (7). In his rebuttal, Thormax claims that "Dissimulation is the most desirable of all qualifications; for though…every one disown[s] it, it is blended with almost every transaction of life; and the tyranny of fashion has rendered it absolutely necessary. The beggar uses it to enforce his supplication; the debtor to keep himself from prison; the bailiff to execute his writ; the creditor to obtain his money; the tradesman to sell his goods; it is the crutches on which the clergy are supported; and it comprises the lawyer's trade; it is the greatest comfort the doctor can bestow; the common cant of the nobility; the minister's merchandise; and the monarch's food" (7–8). He argues that without inauthenticity and imposture, society would not be able to function and that people refrain from stealing not because they respect property rights but because they fear punishment. Hobart "seem[s] much inclined to favour the doctrine of Thormax" (8), who has the last word in the debate, and delights in tormenting his tutor. He applies an irritant to the underside of the Scotsman's wig, which compels his victim "to dance and caper about the room, like a distracted maniac," and on another occasion drops "oil of vitriol" on the tutor's spectacles, which inflicts "acute pain" (10–11). From Thormax the boy learns to despise moral principles and authority figures and to embrace hypocrisy and dissimulation.

Many of Hobart's transgressions result from his inability to restrain his amorous impulses. While still a teenager, he attempts to seduce a woman who is married to a much older man. He mistakenly believes that she has become another man's mistress and vows to seek vengeance on her lover. In a violent scene that prefigures Hobart's rash behavior during his elopement with Miss Spooner, he strikes his presumed rival with "the butt end of his whip" (20) until his opponent slashes him across his forehead with a sword. He later deflowers Miss Green, the married woman's younger sister, who has a miscarriage and dies. Hobart weeps over Miss Green's final letter to him, in which she begs him not to corrupt her older sister, and initially resolves to respect her wishes. But "after a short struggle, passion prevail[s]; and . . . throwing aside all restraint, he determine[s] to leave no means untried to gratify his wishes" (44). His father intervenes, however, and forces his wayward son to abandon his "machinations" (45) and enlist in a loyalist regiment fighting in the Revolutionary War. Although Collard concedes that Hobart's conduct toward Miss Green "exhibits its deformity strikingly," he attempts to extenuate the youth's behavior. He asks the "fair reader" to "suspend for a moment [her] indignation" and recognize "that a want of sufficient power to persevere in our resolutions, is a crime chargeable to the greatest part of mankind" (44). Hobart may be a scoundrel, but he is neither a monster nor irredeemably evil. Thus the lessons that "those who superintend youth" glean from Collard's biography are applicable to "the greatest part of mankind."

After demonstrating bravery in battle and in a duel "with a British officer," Hobart goes "into winter quarters in New York, which [is] . . . the center of gaiety and dissipation" (45). Collard speculates that this is "the critical period which gave a bias to his mind; and, in a great measure, influenced his future conduct." According to him, if an observant preceptor had "artfully divert[ed]" Hobart's mind from making bad choices, the youth might have learned to resist "the allurements of vice" (46). Unfortunately, Hobart squanders his money gambling, becomes infatuated with "a little comic actress" (47), and falls under the influence of the cynical Dr. Torquid, "a professor of physic from England" (50), who advises him to wager systematically. In Torquid's view, pickpockets, skillful gamblers, deceitful salesmen, obfuscating clergymen, dishonest lawyers, and quacks are all robbers, but society only prosecutes the pickpockets. He divides "tradesmen and gamesters" into two classes—honorable "dupes" and "artful" thieves (52)—and tells Hobart that dupes never prosper. Every successful transaction, Torquid continues, has a "double motive": one "feigned" and the other "true." For example, in an advertisement for "a sovereign solvent," the feigned motive is to provide a beneficial product that dissolves bladder stones, but the true motive is to enrich the seller by tricking desperate and suffering customers into "part[ing] with their money freely...in direct contradiction to science, and to common sense." Hobart "imbibe[s] [Torquid's] doctrines...with the utmost rapture" and is "highly gratified also to observe, how compleatly [*sic*] this original could conceal his real character, beneath an impenetrable veil of obscurity" (56). Whereas dupes are transparent, those who exploit them are opaque.

Following Torquid's advice, Hobart romances Mrs. Parsons, a wealthy married woman more than twice his age, and her largesse enables him to purchase the affections of the comic actress. He soon tires, however, of the actress and seduces his patroness's young niece. After Mrs. Parsons discovers Hobart's double infidelity, she gets excessively drunk, and when he arrives at her house, she seizes him with a "masculine grasp," falls on top of him, claws his face, blacks both his eyes, screams "murder!" (61), and vomits on him. She later accuses him of rape. Mortified, Hobart withdraws from society to recover from his injuries and receive treatment for "a certain malady" (63), presumably venereal disease. While he is convalescing, Dr. Torquid regales him "with a short sketch of the early part of the doctor's life" and introduces Hobart to the doctrine of "useful dissimulation": "Some men erroneously affirm, that we cannot appear to be what we are not; it is however certain, there is nothing wanting to succeed, but to join, to the talent of a comedian [i.e., actor], system and proper discrimination" (68–69). Rather than confirming Torquid's doctrine, his "sketch" casts doubt on its validity. He recounts a series of dissimulations that end in disaster rather than success. Pretending to be a devout Christian, he obtains employment with a Methodist preacher but abandons his position after impregnating the preacher's daughter. While working as a waiter in London, he discovers "that dissimulation pervade[s] all ranks of men, and that flattery [is] a most important ingredient" (78). He becomes the servant of a genteel young wastrel who refuses to repay the money he borrows from Torquid. Disillusioned, Torquid "bid[s] adieu to sincerity in public" (85) and steals 40 guineas from his master to compensate himself for his loss. He is eventually imprisoned for this offense, forced to enlist as a soldier, deserts, and is hired by a German named Dr. Folsh to dispense medicines. Dr. Folsh turns out to be a charlatan who performs "cures" on a stage, accompanied by a tumbler and merry-andrew (clown): "this great man owed the eminence of his reputation more to his laced coat, bag wig, and a few common stage tricks...than to any physical knowledge he possessed" (111). From this quack, Torquid learns that "buffoonery" and medicine are "species of the same art, which, in different shapes, might be discovered in a variety of the manœuvres of mankind" (112). Torquid's medical apprenticeship is interrupted, however, when he is arrested for desertion, given ten lashes, and reinstated in the army. After his military service ends, he becomes an old gentleman's servant, travels "with a celebrated empiric" (120) (a physician who relies on experience rather than training), and practices medicine in England until an unspecified "decision in the Court of Exchequer" (121) forces him to flee to America to avoid imprisonment.

Torquid imparts the following maxims to his disciple: "a genteel appearance [is] a better recommendation than intrinsic merit," men of the highest rank possess "the greatest share of dissimulation," "riches [are] sure to command universal respect," "poverty [is] every where abominated," and "all the actions of men [are] influenced by [self-]interest" (118–120). According to him, "what [is] considered honorable in one rank of men, in another class [is] esteemed the direct opposite": "If two puppies of noble birth absorbed in debauchery at a brothel, were to blow out each others brains with a pair of pistols, their juvenile imprudence might be tenderly lamented, but their honor and courage would be treated with respect. But if two Irish hay-makers, indulging in the same laudable amusement, were to decide a similar dispute with their pocket-knives, in a cellar in St. Giles's, they would be termed two vile, blood-thirsty murderers" (119). Society is superficial, duplicitous, mercenary, and snobbish. It condemns pickpockets but condones robberies by gamblers, physicians, lawyers, and merchants. Anyone who possesses "the talent of a comedian," applies "system and proper discrimination," and refrains from "infracting the laws of society" (104) will succeed in the universal masquerade.

Hobart fails, however, to heed Torquid's warning against breaking society's laws. He continues to live beyond his means and embezzles money from his regiment to pay his debts. When the theft is discovered, Hobart is forced to resign his commission, and he leaves for England "about the end of the year 1781" (123). His father dies in 1782, and as an American loyalist Hobart receives compensation from the British government for his lost possessions in Virginia. The young spendthrift has numerous "*amorous adventures*" (121) in England and France, gambles away most of his money, and meets his third evil counselor, a sharper named Caddin:

> Caddin...had, for many years, practised as an attorney in Cheshire, but he possessed such a propensity for depredation, that, though his profession afforded him great opportunity, his genius could not be confined within the narrow limits of professional robbery; in order, therefore, to give ample scope to his faculties, he took up his residence principally in London. This original in iniquity attracted Hobart's notice, and they soon formed a particular intimacy. By him he was informed of the inexhaustible resources within the reach of men of genius, in spite of the flimsy barriers of the law, and instructed in the art of gaming; but Hobart was nowise calculated for a sportsman, and was always a dupe to the knowing-ones. (137)

Hobart and Caddin's partnership resembles Tippy and Fancourt's inconstant alliance in Cowley's *The Town before You*. Under the former attorney's tutelage, Hobart begins his career as an imposter. During their trip to the York races, he "use[s] a travelling name" and, with the help of two servants, poses "as a man of fortune, amongst the first class" (137). While visiting Scarborough, he "assume[s] the character of a person of high rank" and sees the acclaimed comic actress Dorothy Jordan perform the role of Priscilla Tomboy in the operatic farce *The Romp* (1778 premiere). He is "so charmed with the wanton tricks of the little Romp, that he resolve[s] to become a candidate for her favor." Conflating Jordan with the West Indian hoyden she plays, the fake aristocrat imagines that he has "a fair prospect of being blessed with the favors of Priscilla Tomboy" (138) but has to abandon their theatrical fantasy romance when he runs out of cash. He rejoins Caddin, who unveils a scheme in which he draws up bogus writs of execution in the names of imaginary clients to extort money from wealthy misers. The two rogues engage in "a succession of depredations and extravagancies at London, Buxton, Brighton, and many other principal places [that rely] principally upon Hobart's genteel address and assurance" (141). They later operate a profitable faro bank in Paris, where Hobart "assume[s] the title of a British nobleman," but the partnership breaks up when Caddin is arrested for a crime he committed "some time before" (147).[19]

Back in England, Hobart hoodwinks "many genteel females" as a fortune-teller. He continues his criminal activities in Ireland, where he is "detected in shop-lifting, committed to prison, tried, convicted in the name of Redman, and ordered for transportation" (148). At this point in the narrative, Hobart appears to have degenerated into a morally rudderless erotomaniac ready to engage in any illicit scheme that will provide him with cash or merchandise. The reader's assessment of him is, however, complicated by two chapters in which he demonstrates courage, fortitude, and compassion. During his "*miraculous*" escape from Dublin prison, which recalls the legendary exploits of Baron von Trenck, he hides five days on the prison roof, "exposed continually to the weather in a very inclement season" (149–150), and lowers himself down the wall by ropes.[20] Weakened by exposure and hunger, he manages to elude the sentinel and stagger into a sedan chair, which takes him to a friend's house. He returns to England disguised as a manual worker and on the road to Bath encounters Samuel Eyrs, who tells him that he and his family have been victimized by "one of the greatest villains that ever disgraced the law" (155). Coincidentally, the culprit turns out to be Caddin. Eyrs recounts "*an affecting tale*" (153) in which Caddin seduces and abandons Eyrs's young sister and then cheats and bankrupts their father, who is thrown in the county jail. Hobart is horrified by his former associate's cruel practices and cannot "with-hold a tear of pity" (166) when Eyrs receives a posthumous letter from his heartbroken sister. Compared to Caddin, Hobart seems like a minor transgressor, and his humane responses to the archvillain's predations and Eyrs's sufferings suggest that he is capable of moral outrage and sympathy.

But although Hobart repudiates Caddin's ruthlessness, he continues his criminal activities. His impersonations of Lord Massey and the Duke of Ormond briefly empower him and transform the obscure womanizer and small-time swindler into a legendary figure. Temporarily, his chameleonism allows him to experience the deference shown to aristocrats and perhaps fantasize that he is an aristocrat. He is, after all, behaviorally, vocally, and sartorially indistinguishable from them. His impostures also facilitate the swindles that provide him with some of the cash and merchandise he needs to finance his dissolute lifestyle. As a criminal defendant, he inspires widespread public sympathy and fascination and the female adulation he seems to have always craved. During his stay in the Birmingham jail, he is treated like a celebrity: "The concourse of people who went to the prison to see this extraordinary man was astonishing; it was at last ordered that none should be admitted but those who produced ticke[t]s from the peace-officers; after which, during his stay at Birmingham, the constables' levees were nearly as numerous as those at St. James's... He generally appeared very chearful, conversed with foreigners in French, and was very communicative" (Dralloc 196–197). His transfer to Warwick prison inspires "a Lady of Birmingham" to compose and publish "A SQUINT at ELYSIUM; or, DUKE and NO DUKE: a Poem, occasioned by the Commitment of Henry Griffin to Warwick," which he reads with pleasure (Langford 193; *Authentic Memoirs* 15). While awaiting trial, "he ha[s] several sums of money sent him from different quarters; and though fettered and immured so effectually, he still [is] so happy as to be blessed with the soft solaces of the fair" (Dralloc 204). Collard marvels at the well-dressed prisoner's ability to borrow money from tradesmen and even his jailor during his incarceration: "Perhaps there is not a more striking instance of the beguiling influence of genteel demeanour and elegance of dress, than what occurred during Hobart's confinement at Warwick; for though every one knew he stood charged with such three heavy offences, that it was morally impossible he should be acquitted of them all, yet he found means to contract debts with different tradesmen to the amount of more than eighty pounds, while a prisoner, of which he never paid a shilling, and what is not a little singular, the gaoler himself was amongst the number of his principal creditors" (Dralloc 221–222). Hobart appears to enjoy his courtroom triumph at Warwick and revel in his notoriety as the pretended Duke of Ormond. In his subsequent trial, however, he is sentenced to death for forging a money order signed Charles, Earl of Tankerville, and "*uttering it to be true*" (225, italics in original). On the day before his hanging, Hobart stabs himself with a penknife and is suspected of taking poison but fails to end his life. Whereas Price's biographer sneers at the "cowardice" of the Social Monster's self-destruction, Collard's brief description of Hobart's suicide attempt is nonjudgmental.

William Godwin's novel *Things as They Are; or, The Adventures of Caleb Williams* (1794), published in the same year as *The Life and Extraordinary Adventures of James Molesworth Hobart*, also explores the gradual development of an impressionable young man's pliable and socially constructed identity.[21] The benevolent Mr. Collins's evaluation of Caleb could be applied to Hobart: "I consider you a machine; you are not constituted, I am afraid, to be greatly useful to your fellow men: but you did not make yourself; you are just what circumstances irresistibly compelled you to be" (416). Circumstances induce both Hobart and Caleb to engage in a series of impostures: whereas Hobart poses as aristocrats, military officers, and "a decent traveling mechanic [manual laborer]" (153) to commit frauds and evade capture, Caleb disguises himself as an Irish beggar, "the son of a reputable farmer of the lower class" (350), a Jew, and a "twisted and deformed" (366) recluse to escape from his relentless persecutor, Mr. Falkland. The "want of cash" (138) impels the spendthrift Hobart; the determination to free himself from Falkland's tyranny motivates Caleb. Caleb, like Hobart, becomes the protagonist of a criminal biography, a "halfpenny legend" (374) titled "*the* Most Wonderful and Surprising History and Miraculous Adventures of Caleb Williams" (368). Moreover, both Caleb and Hobart demonstrate endurance, determination, and resourcefulness in their escapes from prison. But unlike Hobart, Caleb ultimately rejects chameleonism. He declares that he "was seized with so unconquerable an aversion to disguise, and the idea of spending [his] life in personating a fictitious character, that [he] could not...reconcile [his] mind to any thing of that nature" (391). During the climactic trial scene at the end of Godwin's novel, Caleb recounts "a plain and unadulterated tale" (431) that his antagonist Falkland praises as an "artless and manly story" (432); in contrast, Hobart's speech in his shooting trial is lawyerly and theatrical, and he maintains his stage presence even on the scaffold. While Caleb insists that he has an irreducible core self beneath his disguises, Hobart is a serial imposter, continually adapting to changing circumstances. His identity is more malleable than Caleb's because he is not constrained by morality, and his impostures are predatory rather than self-defensive. Hobart exemplifies the *ancien régime* of identity; Caleb stubbornly clings to the modern conception of selfhood.

Whereas *Caleb Williams* condemns England's laws and legal institutions, *The Life and Extraordinary Adventures* is more cautious. Collard concludes that Hobart's execution is "necessary": the forger possessed qualities "so inimical to society, that he fell a dreadful example to dissipation and licentiousness, and a necessary sacrifice to the offended law." Unfortunately, Hobart "could never be prevailed upon to entertain any just notions of the distinction of property" (247). For both Collard and Godwin, however, imposture and swindling are endemic to things as they are. In *An Enquiry Concerning*

Political Justice (1793), Godwin writes: "Two of the greatest abuses relative to the interior policy of nations, which at this time prevail in the world, will be allowed to consist in the irregular transfer of property, either first by violence, or secondly by fraud. If among the inhabitants of any country there existed no desire in one individual to possess himself of the substance of another, or no desire so vehement and restless, as to prompt him to acquire it by means inconsistent with order and justice, undoubtedly in that country guilt could hardly be known but by report" (3.22). Wealthy individuals who possess "neither brilliant talents nor sublime virtues" use "the splendour of their equipage, the magnificence of their retinue and the sumptuousness of their entertainments" to "keep their inferiors at a distance" and create the illusion of their superiority (3.23). Taught that "integrity, virtue, understanding and industry are nothing, and that opulence is every thing" (3.24), poor men engage in over-expenditure and fraud. The king is the imposter-in-chief: "monarchy is founded in imposture. It is false that kings are entitled to the eminence they obtain...To conduct this imposture with success it is necessary to bring over to its party our eyes and our ears. Accordingly kings are always exhibited with all the splendour of ornament, attendance and equipage" (3.230). As Thormax points out in *The Life and Extraordinary Adventures*, dissimulation is "the monarch's food." English society is based on imposture. When Hobart pretends to be aristocrats, he impersonates imposters.

Collard is profoundly ambivalent about Hobart. On one hand, he emphasizes the sordidness of the swindler's romantic intrigues and his lack of principles and self-discipline.[22] On the other hand, Collard presents his subject as a gallant soldier, an ingenious and resolute escape artist, a sentimental traveling companion, and a charismatic defendant and prisoner who dies with dignity. Intelligent and well-bred, Hobart could have become a model citizen. His embryonic identity is, however, malformed by immoral advice, overmastering desires, and a society that despises paupers and fawns over aristocrats. Therefore he is a victim as well as a perpetrator. Collard indicates that Thormax's, Torquid's, and Caddin's cynical teachings and the absence of a countervailing moral preceptor who might have nudged the young man's mind in the right direction at the crucial moment are important factors in Hobart's metamorphosis into a rake and criminal chameleon. But although *The Life and Extraordinary Adventures* contains moral reflections and denounces both Torquid and Caddin as "original[s] in iniquity" (53, 137), it does not dispute the evil counselors' depiction of society as a corrupt theater of hypocrisy and dissimulation. It suggests that Hobart's impostures differ from those practiced by successful salesmen, gamblers, medical empirics, and lawyers only in their audacity, theatrical flair, and technical illegality.

EPILOGUE: THE BEAUTY OF BUTTERMERE'S VILE SEDUCER

The most notorious criminal chameleon of the Romantic era was John Hatfield, who pretended to be "Alexander Augustus Hope, Member [of Parliament] for Linlithgowshire, and brother to the Earl of Hopeto[u]n" (Coleridge 1.357).[23] In 1802, while visiting the Lake District, he negotiated counterfeit bills of exchange for £20 and £30, defrauded the post office by franking letters with the name of a Member of Parliament, and bigamously married Mary Robinson, the famed "Beauty of Buttermere." An advertisement "issued for apprehending the pretended Colonel Hope, who lately married the Buttermere Beauty" claimed that Hatfield was fond of talking about "Hatfield Hall, and his estates in Derbyshire and Chester, of the antiquity of his family, which he pretends to trace to the Plantagenets; all which are shameful falsehoods, thrown out to deceive" (*The Morning Post and Gazetteer*, November 8, 1802). Among the journalists who reported on Hatfield's imposture was Samuel Taylor Coleridge, who wrote five articles about the swindler's courtship and victimization of the Beauty of Buttermere for the *Morning Post* (October–December 1802). As Russett observes, the story was also recounted in William Wordworth's *The Prelude* (1850), Thomas De Quincey's *Recollections of the Lakes and the Lake Poets* (1834–1840), "four novels (two published in the nineteenth century, two in the twentieth century), numerous brief guidebook entries, popular ballads, pamphlet biographies and rogues' galleries, and a stage melodrama" (91).

Hatfield, like Hobart, was a genteel and charming ladies' man, forger, and imposter who posed as "a man of rank and fortune" (Coleridge 1.358). Both men were extraordinarily poised, even on the scaffold. Hatfield's "Executioner was extremely aukward, and Mr. H. found it necessary to give various directions as to the placing of the rope, and the proper method of driving away the cart" (*The Morning Chronicle*, September 7, 1803). Hobart "approached the awful scene of death with firmness and composure" and helped his executioner loosen his shirt-collar and adjust the rope. Moreover, both chameleons seduced innkeepers' daughters and inspired theatrical characters: Charles Dibdin the Younger dramatized the Hatfield-Robinson scandal in his "Burletta Spectacle" entitled *Edward and Susan; or,*

The Beauty of Buttermere (Sadler's Wells, April 11, 1803 premiere), and Cowley's Tippy was partially based on Hobart. But unlike Hobart, Hatfield was demonized by some of his contemporaries, and his infamy endures to the present day. His unsavory reputation had more to do with his seduction of the Beauty of Buttermere and his abandonment of his prior wife and children than his imposture and forgeries. Whereas Miss Spooner was obscure and forgettable, Mary Robinson was a minor celebrity who had been celebrated for her beauty and charm in *A Fortnight's Ramble to the Lakes* (1792), a popular travel book by Joseph Budworth (Reiman 218–220). Her betrayal by Hatfield was denounced in *The Derby Mercury*: "The address of the accomplished swindler, and the depravity of the hardened villain, are united in this living Zelucco [*sic*],[24] who has become so well known to the public by his baseness to the unfortunate Mary of Buttermere. It affords but a melancholy picture of human nature, to say, that his act of wanton wickedness exhibits only a solitary instance of the daring iniquity which has marked the whole life of this abandoned man . . . The perfect basilisk, he hardly ever saw a woman whom he wished to allure, without success. The history of his seductions and gallantries would form a volume, at which British blood would run cold" (November 18, 1802). In *The Prelude* (1805 version), Wordsworth describes Hatfield as "the Spoiler . . . , 'a bold bad Man' / To God unfaithful, Children, Wife, and Home, / [who] wooed the artless Daughter of the hills, / And wedded her, in cruel mockery / Of love and marriage bonds" (7.323–327).[25] Writing in 1834, De Quincey claimed that the imposter's mistreatment of Robinson sealed his fate: "it was in some measure the heartless part of Hatfield's conduct, which drew upon him his ruin: for the Cumberland Jury, as I have been told, declared their unwillingness to hang him for having forged a frank; and both they, and those who refused to aid his escape, when first apprehended, were reconciled to this harshness entirely by what they heard of his conduct to their injured, young fellow-countrywoman" (71).

The reliability of De Quincey's retrospective account is, however, questionable, and Hatfield's plight aroused sympathy as well as condemnation. As previously noted, forging franks was only one of his crimes, and *Trewman's Exeter Flying Post* reported that rather than demanding the death penalty, "The jury recommended Hatfield to mercy" (September 1, 1803). Visiting Carlisle on the day Hatfield was condemned to death, Dorothy Wordsworth observed that "[h]ere, as everywhere else, the people seemed utterly insensible of the enormity of Hatfield's offences; the ostler told William that he was quite a gentleman, paid every one genteelly, etc. etc." (40). When she and William returned to Carlisle after Hatfield's execution, Dorothy noticed that "[e]verybody spoke of Hatfield as an injured man" (217). Hatfield's popularity mystified Coleridge, who wrote: "It will hardly be believed, how obstinately almost all classes at Keswick were infatuated in his favour, and how indignantly they spoke of the Gentleman who had taken such prudent and prompt measures to bring the imposter to detection" (1.413). Rather than attributing the public infatuation with Hatfield to the imposter's charisma and genteel behavior, Coleridge concluded that the local people were simply too innocent to conceive of Hatfield's unnatural "wickedness" (1.414)

Newspaper accounts praised Hatfield's appearance and conduct during his trial. *The York Herald* reported that "The Prisoner is of a handsome and genteel person, and his behaviour in Court was proper and dignified, and he supported his situation from first to last with unshaken fortitude" (August 20, 1803). Hatfield also impressed *The Bury and Norwich Post*: "He was neatly dressed in black, and his deportment and manner were remarkable for ease and gentility . . . The prisoner heard [his sentence] with firmness, bowed respectfully, and was taken away from the dock, and thence to the goal" (August 24, 1803). After his conviction, Hatfield became devoutly and demonstratively religious. A journalist visiting him in prison remarked on his transformation: "He said he had for some time past been employed in making his peace with the Almighty, whose pardon, he humbly hoped, he should obtain, and who, he fervently prayed, would give him fortitude to bear the last great event that should close this world upon him for ever. I left him in a few minutes after he had expressed this hope, and as I quitted the room I observed him drop on his knees in prayer" (*The Morning Chronicle*, September 2, 1803). It is impossible to determine whether his newfound piety was sincere or feigned, but it probably influenced public opinion in his favor.

Following Hatfield's execution, a remarkably sympathetic report on his final days, possibly by the same journalist who interviewed him in prison, appeared in *The Morning Chronicle*:

> The manner in which he has lately demeaned himself would have commanded respect had his cause been better. From the hour when the Jury found him guilty he has behaved with the utmost serenity and cheerfulness. He received the visits of all who wished to see him, and talked upon the topics of the day with the greatest interest or indifference. He could scarcely ever be brought to speak of his own case. He neither blamed the verdict, nor made any confession of his guilt. He said that

> he had no intention to *defraud* those whose names he forged; but he was never heard to say that he was to die unjustly... Notwithstanding Hatfield's various and complicated enormities, his untimely end has excited considerable commiseration in [Carlisle]. His manners were extremely polished and insinuating, and he was possessed of qualities which might have rendered him an ornament to society. No one so much deplores his fate as the unfortunate object of his seduction—Mary of Buttermere. She has remitted him money, has written him letters, and with the greatest difficulty has been prevented from coming to visit him. She looks upon him as the man who gained her virgin love, and who for her sake was led into all his deviations from rectitude. (September 7, 1803)

The reporter depicts Hatfield as a quasi-tragic figure, an intelligent, eloquent, and courageous man who inexplicably used his talents and charisma to defraud and seduce. His sentimental account recalls Collard's assessment of Hobart: "he possessed many excellent qualities, both natural and acquired."

Hatfield carefully staged his final performance: "The Hangman not having fixed the rope in its proper place, he put up his hand, and turned it himself. He also tied his cap, took his handkerchief from his own neck, and tied it about his head also.——Then he requested the gaoler would step upon the platform and pinion his arms a little harder, saying, that when he lost his senses, he might attempt to place them to his neck. The rope was completely fixed about five minutes before four o'clock, it was slack, and he merely said, '*May the Almighty bless you all.*' Nor did he falter in the least when he tied the cap, shifted the rope, and took his handkerchief from his neck" (*The Morning Post*, September 7, 1803). Responses to his demise were mixed. A squib in *The Morning Chronicle* declared that "[n]otwithstanding [Hatfield's] popular manners, few were ever executed in this place who were less regretted" (September 9, 1803), and *The Newcastle Courant* observed that the imposter "exhibited a strange mixture of villainy and humanity" (September 17, 1803).

During the Romantic period, when chameleonism was linked to libertinism—as it was in Hatfield's case and in Collard's biography of Hobart—it became profoundly reprehensible. As I have pointed out, Hatfield's seduction of the Beauty of Buttermere provoked widespread outrage, and the *Analytical Review* was revolted by the "licentious amours" detailed in *The Life and Extraordinary Adventures of James Molesworth Hobart*. But in spite of Hatfield's and Hobart's many transgressions, a number of their contemporaries sympathized with them and admired their valedictory performances on the scaffold.

Journalists and the public were fascinated with the imposters' charismatic facades but had little interest in their subjectivities or motivations. When Hatfield mentioned that he had been depressed for almost 20 years, the reporter interviewing him in prison was too tactful to insist on an explanation: "he told me that... the world was now and had long been a misery to him; that he had been unhappy in his mind for nearly twenty years. The original cause of that unhappiness I could not learn, nor, as he did not think proper to disclose it, did I press him upon the subject" (*The Morning Chronicle*, September 2, 1803). It does not seem to have occurred to Collard to ask Hobart why he never corresponded with his wealthy mother and siblings in Virginia.[26] In contrast to the German Princess, whose mind was allegedly warped by her youthful readings of "romance and books of knight-errantry" (Rayner and Crook 249), neither Hatfield nor Hobart was psychologized as a fantasist.

The Mirror of Fashion maintained that Hatfield's notoriety surpassed the fame of most great men: "HATFIELD engrosses at present the conversation of the town. Really it in general happens that great men are not so much talked of as great villains; for the former are only known and appreciated by persons of a superior class, while the latter form the subject of discourse in all circles, from the library of the philosopher to the gossiping group at a country fireside, and the villainy requires only to be distinguished to have a distinguished mention in history" (September 6, 1803). Hatfield and Hobart were fantasy figures, commoners who adroitly impersonated men of rank and became instant celebrities. Their gentility, handsomeness, and stylish dress enhanced their public images. For them, the courtroom, the prison, and the scaffold were stages on which they could display their personae. They might have been malicious or mentally unbalanced, but they cut dashing figures in England's theatrical culture.

Chapter 2

Richard Cumberland's Imposters

Sir Fretful Plagiary

Richard Cumberland (1732–1813) was the most prolific and popular dramatist of his era. He composed over 50 plays, including six that were theatrical hits: *The Brothers* (1769), *The West Indian* (1771), *The Fashionable Lover* (1772), *The Jew* (1794), *The Wheel of Fortune* (1795), and *False Impressions* (1797).[1] His prickly response to critical reviews of *The Fashionable Lover* led David Garrick to dub him "the man without a skin" (Cumberland, *Memoirs* 175), and Richard Brinsley Sheridan satirized him in his comedy *The Critic* (1779) as Sir Fretful Plagiary, a posturing, hypersensitive, and egocentric playwright.[2] During the late eighteenth century, Cumberland was the leading purveyor of sentimental comedies, a dramatic subgenre inaugurated in 1696 by Colley Cibber's *Love's Last Shift; or, The Fool in Fashion*. The English sentimental comedy "was a vigorous protest against the accepted view in comedy that ordinary human nature was a target of ridicule" (Williams 414). In most of Cumberland's sentimental comedies, the focus is on middle-class characters and bourgeois values. Virtue always prevails, tears are frequently shed, villainous characters usually repent, and the humor is never bawdy.

Cumberland considered himself a moralist. In his *Memoirs* (1806), he argues that it is the dramatist's duty "to reserve his brightest colouring for the best characters, [and] to give no false attractions to vice and immorality." He condemns the licentious plays of his Restoration predecessors:

> Congreve, Farquhar, and some others have made vice and villany [*sic*] so playful and amusing, that either they could not find in their hearts to punish them, or not caring how wicked they were, so long as they were witty, paid no attention to what became of them: Shadwell's comedy is little better than a brothel. Poetical justice . . . has not left the comic writer without his instruments of vengeance; for surely, if he knows how to employ the authority that is in him, the scourge of ridicule alone is sharp enough for the chastisement of any crimes, which can fall within his province to exhibit. (141)

Cumberland worried about the moral influence of private as well as public theatres. During the Georgian period, private theatricals proliferated throughout England (Brooks 1). As the *St. James's Chronicle* observed, "[T]he Rage for dramatic entertainments in private Families has increased astonishingly; scarce a Man of Rank but either has, or intends to have his petite Theatre, in the Decoration of which the utmost Taste and Expence are lavished" (November 2–5, 1776). In "Remarks upon the Present Taste for Acting Private Plays" (1788) Cumberland writes that "[t]here are many and great authorities against this species of entertainment, and certainly the danger is great, where theatrical propensities are too much indulged in young and inexperienced minds . . . Young women of humble rank and small pretensions should be particularly cautious how a vain ambition of being noticed by their superiors betrays them into an attempt at displaying their unprotected persons on a stage, however dignified and respectable" (118). He argues that private theatricals endanger the virtue and inflame the vanity of amateur players and thus should be carefully regulated. "[T]he theatrical mania" that pervaded fashionable society also alarmed Vicesimus Knox, who claimed that "the taste for acting contributes much to the encrease of vanity and folly, the transition from which to vice and misery is too easy" (36).

However, although Cumberland was morally conservative and staunchly anti-Jacobin, his views regarding marriage and social prejudice were progressive.[3] Two of his female characters condemn legal prostitution, the widely accepted practice of marrying for money or social rank rather than for love. In *The Fashionable Lover*, Cumberland's destitute heroine proudly rejects the rakish and wealthy Lord Abberville's marriage proposal and informs him that "there may be a legal prostitute as well as a licentious one" (III.iii.37).[4]

Similarly, in Cumberland's comedy *The Imposters* (1789), the female protagonist indignantly refuses to "barter the freedom of [her] condition and sacrifice the affections of [her] soul" to obtain "equipage, attendants, pleasures, palaces" (III.48–49). Legal prostitution was also denounced by feminist writers such as Mary Wollstonecraft and Mary Robinson. In *A Vindication of the Rights of Woman* (1792), Wollstonecraft complains that "[t]o rise in the world, and have the liberty of running from pleasure to pleasure, [women] must marry advantageously, and to this object their time is sacrificed, and their persons often legally prostituted" (64). A character in Robinson's *Angelina; A Novel* (1796) refuses to wed an aristocrat whom she abhors and validates her decision by quoting from Cumberland: "One of our most celebrated dramatic writers says, 'There may be a legal prostitute, as well as a licentious one'" (20–21).

Along with repudiating the commodification of women, Cumberland champions persecuted and negatively stereotyped ethnic groups in his comedies. He discusses his project to counteract social prejudices in his *Memoirs*:

> I perceived I had fallen upon a time when great eccentricity of character was pretty nearly gone by, but still I fancied there was an opening for some originality, and an opportunity for showing at least my good-will to mankind, if I introduced the characters of persons who had been usually exhibited on the stage, as the butts for ridicule and abuse, and endeavored to present them in such lights as might tend to reconcile the world to them, and them to the world. I thereupon looked into society for the purpose of discovering such as were the victims of its national, professional, or religious prejudices; in short, for those suffering characters which stood in need of an advocate, and out of these I meditated to select and form heroes for my future dramas, of which I would study to make such favorable and reconciliatory delineations, as might incline the spectators to look upon them with pity, and receive them into their good opinion and esteem. With this project in my mind...I took the characters of an Irishman and a West Indian for the heroes of my plot, and began to work it out into the shape of a comedy [*The West Indian*]. (141–142)

The Fashionable Lover features Colin Macleod, a kind-hearted Scottish servant who comes to the aid of the cast-off heroine and tries to reform his libertine master, and in *The Jew*, Cumberland tries to atone for his earlier bigoted representations of Jews through his sympathetic portrayal of Sheva, an altruistic broker. Sheva lives austerely to save money for the needy. One of his beneficiaries describes him as "The widow's friend, the orphan's father, the poor man's protector, the universal philanthropist" (V.73). Montagu Modder argues that *The Jew* "had considerable influence over the more serious drama of the period...Other dramatists copied Cumberland's Sheva. Songs about Sheva became popular, and for a number of years the character of Sheva helped in promoting the spread of a more generous feeling towards the Jews among the theater-going public" (121–122). Moralistic and egalitarian, Cumberland's sentimental comedies celebrate principled characters who possess the capacity for disinterested benevolence, regardless of their social, ethnic, or gender identities. As a character observes in *The Fashionable Lover*, "a virtuous individual is of no sex, no country" (III.38).[5]

Given Cumberland's commitment to moral reformation and his disapproval of playwrights who make villainy seem "playful and amusing," one would expect his dramatic portrayals of imposture to be overwhelmingly negative. His chameleonic rogues are, however, witty and entertaining and regard their impostures as venial offenses. In *The Imposters*, a valet de chambre named Harry Singleton impersonates his master, Lord Janus, to woo an upper-class heiress. Singleton asks why he should "alone be call'd an Imposter for a mere flaw in [his] title, when there are so many worse imposters about the world, who counterfeit love before marriage and turn tyrants after it?" If his scheme succeeds, he vows to become "a most loving husband," "retire from the gayeties of the world, and live like a plain country gentleman in [a] plain country house" (V.73, I.14). In *The Box-Lobby Challenge, a Comedy* (1794), Jack Crotchet, an uneducated and shiftless printer's son who poses as "a scholar of the first class at Cambridge," "a man of fashion," and the descendent "of the Crotchets of Cornwall, a Saxon family, long antecedent to the Norman Conquest" (I.i.4, I.ii.13, II.ii.19), is an opportunist whose dissimulations are pardoned by most of the play's characters. Like James Molesworth Hobart, he is a charming and paradoxical figure. His bewildered fiancée describes him as "a strange mixture...of good and bad, honesty and deceit, reason and rhodomontade [*sic*]" (V.55).

In this chapter I argue that Cumberland, like many of his contemporaries, is both fascinated with and anxious about imposture. He relishes and exploits the comic appeal of self-consciously theatrical characters who revel in their transgressive performances and deliver wry asides, but as a moralist he finds their behavior problematic.[6] *The Imposters* and *The Box-Lobby Challenge* offer contrasting portraits of chameleons striving to improve their economic and social positions by assuming false identities. Whereas in *The Imposters* impersonation is condemned as a perversion of talents that must be rigorously punished, in *The Box-Lobby Challenge* the protagonist's imposture results in his financial security, three marriages, and "a general reconciliation" (V.iii.61). Unlike the valet-turned-viscount of *The Imposters*, Jack Crotchet possesses at least some scruples: he misrepresents himself to trick a wealthy 50-year-old woman into agreeing to marry him, but he insists that she leave her fortune to her rustic nephew. In contrast, Singleton despises the people he hoodwinks, slanders the woman he hopes to marry, and turns on his accomplice. Whereas Crotchet is redeemable, Singleton is not. In Cumberland's comedies, imposture allows marginalized and financially disadvantaged individuals to reinvent themselves. But they are eventually unmasked and held accountable for their performances.

PLAUSIBLE JACK'S TWO VOICES

The Imposters had a modest run of six performances at Drury Lane (Genest 6:530; Hogan 2:1125, 1128–1129) and "met [with] sufficient favor to be published and run through three editions" (Borkat, "Notes to *The Imposters*" 1).[7] Although reviews of the play were lukewarm, the acting was highly praised, and the *Times* reported that the comedy was applauded "with the most unbounded marks of approbation" by "a brilliant audience" (January 27, 1789).[8] John Palmer (1744–1798), nicknamed "Plausible Jack," was the perfect choice to play Singleton. Palmer excelled at using asides to make the antipathetic characters he represented more palatable to audiences.[9] In Charles Lamb's essay "On Some of the Old Actors" (1823), he describes Palmer as a double-voiced behavioral hybrid: "In sock or buskin there was an air of swaggering gentility about Jack Palmer. He was a *gentleman* with a slight infusion of *the footman*… When you saw Jack figuring in Captain Absolute [in Sheridan's *The Rivals* (1775)], you thought you could trace his promotion to some lady of quality who fancied the handsome fellow in his top-knot, and had bought him a commission… Jack had two voices—both plausible, hypocritical, and insinuating; but his secondary or supplemental voice still more decisively histrionic than his common one. It was reserved for the spectator; and the *dramatis personæ* were supposed to know nothing at all about it" (159). In *The Imposters*, Singleton addresses a rueful aside to the audience after Eleanor Sapient spurns his facile gallantries: "She has fairly put me down; I have not a word to say for myself" (III.49). Palmer's "supplemental voice" invited theatergoers to sympathize with his character's romantic inadequacy even as they condemned his exploitative scheme.

Richard J. Dircks observes that *The Imposters* "borrowed the familiar idea of two ambitious frauds who attempt to find wealthy wives" and dismisses the comedy as "a pale treatment of the same theme that was brilliantly treated by George Farquhar in *The Beaux Stratagem* (1707)" (68–69). Dircks overlooks, however, the significant class difference between the two sets of imposters: whereas Farquhar's Aimwell and Archer are destitute men of fashion, Cumberland's Singleton is a former domestic and his accomplice Polycarp was previously "a starving usher in a country school" (V.78). Inasmuch as Singleton attempts to rise from the serving class to the aristocracy through fraud, he is a much more ambitious and subversive figure than Aimwell, whose imposture turns into reality when he becomes "the true Lord Viscount Aimwell" (V.iv.93) following the death of his elder brother. Moreover, while Aimwell falls in love with the heiress he romances, Singleton is mercenary and exploitative. After Dorinda agrees to marry him, Aimwell confesses his imposture to her: "I'm all a lie, nor dare I give a fiction to your arms; I'm all counterfeit except my passion . . . I am no Lord, but a poor needy man, come with a mean a scandalous design to prey upon your fortune:—But the beauties of your mind and person have so won me from my self, that like a trusty servant, I prefer the interest of my mistress to my own" (V.iv.90). In contrast, Singleton never permits his amorous impulses to distract him from his pursuit of wealth. He tells Polycarp that he might have loved Eleanor "for her person" if he "had not such an uncontroulable [*sic*], inexpressible passion for her fortune" (I.15). Polycarp, like his confederate, is an acquisitive social climber; he courts an older, upper-class woman whom he detests to enrich himself. Whereas *The Beaux Stratagem* represents imposture as a harmless ruse that upholds rather than undermines the class system—in the comedy's final act, an upper-class heiress becomes engaged to a lord—*The Imposters* portrays imposture as criminal and socially destabilizing. Polycarp forges marriage deeds, and he and Singleton attempt to form misalliances that would enable them to infiltrate the ranks of the landed gentry.

Throughout *The Imposters* the stage directions identify Singleton by his alias, Lord Janus, rather than by his real name. In Roman mythology, Janus is a god with two faces that looked forward and backward; by the eighteenth century he had come to symbolize both wisdom—the ability to consider simultaneously the past and the future—and duplicity. The playwright George Colman the Elder praises Janus as an exemplar of prudence in his periodical *The Connoisseur* (1754–1756): "The medals, on which the image of this Deity was engraved, bore two faces, . . . one looking forwards, as it were, into futurity, and the other taking a retrospective view of what was past. There cannot be devised a stronger, or more sensible lesson of moral instruction, than this figure teaches us. This double view comprehends in itself the sum of human prudence; for the most perfect reason can go no higher than wisely to guess at the future, by reflecting on the past" (225). The two-faced god has, however, sinister connotations in Cumberland's *The Battle of Hastings, A Tragedy* (1778), in which the treacherous Waltheof boasts of his ability to manipulate others:

> I . . . make all men mine own,
> And still conforming to these changeful times,
> Like ancient Janus double-fac'd, at once
> Follow the setting, meet the rising sun. (III.i.45)

During the battle of Hastings, the "still veering traitor" (V.82) abandons his king and joins the Norman invaders.

In *The Imposters*, Janus's two-facedness is reflected in the contrasting personalities of the actual Lord Janus and his impersonator and in Singleton's dual identity as a devious valet pretending to be an honorable aristocrat. Singleton's surname, which implies a unitary, monomorphic identity, is a misnomer. Even when he is not dissembling, Singleton envisions himself as Janus-like: he tells Polycarp that if his gambit fails, he will "sit like the real Janus, with a Melancholy face looking backwards on the world, and meditating on the quick transitions of all human grandeur" (IV.54). The fatuous, wealthy, and ironically named Sir Solomon Sapient, who wants his daughter Eleanor to marry Lord Janus, extols the viscount's title and heraldic devices: "the title of Janus proves the circumspection of his ancestors; 'tis as much as to say they had all their eyes about 'em: his armorial bearings are typical of sagacity; two vizors in a wreath of serpents: his supporters are an allegory; on the dexter side a fox, denoting cunning; on the sinister a goose, which is the emblem of wariness" (I.4). Janus's armorial bearings seem, however, to represent guile rather than sagacity and the two-faced Singleton rather than his honest former master: visors are masks, serpents are proverbially treacherous, and the cunning fox suggests intrigue. Although Singleton assumes his erstwhile employer's name and title, he does not imitate the peer's self-effacing manner. Whereas the real Lord Janus, who never appears in the play, "is too apt to intercept his good qualities and keep them out of sight, . . . is much too modest and well-bred to affect the man of wit and acuteness; [and] is of the gentlest manners and diffident almost to a failing," his flamboyant impersonator "has a fluency of expression, a very happy command of his features, [and] a ready address in setting himself off to advantage" (I.22). Singleton thinks that to perform the role of viscount convincingly and marry "Miss Eleanor the heiress" (I.14) he must dress elegantly, speak effusively and gallantly, and make dramatic gestures. His imposture hoodwinks Sir Solomon, who imagines that he has "intuitively develop'd all the latent virtues of [Lord Janus's] heart" (I.4). When Captain George points out that "[h]is lordship's suite is not very splendid," Sir Solomon replies that "Lord Janus does not affect pomp; he travels as it were incognito" (I.3).

A used-clothes salesman and Lord Janus's wardrobe assist Singleton's impersonation. As Polycarp observes, the fake viscount has been "equipt at all points like a lord" and "handsomely metamorphos'd by the help of little Moses the French Jew." Adopting the alias Philibert, Moses becomes Singleton's valet de chambre and "brushes every coat *con-amore* with a fellow-feeling for it's future good appearance in Rag-Fair." Polycarp and the pretend Lord Janus discuss the transferability of clothes and identity:

> *Polycarp*... I have some slight traces in my memory of the very suit now upon your lordship's back.
>
> *Lord Janus.* Very likely; I dare say I'm not the first lord that has worn it.
>
> *Polycarp.* Nor the first lord's valet perhaps, who has made free to borrow it.
>
> *Lord Janus.* I know when I was in that post in Lord Janus's service, I so often wore his cloaths, that I thought it for his honour to wear his name too.
>
> *Polycarp.* 'Tis a pity but you cou'd wear his face also.
>
> *Lord Janus.* Why, as he has two by his title, it wou'd be no great robbery if I did.
>
> *Polycarp.* It must be the face that looks backwards then, for 'tis more than probable that is the way you must take your last journey out of life. (II.24–25)

For Singleton, identity is conferred by clothes and names.[10] He echoes Bronze, an ambitious valet in Hannah Cowley's comedy *The World as It Goes; or a Party at Montpelier* (1781 premiere), who declares that he "may as well use [his master's] Name as his Coat" and play "the Gentleman at a French Countess's" (III.iii.53–54). As Kristina Straub points out, during the eighteenth century, "Polemical literature on 'the servant problem' is filled with diatribes against servants' 'dressing up' to appear like their masters" (183). Male servants who dressed above their station were not, however, as vilified as female domestics who wore their mistresses' cast-off clothing (Straub 184). Polycarp agrees that clothes are transformative but reminds Singleton that faces are also an important signifier of identity: anyone who has seen the real Lord Janus can expose the fake one. He also implies that Singleton's fraud could lead him to the gallows. Focused on appearances, the imposters discount the significance of personality, education, and intrinsic merit. They imagine that if Singleton could somehow wear Lord Janus's face, his false identity would be unassailable.

Singleton's scheme begins to unravel when Lord Janus's friend Sir Charles Freemantle arrives on the scene, sees Eleanor falling from a plunging horse, and rescues her. Although Eleanor is disappointed that her savior is a baronet rather than a lord, they immediately fall in love. The play's eighteenth-century audiences would have identified Sir Charles as a stereotypical sentimental hero, and his romantic avowals are nearly as perfervid and stylized as Singleton's hypocritical declamations. He tells Eleanor that if he speaks with her "five minutes longer," he will "be absolutely and irrecoverably in love with [her] for life" (II.18) and rhapsodizes about her in a soliloquy: "I am fascinated, fixt, spellbound by the wand of an enchantress: the place is full of charms and filtres; she has sprinkled love powder in the air and every breath I draw brings infection to my heart" (II.19). When Sir Charles is told, however, that his friend Lord Janus has a prior claim on Eleanor, he reluctantly withdraws his suit.

Whereas Sir Charles is restrained by his gentlemanly ethics, Lord Janus's impersonator attempts to seduce Eleanor with "equipage, attendants, pleasures, palaces." She resents his infantilization of her: "I protest this is a very amusing inventory, and shews how well you understand to chuse out playthings for a child" (III.48). More perceptive than her father and uncle, she recognizes "the false character and sham pretensions of a counterfeit" (V.71). Singleton fails to grasp, until it is too late, that Eleanor finds Sir Charles's displays of chivalry and rectitude more attractive than the fake viscount's performance as a man of fashion and his "pedlar's courtship" (III.50). Desperate and running out of clichés, he boorishly attempts to embrace Eleanor, and she shouts, "Stand off!" (III.49). Rather than instructing the bogus Lord Janus to behave sincerely or naturally, Eleanor tells him to go to his rival and "by copying his manners learn to make [himself] more acceptable to [her]." She objects to his performance rather than his inauthenticity. Singleton confesses his shortcomings in a series of metatheatrical asides and admits that his chameleonism is limited: he "can act the lord, but...cannot counterfeit the lover" (III.50). While he can simulate the appearance, pretentiousness, and gallantry of a fashionable aristocrat, he cannot replicate Sir Charles's knight-errantry and refined sensibility.

Because Sir Charles knows what the real Lord Janus looks like, he poses a grave threat to Singleton's imposture. After Sir Solomon mentions his encounter with the baronet, Singleton has "an ague-fit," calls Sir Charles his "evil genius" (III.34–35), and demands Sir Charles's instant expulsion from the premises. Singleton's and Polycarp's vague innuendos make the impressionable Sir Solomon wonder if Eleanor's rescuer is "other than he pretends to be; a cheat, an imposter" (III.37). Informed by Captain George that his presence is unwelcome, Sir Charles agrees to leave but insists on an interview with Lord Janus so he can clear himself "from all suspicion of such mean clandestine measures, as one competitor [for a woman's affections] will sometimes enviously practise to degrade and level his superior" (III.44). To get rid of Sir Charles, Singleton decides to speak with him, but not as Lord Janus. He changes his clothes and resumes his previous identity, "a character [he is] more perfect in than that of his lordship" (IV.52), and when Sir Charles arrives at the appointed meeting place he is surprised to encounter the valet rather than the viscount. Singleton pretends that he has been dispatched with a message from his master announcing that Eleanor has consented to marry Lord Janus and persuades Sir Charles that she is deceitful and "a wanton" (IV.60). The exultant imposter jeers at the baronet's credulity in asides: "Oh! you are a precious gull!...A fair wind to your small cargo of wits" (IV.61). Convinced that Eleanor is "the arrantest coquette in nature" (IV.59), Sir Charles insults her and quarrels with her uncle, who accuses him of lying:

> *George*... Did Lord Janus assert he had her consent to marry him?
> *Sir Charles.* I have not seen Lord Janus.
> *George.* For shame! for shame! I blush to hear you so prevaricate: such meanness let me tell you, scarce deserves a gentleman's resentment.
> *Sir Charles.* Meanness! prevaricate! what language is this? I tell you once again I have not seen Lord Janus.
> *George.* 'Tis false! I know 'tis false.
> *Sir Charles.* Intolerable insult! Draw! (*they draw.*)
> [Eleanor *runs in between them.*]
> *Eleanor.* For heaven's sake, hold your hands! I'll die between your swords.
>
> (IV.66–67)

Singleton temporarily casts both Eleanor and Sir Charles as dissemblers, and the confusion caused by his double identity nearly precipitates a duel. His imposture is, however, doomed by his facial recognizability. Eleanor's emotional gesture convinces Sir Charles of her sincerity, and they and George soon realize that a rogue valet has been posing as Lord Janus. Incensed by Singleton's vile conduct, George resolves to humiliate as well as punish him by stage-managing his arrest.

The play provides insights into Singleton's character and somewhat distorted self-conception. According to Polycarp, Singleton is a man of enormous potential whose decision to engage in imposture is perverse and self-destructive: "Thou has every quality of a gentleman about thee, but the principles of one; birth, that shou'd not have been disgrac'd; education, that ought not to have been abus'd; and talents, which it is a scandal to pervert; had you applied them as you ought, instead of sinking into the menial drudgery of service, you might have rais'd yourself to a level with that station, which you treacherously counterfeit" (IV.53). For Polycarp and the biographers of Semple, Hobart, and Hatfield, an ingenious male imposter is a puzzling phenomenon: why does an educated and talented man resort to fraud when he might have used his natural and acquired abilities to achieve success legitimately? In Singleton's case, he believes that imposture will quickly and effortlessly enable him to escape his life of "menial drudgery" and join the leisure class. After returning from his interview with Sir Charles, he rejoices in his self-reinvention and rationalizes his transgressions:

> Now then I am a man again, a man of my own making, a peer by my own patent, lord of my own ascendant; and who suffers by my good fortune? who sinks that I may swim? Not Sir Charles Freemantle, for him I have dispatch'd upon his travels, and 'twill be hard if he does not come home a wiser man than he set out; not grave Sir Solomon, for he is a fool of his own making; not even fair Eleanor herself, for I will make her a most loving husband; and why shou'd I alone be call'd an Imposter for a mere flaw in my title, when there are so many worse imposters about the world, who counterfeit love before marriage and turn tyrants after it? (V.73)

Singleton attempts to justify himself by arguing that his fraud is victimless and there are worse hypocrites than him. Despite the fact that Eleanor has seen through his artifices, he fantasizes that he has succeeded in refashioning himself into a viscount and his imposture can be sustained indefinitely. He later describes himself to Polycarp as a nobleman who masquerades as a servant to amuse himself: "I have made a short step out of character, like many of my brother peers, to regale myself with the humours of the vulgar, and now step into it again to laugh at those I have cajol'd by it" (V.76). For Singleton, identity is performative, and he enjoys switching back and forth from valet to viscount. He despises "the vulgar" Sir Charles, whose identity is unitary and who is incapable of subterfuge. According to Singleton, "of all the fools, honesty ever made, [Sir Charles] is best intitled to wear the cap" (V.77).

Polycarp, like his fellow imposter, is double-voiced as well as two-faced: he lies to his dupes while delivering frank asides to the audience. The standard etymological definition of the word Polycarp is much fruit, but in *The Imposter* the name (probably an alias) seems to signify much carping.[11] Polycarp appears to have been driven to imposture by grim economic necessity—Singleton claims that he extracted the "starving usher" from "the gripe of poverty" and "the very jaws of famine" (V.78)—and he regards himself as "a novice in iniquity" (III.38). Posing as a lawyer and business agent, Polycarp makes love to Mrs. Dorothy, Sir Solomon's middle-aged cousin. When the fake Lord Janus boasts about his generous marriage deeds, Polycarp's hypocritical assent is followed by a sardonic aside: "Yes, truly, were all men's deeds like your lordship's, there wou'd be little employ for the conveyancers—The hangman's office would have all the custom. [*aside*]" (I.8). He continues his acerbic commentary throughout the marriage settlement negotiations:

> *Lord Janus.* [Janus Castle is] a substantial edifice, and in good repair; I can't complain of my expences in keeping it up.
> *Polycarp.* I should wonder if you did. [*Aside.*]
> *Sir Solomon.* I have heard much of its magnificence, and I confess my expectations run very high.
> *Polycarp.* Your disappointment will soon overtake 'em. [*Aside.*]
> . . .
> *Lord Janus.* Honor, my good Sir Solomon, is the very oath and bond of a peer; I must forfeit my title before I can falsify my word.
> *Polycarp.* I rather think you'll do both at the same time. [*Aside.*]
> (III.33–34)

Polycarp's ironic counter-discourse mocks both Singleton's hypocrisy and Sir Solomon's gullibility and reflects his conflicted attitude toward imposture. He is less delusional than Singleton and repeatedly predicts that his accomplice will end up on the scaffold. Desperate "to marry and be honest" (I.12), he woos Dorothy with extravagant flattery, comparing her to Juno, Minerva, and Venus and begging her to "fix...an early moment for [his] happiness, or expect to see [him] pine away into an atrophe [*sic*]" (IV.57). His dream of financial security evaporates, however, after Singleton reveals to Sir Solomon and Dorothy that Polycarp is only a humble assistant schoolteacher whose "fine speeches were taken out of [his] schoolboy[']s copybooks" (V.80). The snobbish Dorothy frostily informs her lowborn suitor that "[i]t is not in the nature of things...to suppose a person of [his] sort cou'd have serious hopes of marrying [her]." In response, Polycarp tells her than he would rather be hung than marry "a tough old woman, whose plagues there is no end to" (V.81) and parodies his sycophantic courtship of her with a series of transparently ironic compliments. After the imposters are exposed, Polycarp sneers at Singleton's plea for mercy: "Canting rascal! I always thought you wou'd die dunghill at the last."[12] Disillusioned with imposture and his treacherous co-conspirator, the lapsed usher refuses to make excuses or simulate remorse, and Captain George praises his "sturdy spirit" (V.89).

The comedy's metatheatricality reaches a climax in the final act, in which both Singleton and Captain George pretend that they are staging plays. Outraged by Polycarp's perfidy, Singleton assaults him, and Sir Solomon and his servant Oliver burst into the room. After George arrives, Oliver mimics Singleton's furious speech to Polycarp: "*Villain! Informer! do you threaten to impeach me? I'll tear your throat out first*" (V.84, italics in original). The false Lord Janus swiftly recovers his composure and pretends that they were only rehearsing a play:

> *Lord Janus.* you...thought me in a real passion—you cou'd not flatter me more. I believe, Captain, you did not come in time to see the rehearsal.
>
> *George.* No, but I hope I am not too late for the conclusion.
>
> *Lord Janus.* Well, Polycarp, methinks we came pretty well off in our quarrelling scene this time: we shall get up this play with some eclât [*sic*].
>
> *Polycarp.* If too many rehearsals don't spoil it.
>
> *Sir Solomon.* What the dickens! were you only acting a play all this while?
>
> *Lord Janus.* Only acting a play, Sir Solomon! What else is the whole beau monde employ'd about? I do but as the rest of my brother nobles: I am fitting up the great hall in Janus Castle for my theatre: there's an end of all old-fashion'd customs, instead of dinners of five courses, we serve you up dramas of five acts; feast your ears, and fast your stomachs. (V.85)

As I have already noted, Cumberland believed that private theatricals negatively influenced the morals of amateur players and needed to be carefully supervised. Singleton envisions a vertiginous world devoted to private theatricals, in which scripted performances are virtually indistinguishable from genuine social interactions. He tries to dispel his audience's suspicions by pretending that he and Polycarp are gifted actors who have convincingly simulated homicidal rage and that their violent altercation is an episode from a play. George has, however, discovered Singleton's previous identity and is not fooled by his impersonation of a passionate thespian.

Unfortunately for Singleton, George takes control over the comedy's final scene by announcing his own private theatrical. Noting that the imposters "have had [their] play," he begins his: "the performers are all ready, and only wait the prompter's signal; I'll touch the bell, and let 'em enter" (V.87). Sir Charles, Eleanor, and the constables appear, and George explains the drama's characters and plot: "Very capital performers some of them; these worthy fellows play the parts of constables; the ladies were to have been married in the play to a pair of the most infamous sharpers in the kingdom, but they have escap'd out of their clutches; this gentleman, who is nothing better than a lord's lacquey, plays the part of his master; this other gentleman, who is his brother in iniquity, has been seized by the throat in the play, and by the throat will be seiz'd when it is over: the manager and director of the whole movement, to whom alone we are indebted for the happy turn of the plot, you behold in this worthy baronet [i.e., Sir Charles], the benefactor, friend and preserver of us all" (V.87–88). Rather than a frivolous patrician pastime, George's private theatrical is a regulatory regime. He shatters Singleton's fantasy that a servant can reinvent himself as an aristocrat through performance. In George's play the "capital performers" are not actors, and the plot is determined by the squirearchy rather than plebeian imposters. His allusion to hanging hints at the grim reality facing Singleton and Polycarp: although imposture was not a capital offense, forgery was, and they have forged and uttered marriage deeds. Neither Sir Charles nor Dorothy appears willing to show the miscreants any mercy.

Even after Singleton has been unmasked, he impudently defends his conduct:

> *Sir Charles*... Now, Mr. Harry Singleton, stand forth! What have you to say for yourself?
>
> *Lord Janus.* Very little, Sir Charles. I have certainly made free with his lordship's title; but I have endeavoured to do it all the honor in my power.

Sir Charles. You do it honor, sirrah! how can that be?
Lord Janus. By bestowing it on the most amiable young lady in the kingdom.
Sir Charles. Well, Sir, there is some ingenuity in your defence, but it would be an injury to mankind to let such a fellow loose upon the world; Sir Solomon, you are an acting magistrate, you will make out his commitment. (V.88–89)

Verbally manipulative to the end, Singleton adroitly shifts from gallantry to pathos: "I beseech you to take pity upon a poor young fellow, who has known better days,...put me into any humble way of life, and I will be honest." He blames his corruption on "the evil habits of that fraternity, into which his hard fortune enlisted him" (V.89). However, his antagonists ignore his maudlin final performance, and Polycarp accuses him of cowardice. Although George grudgingly admits that Singleton's "ingenuity almost excuses his iniquity" (V.85), Sir Charles refuses "to let such a fellow loose upon the world." An unscrupulous valet who can impersonate a viscount poses an intolerable threat to the social hierarchy. Singleton is enterprising, eloquent, and cunning, but his virtuous adversaries have rank, wealth, and the constabulary on their side. They debunk his performances and compel him to bring "his drama to it's [*sic*] catastrophe" (V.90).

THE BOX-LOBBY LOUNGER

The Box-Lobby Challenge was more theatrically successful than *The Imposters*, running for 12 nights at Haymarket (Genest 7:148). However, a review published in the *Morning Post* excoriated the comedy's immorality: "[the play's] only attempts at humour consist in a repetition of stale and vulgar witticisms; and its only exhibition of Character is highly immoral. Young Crotchet the principal character, is painted as guilty of irreverence to his parents, ingratitude to his friend, seduction to his mistress; a coward, ignorant and debauched, and yet succeeds to a situation seldom the reward of virtuous and persevering merit" (February 24, 1794).[13] Because the wayward protagonist is enriched rather than punished, the reviewer concluded that the play condoned his transgressions. In contrast, the *Public Advertiser or Political and Literary Diary* refrained from moral judgment and reported that the audience "laughed heartily and applauded greatly, and crowned the conclusion of the Comedy with the strongest stamp of general approbation, which the custom of a modern theatre recognizes" (February 24, 1794).[14] *The Box-Lobby Challenge* is less sentimental and more socially egalitarian than *The Imposters*, and its attitude toward imposture is more indulgent. Although Jack Crotchet misrepresents himself through much of the play, in the final scene he confesses his "crimes" (V.60) and asks for forgiveness. Whereas Singleton and Polycarp are vilified and arrested for their misdeeds, Jack's dissimulations are pardoned, and a wealthy woman agrees to marry him. In *The Box-Lobby Challenge*, Cumberland suggests that a lowborn imposter who is not innately vicious can be reformed and integrated into fashionable society.

At Haymarket, Jack Crotchet was performed by John Bannister (1760–1836), one of the Romantic period's most popular and versatile actors: "The comedian George Bartley, one of the several who half-seriously addressed Bannister as 'father,' said that in 30 years' acquaintance he never saw John without a smile on his face. Bannister possessed a guileless joyousness which drew to him people of all kinds. His list of acquaintances, from king to charwoman, may have been the longest in London" (Highfill, et al., "Bannister, John" 1.271). According to Lamb, "Jack was . . . *beloved* for his sweet, good-natured, moral pretensions . . . Your whole conscience stirred with Bannister's performance of Walter in [Thomas Morton's] the Children in the Wood [1793 premiere]" (158). It seems likely that Bannister's charm distracted many audience members, although obviously not the *Morning Post* reviewer, from Jack Crotchet's moral failings.[15]

The comedy's title refers to a quarrel that occurs before the drama begins in the theater lobby that leads to the boxes. Thomas Rowlandson's drawing *The Box-Lobby Loungers* (1785) portrays the late-eighteenth-century box-lobby as an interstitial, quasi-theatrical space that featured sexual intrigue and harassment and in which plebeians and the social elite intermingled. While drunkenly loitering in the box-lobby, Jack insults Laetitia Rayner as she passes by and is kicked and challenged to a duel by the gallant Captain Waterland.[16] Jack explains to his father ("Old Crotchet") that when Waterland demanded his card, he gave the Captain a friend's "ticket":

> *Jack.* Box-lobby quarrel, nothing more, gave him my card—never put up with an affront, damme.
> *Crotchet.* What do you mean by your card?
> *Jack.* Sword and Pistol.
> *Crotchet.* Zooks! we shall have a duel in the house.
> *Jack.* No, no, no, you wont; there'll be no duel, unless the gentleman, whose name is on the ticket, chuses to fight—always make free with a friend on those occasions.—Borrow'd this frock-suit—found the owner's ticket in the waistcoat pocket—carried it off

> with spirit—left the house with a high hand—foot slipt, tumbled over a fruit-woman—sav'd half-price, and pocketed three oranges in the scramble.
>
> *Crotchet.* You'll scramble to the gallows. (I.i.5)

Borrowing another person's suit and identity, Jack poses as a man of honor and acts "with spirit" and "a high hand," but he is neither courageous nor foolish enough to fight a duel with an army officer. His surname, Crotchet, implies eccentricity and trickiness, and his fluid identity enables him to extricate himself from tricky situations and capitalize on opportunities throughout the play. He believes that all he needs to reinvent himself is a confident manner and "a fashionable suit" (I.i.6).

The man Jack impersonates in the box-lobby quarrel is Fulsome, who is also a poseur. Old Crotchet, who prints Fulsome's books, describes his client: "He has cunning... Fulsome was usher to a country school, he married the *femme de chambre* of a rich dowager, who took him into her family, and made him bear-leader [traveling tutor] to her booby son; he danc'd him a tour thro' Europe, and publish'd it in two quarto volumes at his return, pirated from the journals of other travelers, and stuffed with drawings of temples, bridges, aqueducts and amphitheatres, most of which he had never seen, and none of which he had ever examin'd: The book sold, and with the profits of that and a small pension Fulsome makes shift to live" (I.i.2). Fulsome is, like Polycarp, an erudite, bombastic, and duplicitous former usher who is determined to rise above his humble beginnings. Besides his plagiarized travel book, he has composed "A Treatise on Education" (I.i.2). He tells Jack's parents that his wealthy and pedantic patroness, Mrs. Diana Grampus, is searching for a "bear-leader" for her rustic nephew, Squire Robert Grampus, and that he has recommended Jack for the post. Although Jack has not even received a grammar-school education, he is confident that he can pass for a tutor and plans to marry Diana, despite the fact that she is twice his age. Both he and Polycarp are mercenary lovers, but Diana proves to be less snobbish and more forgiving than Dorothy.

Fulsome creates a fictitious identity for Jack, informing Diana that he "was a scholar of the first class at Cambridge, carried all the prizes, all the medals" (I.i.4), descends from "an ancient house in Cornwall" (II.ii.22), and is "strictly moral" (II.ii.19). During Jack's interview with Diana, she asks him who his favorite Roman poet is, and the printer's son replies that "Elzevir is the fairest type" (II. ii.22)—Elzevir is a

Dutch publishing house and a typeface. Fulsome claims that Horace is Jack's favorite poet, and when Diana instructs Jack to recite one of Horace's odes, Fulsome cleverly pretends that he has been trying to cure his protégé of pedantry:

> *Fulsome.* Now Crotchet, I stand a fair chance of my penalty, and if you spout one line of Latin in this lady's company, before Heaven I'll exact it.
> *Diana.* What do you mean by that, may I ask?
> *Fulsome.* Only that he is bound to me, Madam, in the penalty of an hundred pounds if he talks Latin in the ladies company. 'Twas a trick he had when he came fresh from college, and so to break him of it altogether, I laid him under this forfeiture; Now as I think he can hardly resist your commands, I stand fair for my hundred pounds.
> *Diana.* On no account will I permit it; I withdraw the Ode of Horace, and think that if there was a trace of pedantry in your friend's character, you cou'd not take a better method for curing a bad habit. (II.ii.22)

In spite of his ignorance of Latin, Jack is hired.[17] But his situation becomes awkward when Diana's niece, Laetitia Rayner, notices that he is the person who annoyed her in the box-lobby and relays this information and the fact that Jack "has undertaken to provide a fencing master for his pupil" (III.i.25) to her would-be suitor, Captain Waterland. Diana has prohibited Waterland's visits, so he decides to pose as a fencing master and force Jack to hire him: "I'll run home…, dress myself in character, take my foils under my arm, post away to aunt Di, send for my Box-Lobby Challenger, make him swear I'm the best master living, or ring off his ears close to his head and baulk the pillory of its prey" (III.i.26). Terrified, Jack readily agrees to Waterland's ultimatum and promises to be the Captain's "everlasting friend, and most devoted humble servant till death" (III.ii.28). Because Waterland adopts his false identity to be with the woman he loves, the other characters condone his imposture.

In his pursuit of Diana, Jack abandons his previous love, Lindamira, who is a novelist. Cumberland contrasts Jack's playful skepticism with Lindamira's overwrought sentimentality:

> *Jack.* The modest eye of day! From what conceited, canting, coxcombly, drab-compos'd novel have you filch'd that silly phrase?
> *Lindamira.* I filch from none; my phrases are original, my scenes are Nature's self, my stile [the river] Pactolus rolling over golden sands.

> Here is my manuscript; a novel, picturesque, descriptive.—Salvator, Claude, Poussin, Vernet, may blush to see themselves out done: My sun, moon, stars; my mountains, hills, vales, rivers, lakes; my woods, heaths rocks and ruins, are not dawbings [*sic*] upon canvas, but all embroidered upon cloth of gold.
>
> *Jack.* I would not give you one farthing for the sum total of them; I abominate descriptions. Have you nature, humour, wit, character? Is your hero a man or a monster? Your heroine a woman or an angel? Do your people make love, Lindy, as you and I have made it, according to the rules of flesh and blood; or as Sylphs and Sylphines do out of æther and gas? (I.i.7)

Although Jack is inauthentic and dishonest, he is not delusional, and he expects fiction to portray genuine human behavior rather than picturesque fantasies. Later in the play, Lindamira claims that she has incorporated Jack's infidelity into her novel: "The faithless perjur'd lover after all his promises, forsakes the fond believing fair to wed with ugliness and age for sordid gold, and leaves her to expire with grief and disappointment." Jack again objects to her unnatural writing, declaring that "no ladies die of grief," but Lindamira pointedly insists that "examples" of "gentlemen marry[ing] for money" and women dying of broken hearts "are to be found" (IV.iii.49–50). After she takes revenge by exposing Jack's imposture, he mocks her self-righteousness and histrionic language: "Taking your word for truth, that I am a base and perfidious monster, a cool deliberate villain, I really have not the face to approach so pure a being as you; your virtues awe me" (V.i.53). Rather than expiring with grief, Lindamira elopes with Fulsome. Both writers are attitudinizing and imitative hacks who abscond without paying their printing bills. Although Jack is, like Fulsome and Lindamira, a fraud and an arriviste, he refuses to identify with them and ruthlessly deflates their pretensions. To refashion himself as a gentleman, he must repudiate his former associates.

Jack Crotchet is a more complicated character than Singleton or Polycarp, whose mercenary motives are relatively straightforward. His identity fluctuates throughout *The Box-Lobby Challenge*, and it is difficult to separate his performances from his self-revelations. Initially, Jack's courtship of Diana recalls Polycarp's hypocritically gallant wooing of Dorothy, but when she agrees to marry him his mood shifts from rapturous to phlegmatic. In the amorous phase of the courtship, he calls Diana "an angel" (III.iii.30) and the "first only idol [his] soul 'ere worshipt" (III.iii.33). Always self-consciously theatrical, he delivers performances designed to "melt [her] heart"

(III.iii.34) and to secure her forgiveness after his imposture has been revealed. He arouses Diana's passion by pretending to mimic his pupil's improper behavior toward young women:

Jack. In the first place then—when a handsome woman falls in his way, instead of regarding her with a look, such as I now address you, modest, respectful, unimpassion'd; on the contrary he stops, stares, rivets his eyes on her's in an eager manner, as for example's sake I do on your's, and looks as he would look her through.
Diana. Oh Heavens! can he look so?
Jack. Now that you know is not proper and decorus [*sic*].—
Diana. There's a very sensible difference between one look and the other as you rightly exemplify. But surely in your case the copy far outgoes the original; his eyes have no expression, your's are all on fire.
Jack. 'Twas caught from what they look'd on: there was a sympathetic glance went to my heart. We must not practise that again; I shall offend.
Diana. And I shall pardon;—pray proceed.
Jack. So, so! the old touch wood has caught fire [*aside*].[18]—Then again, if he is to take a lady's hand for the purpose of conducting her out of the room, or to her carriage, we'll say—ought it not to be touched lightly, delicately, devoutly, in this fashion with one hand; and not seiz'd violently with both in this warm impetuous manner, as if he was going to hurry her into a post chaise for an elopement?
Diana. Just so; I feel what you mean exactly—and then his boisterous mode of saluting—. . .
Jack. What! thus for instance—
Diana. No, no; worse than that.
Jack. Oh horrible! what, quite as bad as this?
Diana. Yes, quite as bad. He must be broke of that.

Abruptly ending his pseudo-imitation, Jack casts himself at Diana's feet and declares that he refuses to go to Italy with his pupil and "be exiled from [her] sight" (III.iii.33). He admits to her that he is an imposter, but his confession is a yet another fabrication: "loveliest of women, for your sake I am an imposter, falsely pretending to stoop my proud spirit to the servile office of tutoring a dunce, when my ambition was to approach a divinity, whom I had hitherto only admired at a distance. This was the deceit I practis'd, and know that one, who carries up his pedigree to centuries above the conquest, never will descend to barter independence for an office, scarcely above menial." Diana raises him from the floor, and he unfolds a fictitious life history in which he was "born to better hopes, educated by the most indulgent parents with the fondest care" but was devastated by the loss of his beloved "father, whose public spirit drew him forth into the post of danger, and after raising him above the heads of his admiring countrymen, exposed him... upon a scaffold, to the taunts and malice of his unrelenting enemies... he fac'd his foes and fell" (III.iii.34).

Jack's protestations to Diana, like Singleton's declarations to Eleanor, are interspersed with asides that underscore the imposter's self-conscious performativity. He portrays himself as a sentimental hero, the blue-blooded son of a heroic patriot who died tragically. But he follows his melodramatic tale with an ironic aside: "I think the pillory owes me a good turn for that panegyrick. *(aside.)*." When Diana offers him a ring and her hand in marriage, Jack tells her not to "name [her] fortune" because his "soul disdains the sordid lures of interest" (III.iii.34). However, after she agrees to dispense with "worldly offers," he regrets his idealistic rhetoric: "Egad! I am a little sorry for that though—I have gone too far—*(aside.)*... I wish I had not thought about my soul at that moment. *(aside.)*" (III.iii.35). At this point in the play, Jack seems like a mercenary fraud playing the part of a gallant lover, but he is not completely selfish. He helps his newfound friends by convincing Diana to allow Laetitia to marry whom she likes.

Jack's behavior toward Diana alters after she gives him a marriage deed that obliges her to marry him or forfeit £10,000 and names his pupil, Squire Robert, "heir to all [her] property" (IV.ii.43) except for an annuity of £400 granted to her prospective husband. No longer an ardent suitor, Jack presents himself as an unsentimental and plainspoken man who has many faults but who is not "an interested, sordid, sneaking fellow." Apparently, his previous identity as a cunning and acquisitive opportunist is "a character" that he "hold[s] in sovereign contempt." "Covetousness," he informs Diana, "has not even the credit of being the vice of a gentleman." Diana is appalled by his dispassionate and prosaic rhetoric:

> *Diana.* Mr. Crotchet, are you serious? Your stile is really so new to me, so very much unlike what you held in our first conversations, that you alarm me most exceedingly: Tell me what you are aiming at by this kind of discourse?
>
> *Jack.* To let you into my character, and get a peep at your's: We have pass'd the stage of love, and there's no longer any call upon us to deceive each other.

Jack implies that lovemaking is inherently dishonest and argues that since the romantic stage of their relationship is over they should speak candidly. He envisages a marriage that is acidic as well as sweet and in which his wife is "a woman of spirit" who enumerates his "faults over and over again" (IV.ii.43). Diana prefers, however, the gallant dissembler to the matter-of-fact fiancé: "He's chang'd, transform'd; no longer like the man he was—no warmth, no gratitude, no tenderness—not so much as a look—I thought to have seen him kneeling at my feet, gazing upon me with uplifted doating eyes, then starting up with rapture on the sudden and unfolding me in his arms" (IV.ii.44). Like Lindamira, she derives her conception of love from sentimental literature.

Jack's sudden transformation into a pedestrian lover appears to be prompted by his possession of the marriage deed, his conviction that Diana is inalterably in love with him, and his desire to adopt a new identity. As he explains to his parents, the deed guarantees him "some forty thousand pounds, with the incumbrance of a wife, or a neat ten with a clear acquittance" (IV.iii.48); thus he will be generously compensated even if Diana breaks off the engagement. But he is confident that she will marry him in spite of her disillusionment: "old Di... [will] not pay forfeit, but start the race, and run it through even to the last" (IV.iii.49). Moreover, Jack seems determined to reinvent himself as a gentleman who despises covetousness, subterfuge, and self-interestedness.

Much to Diana's horror, Sir Toby Grampus informs her that her "fine fashionable fop of a tutor... Jack Crotchet, is a pick-pockety imposter, and instead of being the son of William the Conqueror, and the Devil knows who, is the spawn of a pillory-printer" (IV. ii.45). But even though Jack is obviously an imposter, Diana insists that he is reformable: "he's not a sordid, sneaking, wor[ld]ly-minded huncks:—He's only a rake, and I'll reform him; he's only a young rantipole young libertine, and I'll marry him" (IV. ii.46).[19] When Sir Toby scoffs at Jack's parentage, the printer's son responds with an egalitarian speech that was censored by the Examiner of Plays and never performed because it "portrayed the aristocracy too unfavorably" (Borkat, "Notes to *The Box-Lobby Challenge*" 1):

> *Jack*... we that cannot count up our generations have oftentimes the sense to outwit you, whose ancestors hang by the wall from Hildebrand, the great Grampus in King Arthur's day, down to little Toby the sprat, in good King George's day... One of your

> forefathers perhaps cou'd eat a whole venison pasty for his breakfast; another cou'd bend a kitchen-poker across his arm, a third might keep hawks and greyhounds; what are they but a catalogue of insignificants? One printer, one compositor, one poor corrector of the press, is worth them all, and his country gains more credit by his labors. (V.i.54)[20]

Previously, Jack mocked Old Crotchet's humiliation at the pillory and pretended to be the descendant of a noble family, but in his exchange with Sir Toby he maintains that printers are more beneficial to society than the rural gentry and celebrates their intelligence and industry. He endorses a value system based on cultural and commercial worth rather than ancestry. Impressed by Jack's eloquence, Sir Toby decides that "a little printer's ink mixt with [the Grampus] blood wou'd do the family no harm" (V.i.54). Jack's defense of his father's profession may be, however, self-serving rather than sincere: he wants to persuade Sir Toby that he is eligible to marry Diana and succeeds in doing so.

Jack describes himself to Diana as "an odd unsettled fellow, made up of contraries" who has no control over his destiny: "'tis mere chance which way the tide turns [him]." Whereas "good sense and good humour in a wife wou'd guide [him] to happiness, a fool or a shrew wou'd shipwreck [him] and herself" (V.i.55). In the comedy's metatheatrical final scene, Jack assumes the role of defendant in a mock trial presided over by Diana. He begins the proceedings by addressing the judge: "your criminal presents himself for judgement; try me with candour, but decide with justice. I pray call your Counsel into Court" (V.iii.58).[21] The "Counsel" consists of Diana's brother, nephew, and niece, the Waterlands, and Lady Jane Danvers. Jack confesses to Diana that he is the son of a printer and not a highborn gentleman, scholar, or educated man and that he broke his engagement to Lindamira. To counter Diana's objection to his parentage, Jack summons Old Crotchet, and his father reveals that he was pilloried for Fulsome's libel: "It is a printer's honour not to give up his principal [*sic*], the rascal was the author of a libel, for which I stood the pelting" (V.iii.60).[22] As Dircks points out, *The Box-Lobby Challenge* "reflects [Cumberland's] awareness of the inherent dignity of lower-class people and their potential for treatment in the theater" (71). Old Crotchet turns out to be an honorable tradesman who heroically defends his principles.

Having acknowledged "pretty nearly the sum total of [his] crimes" (V.iii.60), Jack ends his defense with a dramatic gesture that clinches his acquittal. He tells Diana that he will not execute the marriage deed that she compelled him to accept:

> *Jack.* I suffer'd you to force a bond upon me, by which you guarantee'd your marriage on the penalty of ten thousand pounds. I did not think you likely to incur the forfeiture, and therefore disregarded the amount: Now, Madam, though I am not worth a doit, I have a spirit, that disdains to punish any lady, who repents of having lik'd me.—Your nephew has the bond—I never shall enforce it.
> *Crotchet.* The fellow's a fool.
> *Squire.* Here, here it is aunt Di. Now who says Jack Crotchet is not a noble fellow?
> *Diana.* This act indeed is noble. (V.iii.60–61)

Jack's renunciation of the bond completes his transformation from box-lobby lounger to "noble" gentleman. But has Jack reformed, or is he just a more adaptable and less rapacious version of Polycarp? His hyperbolic declarations to Diana in act III, his altered behavior toward her after she gives him the marriage deed, and the fact that she is twice his age suggest that his motivation for marrying her may be mercenary rather than romantic, and his repudiation of the deed could be interpreted as a calculated gamble. Moreover, given that he is "an odd unsettled fellow, made up of contraries" who floats where "the tide turns" him, it is possible that he may revert to his earlier behavior or abandon Diana as he deserted Lindamira. Jack convinces, however, the play's upper-class characters that he has reformed, and they welcome him into their circle. Unlike Singleton, he is able to stage-manage his mock trial and charm the judge and counsel into pardoning him and inviting him to join their social circle. He is capricious, malleable, and "a low-born . . . beggar," but he is also "airy, gay, genteel [and] well-drest" (V.iii.58), which, in Diana's opinion, compensates for his lack of a pedigree. Thus *The Box-Lobby Challenge* privileges social progressivism over didactic moralism. Cumberland's egalitarianism, which reached its apogee in *The Jew*, is manifested in his sympathetic portrayal of the chameleonic pillory-printer's son and Jack's censored critique of the unproductive landed gentry.

In Cumberland's tongue-in-cheek epilogue to *The Battle of Hastings*, he asserts than everyone acts a part and that artificiality inevitably triumphs over nature:

> From ancient Thespis to the present age
> The world hath oft been term'd a public stage, . . .
> Are we all *actors* then?—yes, all from Adam,

And *actresses*?—I apprehend so Madam:
Some fill their cast with grace, others with none,
Some are shov'd off the stage, and some shov'd on;
Some good, some bad, still we all act a part,
Whilst we disguise the language of the heart;
Nature's plain taste provides a simple treat,
But art, the *Cook*, steps in and mars the meat. (1–2, 11–18)

Cumberland speculates in his "Remarks upon the Present Taste for Acting Private Plays" that "[i]f the present taste for private plays spreads as fast as most fashions do in this country, we may expect the rising generation will be . . . one entire nation of actors and actresses" (115). In his comedies, even honorable characters like Captain Waterland and Harry Algernon (in *False Impressions*) assume fictitious identities to be with the women they love. In *The Imposters* and *The Box-Lobby Challenge*, Cumberland explores the moral and social implications of performative self-fashioning. These plays mirror late-eighteenth-century Britain's stagestruck culture, in which public and private theatricals were "overlapping and interactive" (Brooks 5). The sham Lord Janus, Polycarp, and Jack Crotchet seek their fortunes in a society in which dress is the key marker of identity, wealthy snobs are easily duped, and dissimulation is ubiquitous. Unlike Singleton/Lord Janus, Jack is able to stage-manage his mock trial and convincingly perform sincerity. As a result, Jack joins the upper class. Although class boundaries are porous and identities are labile in both comedies, *The Box-Lobby Challenge* portrays social mobility and imposture more sympathetically. In a nation of actors and actresses, authenticity is unfashionable, and the subterfuges of a charming rogue like Jack Crotchet are easily forgiven.

Chapter 3

Thomas Holcroft's Politicized Imposter and Sycophantic Chameleon

Jacobin Imposter, or Not?

Harry Monrose, the louche protagonist of Thomas Holcroft's comedy *Knave, or Not?* (1798), is the theatrical descendent of Richard Cumberland's comic imposters, Lord Janus/Harry Singleton in *The Imposters* and Jack Crotchet in *The Box-Lobby Challenge*.[1] "Plausible Jack" Palmer played both Singleton and Monrose. Like Singleton, Monrose is a clever and cynical commoner who poses as an aristocrat and seeks make his fortune through marriage; like Crotchet, he pretends to be highborn to get hired as the tutor of the loutish but good-natured heir apparent of an upper-class family. While the valet de chambre Singleton impersonates an English viscount and the working-class Crotchet passes himself off as the descendent of "a Saxon family, long antecedent to the Norman Conquest" (II.ii.19), Monrose, a poor curate's son, masquerades as "a foreign Count" (I.i.3). In defense of their behavior, Singleton and Monrose claim that since imposture is omnipresent in English society their behavior is normative and implicitly condoned. All three comedies end with metatheatrical mock trial scenes, but in *Knave or Not?* the imposter becomes the prosecutor.

Performed before the French Revolution began, *The Imposters* was politically uncontroversial. In the politically charged 1790s, however, conservative theatergoers fiercely objected to plays that featured egalitarian speeches, mocked the aristocracy, or criticized the government.

John Larpent, the Chief Examiner for Plays, censored antiaristocratic passages in *The Box-Lobby Challenge* and *Knave, or Not?*, and during the premiere of *Knave, or Not?* audience members angrily hissed at Monrose's critiques of patrician, judicial, and governmental corruption and damned the play. To appease spectators and reviewers, Holcroft cut the offending passages from the script, and subsequent performances of the comedy met with less opposition.[2]

In this chapter I will argue that the opening-night repudiation of *Knave, or Not?* reflected not only the audience's hostility toward Holcroft's supposed political ideology but also revolutionary-era anxieties over chameleonic political subversives. These anxieties had been stoked by the Pitt administration, which in 1794 charged Holcroft and other reformists with treason, alleging that they had allied themselves with French Jacobins and were part of a vast and clandestine conspiracy to overthrow the British constitution and monarchy.[3] As I pointed out in the introduction, a number of Romantic-era writers envisioned Jacobins as predatory chameleons who constantly metamorphosed themselves to further their nefarious schemes. An anonymous biographer denounced the Scottish swindler James George Semple as "an emissary to Robespierre" and a "perfect cameleon...without any fixed principle, except a propensity for blood and rapine": "In the same instant he changes his affected countenance of affability and goodness, to that of rage and fury; and when he is expressing the most violent love in his eyes, either the poniard of the assassin is in his hand, or a warrant from the executioner's axe is in his pocket" (*The History of...James George Semple* 134).[4] On September 8, 1795 *The True Briton (1793)* published "A Letter from *Avranches*" that describes a French Jacobin "named GAUCHET" as "a known Terrorist [and] a Cameleon, who has been successively a Monk, an Attorney, a Soldier, a Parson, and a Commissary." Mary Robinson's novel *The Natural Daughter* (1799) depicts the revolutionary agitator Jean-Paul Marat as a bloodthirsty libertine who adopts a series of personae—polite, licentious, threatening, and "demonian"—to manipulate an imprisoned British woman into becoming his mistress (73). In a virulent attack against Holcroft, Robinson, and other reformist writers published in 1800, the loyalist Robert Bisset also linked Jacobinism to chameleonism: "One prominent feature often mentioned in Jacobinism is its versatility; totally unrestrained by any principle of morality or religion, it scruples not to assume any form which may promote its general purpose of involving every country in anarchy, to facilitate schemes of plunder and desolation...As [the Jacobin] has no moral or religious principles of his own, he will pretend to assume those of persons whom he conceives likely to prove easy dupes and useful instruments" (2.242–243). In *Knave, or Not?*, Monrose's "versatility" allows him to pose as a foreign nobleman while harboring radical views. He has "visited the Continent" (II. xx.42), reviles the aristocracy, advocates social mobility, and claims that "[a]ny man may be created a Count, abroad" (I.i.3). Much to Holcroft's chagrin, during the opening night of *Knave, or Not?* his duplicitous and egalitarian protagonist triggered the audience's anti-Jacobin paranoia.[5] However, after Monrose's most blistering social critiques were cut from the script, he sounded less Jacobinical and became less controversial. Holcroft concluded from the reaction to *Knave, or Not?* that any play associated with him would be automatically condemned, and his next comedy, *He's Much to Blame* (1798), was presented as the work of his friend John Fenwick. *He's Much to Blame* features chameleonic characters—a woman posing as a man and a baronet who imitates whomever he is with—but its social satire is relatively oblique.

After reviewing the licensing manuscript of *Knave, or Not?*, Larpent ordered the excision of a passage in which the protagonist speaks disrespectfully of the aristocracy (II.xx.43).[6] This deletion did not, however, prevent the play from being damned when it opened at Drury Lane on January 25, 1798. According to the historian and biographer John Adolphus, Monrose's sentiments "would have passed some years before as mere common-place, or as the ravings of a moody misanthrope; but in the existing state of politics, and from such a writer, every unfavourable conclusion was adopted" (2.18).[7] A review of the premiere of *Knave, or Not?* deplores the comedy's critique of English society and reports that the audience hissed throughout the performance:

> It was an attempt to render every man dissatisfied with the existing state of Society, in whatever rank of it he might be placed. It was a representation of human nature in a more odious light than, we trust, it is any where to be found, except in that Country where, the Author tells us, a title may be purchased for a Guinea, and which he has dared to call happy. The situation of the poor in England, and the oppressions of the rich, are subjects studiously introduced, to add to the melancholy impression which it was intended that *Knave or Not* should convey. The audience, unwilling that the catalogue of human misery should be incomplete, and that the Author should be without his share, hissed the Piece incessantly through the first four Acts, and damned it before the conclusion of the fifth. (*Sun*, January 26, 1798)

As Amy Garnai and Jane Moody have demonstrated, the audience that attended the comedy's first performance was much more politically censorious than the Chief Examiner and compelled Holcroft to cut speeches criticizing aldermen, magistrates, lords, the wealthy, and men of fashion from the script (Garnai 476; Moody, "Censorship of Jacobin Theatre" 208–209). Holcroft reinstated the deletions in the published version of the play and highlighted them by printing them "between inverted commas" (Advertisement iii). In addition, he defiantly expanded the speech criticizing the aristocracy that had been censored by Larpent (II.xx.43). Predictably, *The Anti-Jacobin Review* denounced the unexpurgated text as "a vehicle of pernicious principles" (Review of *Knave or Not* 52).

Holcroft blamed the opposition to *Knave, or Not?* on the misperception that he was a radical Jacobin and the audiences' assumption that the character Harry Monrose speaks for him. In 1792, Holcroft had become a member of the reformist Society for Constitutional Information, and in 1794, at the height of the governmental oppression of political dissidents, he was indicted for high treason. Although the case against him was ultimately dropped by the prosecution, he believed that he and his codefendants had been permanently branded "acquitted felons" (Holcroft and Hazlitt 2.77). In his prefatory "Advertisement" to *Knave, or Not?* Holcroft complains that accusations that his writings promoted the "spirit of faction, commotion, and anarchy" destroyed his theatrical career:

> The unrelenting opposition which the productions of the author of the present comedy have experienced for several years is well known, to those who pay attention to our public amusements... Since the appearance of The Road to Ruin [1792], his comedy of The Deserted Daughter [1795] only has escaped; and that, as he imagines, because it was not known on the night of its first performance by whom it was written. Love's Frailties [1794], The Man of Ten Thousand [1796], and Knave or Not? have sustained increasing marks of hostility: so that the efforts made to afford rational amusement to the public, emolument to the author, and improvement to morals, have been rendered feeble and ineffectual. (iii)

The *Critical Review* agreed that *Knave, or Not?* had been attacked because of its author's notoriety: "As Mr. Holcroft is obnoxious to the predominant part, the play has sustained strong and 'increasing marks of hostility.' When we see what comedies succeed upon the stage, we hesitate not in ascribing the failure of this piece to an unjust and ungenerous spirit of faction" (233–234).[8] An editorial barb in the *True Briton (1793)* exemplifies Holcroft's demonization by the conservative press. Referring to the interrogative title of *Knave, or Not?*, the newspaper sarcastically quipped, "The Author...did not, as reported, intend the Hero of the Piece for a portrait of himself, for in that case there could have been *no doubt*" of the hero's knavery (January 30, 1798).

Contemporary reviews suggest, however, that the cuts in the script mollified many of the spectators, and the comedy's run of six nights was, by late-eighteenth-century standards, disappointing but not abysmal. Holcroft blamed the play's demise on an arbitrary decision by the proprietors of Drury Lane, who "ceased, without any apparent cause, to play 'Knave or Not?,'" rather than low ticket sales (Holcroft and Hazlitt 2.191). Other plays that were "damned," such as Hannah Cowley's *The World as It Goes; or a Party at Montpelier* (one performance), Lady Eglantine Wallace's *The Ton; or, Follies of Fashion* (1788) (three performances), Mary Robinson's *Nobody* (1794) (three performances), and William Godwin's *Antonio; or, The Soldier's Return* (1800) (one performance), had significantly shorter runs. In 1789, Cumberland's less controversial *The Imposters* was also performed only six times. Moreover, it seems likely that the pairing of *Knave, or Not?* with George Colman the Younger's incredibly popular afterpiece *Blue-Beard; or, Female Curiosity!* (1798) attracted large audiences.[9] An article in *London Chronicle* assesses the comedy's second performance:

> The new Comedy of *Knave or Not* was repeated last night to a very orderly audience, there being a general convention of the Author's friends. Several judicious alterations and necessary omissions having taken place in the dialogue, the whole presented itself in a less objectionable shape, but the *cloven foot* has not yet been amputated, and the *Knave* continues to strut about in monstrous pace, marked with many of his original unnatural deformities: some of his most forbidding features have assumed a more mild and conciliating appearance; but the mask which has been thrown over his hateful nature, only serves to cover the exterior blemishes of his character, not to hide the hideous colours of his heart. The Performers were all in high spirits, and the ardor with which they exerted their respective talents, was much applauded by the audience. Previous to the commencement of the piece, Mr. Wroughton [who played the sentimentally altruistic Sir Guy Taunton] came forward, and read a few lines which he had received from the Author, in which he disclaimed any particular allusion, and

> begged the indulgence of the audience to hear the Play with calmness before they delivered their decision upon its merits. This request was well received, and strictly complied with. The whole was dispassionately heard, and, on the third representation being announced, a division took place, when the ayes appeared to have a decided majority.—The epilogue, was well as the dialogue of the Piece, has undergone some alteration. (January 25–27, 1798)

While the review claims that the play's diabolical deformities have been masked rather than eradicated, it notes that the audience, which included "a general convention of the Author's friends," was orderly, and that those who favored another performance were in the "decided majority." According to the *Oracle and Public Advertiser*, the revised comedy was well-received: "The New Comedy of *Knave or Not*, after the exercise of the pruning-knife, in those passages most exceptionable, was last night received with much commendation. It still, however, wants some more bustle or incidents to render it more agreeable. The greater part of the Dialogue is far superior to most of the flippant ribaldry of modern *long Farces* called Comedies" (January 27, 1798). The debate over the merits of *Knave, or Not?* resumed on its third night: "The new Comedy of the *Knave* was presented, for the third time, on Saturday evening. On its being announced for a fourth representation, some opposition, as usual, was manifested, but a large majority of the audience carried the question in the affirmative" (*London Chronicle*, January 27, 1798). Although Holcroft regarded the play as a failure, in its censored form *Knave, or Not?* won the approval of many of its viewers. Palmer's charm and popularity seem to have mitigated the audience's disapproval of the character he played. The *Sun* noted that "[f]ew Plays have received more support from good acting, where the opportunity for such support was afforded, than the unsuccessful Drama of last night.—Palmer, in the character of *Harry Munrhose* [*sic*], was often tolerated, where the sentiment, in the mouth of a less able Performer, would have drawn forth the strongest expressions of dissatisfaction" (January 26, 1798).[10] Theatergoers were clearly divided over whether or not the revised play and its upwardly mobile protagonist were politically objectionable.

In his somewhat disingenuous "Advertisement," Holcroft attempts to dispel the notion that Monrose speaks for him: "It was imagined that the author himself was as unqualified a libeller of mankind as Monrose; in which character the writer's individual sentiments were supposed to have been incorporated." He claims that through

Monrose the play explores the ways in which "guilty men" rationalize their conduct:

> Persons, who have made the human mind their study, have discovered that guilty men exert the whole force of their faculties to justify their own course of action to themselves. To this principle the writer was strictly attentive, in pourtraying [*sic*] the character of Monrose. His design was to draw a man of genius, misled by his passions, reasoning on his actions, systematizing them, condemning them in principle, but justifying them in practice, and heating his imagination by contemplating the crimes of others; that he might still maintain that respect for himself of which the strongest minds, even in the last stages of vice, are so tenacious. (iii)

According to Holcroft, Monrose should be regarded as an ethical and psychological case study rather than a Jacobin ideologue. He characterizes Monrose as "a man of genius" whose thinking is "misled by his passions" and heated by his imagination. As Philip Cox points out, however, "Monrose's pronouncements have a satirical thrust that is supported by the author" (95). And like Holcroft, a cobbler's son who transformed himself into a famous playwright and public intellectual, Monrose is adept at "cross-class 'passing'" (Wallace and Markley 6). But whereas Holcroft believed that humans are "capable of gradations of virtue, which others affirm that they can never attain" ("Advertisement" iii), his misanthropic protagonist insists that "it is a depraved, oppressive, despicable world; and . . . he who would not be trodden under foot must be like it" (III.viii.33).

Intelligent, cosmopolitan, and fiercely judgmental, Monrose is a much more conflicted character than Cumberland's opportunistic imposters. His virtuous sister Susan serves as his conscience and urges him to abandon his imposture. In response, he explains that in a mercantile society, fraud is "the common calling": "From high to low 'tis all bargain and sale. And what is bargain and sale? Why to display the good side, and conceal the bad: that is, to cheat and lie!" The "rewards" of cheating, he declares in a censored passage, are the alderman's "Fur gowns, gold chains, and white wands."[11] According to him, "Fools and knaves are the two grand classes: for the honest men are too insignificant, and too few, to form a class. Poverty and disgrace are got by keeping them company; and he that would thrive must shun them, as he would the plague" (I.i.2). His cynical worldview recalls the teachings of Dr. Torquid, who argues in *The Life and Extraordinary Adventures of James Molesworth Hobart* that "the great mass are dupes to a few knaves of the first class, from which a gradation of knavery may be traced to the humblest efforts, where there is not sufficient skill to escape detection" (Dralloc 50–51). But unlike Torquid, Monrose sees himself as engaging in class warfare and defending himself against the depredations of the wealthy: "He that would make the rich his tool must worm out their secret vices: he then has them in his gripe, and the tyrant becomes the slave . . . I act but on the defensive, and turn the weapons of oppression against itself" (I.i.5). Monrose discovers that his affluent employers, Sir Job Ferment and Lady Ferment, both have "secret vices" that he can exploit. While Sir Job has embezzled an heiress's fortune, Lady Ferment has had an adulterous tryst at a masquerade with a man disguised as a "gallant Highlander" (II.x.34). He regards himself as a knave exploiting worse knaves.

Monrose's imposture does not require much acting. His performance as an aristocratic tutor is minimalist in comparison to Singleton's flamboyant impersonation of a viscount. Whereas Crotchet must pretend to know Latin to secure his tutorship in *The Box-Lobby Challenge*, Monrose, who has "travelled, [and] know[s] the world" (I.i.2), is clearly qualified to instruct his oafish pupil. Although Monrose claims to be a foreign count, he does not identify his nationality, attempt to behave like an aristocratic émigré, or speak with a foreign accent. Because Lady Ferment fears that he may blackmail her, she does not dispute his "gentility" (II.x.33) even when she is confronted with his sister's nonaristocratic and non-foreign "Cheshire dialect" (II.xv.37) and country bumpkin manners.[12] Monrose does not have to be a skillful or even credible performer to manipulate his hypocritical and corrupt employers. He does not even need to be charming. To maintain his false identity he relies on the collusion of his fellow rogues: if they do not expose his imposture, he will not reveal their misdeeds. Until the play's final act, there is an unspoken agreement among the comedy's masqueraders that they will not unmask each other.

Monrose informs Susan that he plans to marry the cheated heiress, Aurelia Roland, and "secure her fortune" (II.xix.41) despite the fact that Aurelia appears to be in love with Oliver Ferment. After Susan exits, Monrose delivers a soliloquy that is reminiscent of Singleton's self-justifying soliloquy in *The Imposters*, in which the valet de chambre boasts that he is "a peer by [his] own patent" and asks why he "alone [should] be call'd an Imposter for a mere flaw in [his] title, when there are so many worse imposters about the world, who counterfeit love before marriage and turn tyrants after it?" (V.73).

Both imposters are provocatively egalitarian, but unlike Singleton, Monrose overtly critiques the aristocracy, which prompted the Chief Examiner for Plays to censor part of his soliloquy. This was consistent with Larpent's decision in 1794 to censor a speech in *The Box-Lobby Challenge* in which Jack Crotchet proclaims that "[o]ne printer, one compositor, one poor corrector of the press" (V.i.54) is worth many generations of baronets. In the following passage, the lines that Larpent proscribed are struck through and the words that were added by Holcroft to the print version of the play are italicized:

> MONROSE... my cursed querulous conscience takes part with my sister, and upbraids me for being an imposter. Absurd! Who are not imposters? Is any man the thing he seems? And, if feign we must, is it not better to feign something that the world respects, than something that it despises? The son of a curate, I have dashed into life, met variety of adventures, visited the Continent, and assumed the airs of a foreign Count. I have certainly disgraced myself; but the world does not think so. Who would shew his naked face when a mask is so pleasant, so profitable, and so easily put on? My father gave me education, Nature gave me desires, and I have given myself a title. Why not? ~~If I am not a lord, it seems I ought to have been. I find no difficulty in being as extravagant as a lord, as proud as a lord, as idle as a lord~~, *and as impudent as a lord. I could game like a lord, be duped like a lord, run in debt like a lord, and never pay, as naturally as if I had been born a lord.* ~~Let lords look to it, then~~, *and reform.* ~~Let them be as superior to the poor in virtue as they are in power, and I will blush for being an imposter~~. (II.xx.42–43)

The play's published text adds impudence, gambling, foolishness, improvidence, and irresponsibility to the list of patrician vices. Monrose says that if lords want to prevent aristocratic imposters like him from misbehaving, they should reform and stop being such terrible role models. In London society, masks are pleasant, profitable, and easily donned. But while Monrose claims that imposture is advantageous and universally practiced, he believes that he has "certainly disgraced" himself, even if "the world does not think so." In contrast to the comedy's patriarchal villains, Sir Job and Mr. Taunton, who rob an orphan and then convince themselves that they "acted like honest men" (III.i.44), Monrose possesses a "querulous conscience" that ultimately compels him to repudiate his knavery. Whereas Singleton revels in his imposture, Monrose "is all a contradiction." He eventually realizes that "[h]e that would succeed in knavery, must be wholly knave" and that his inability to "shake off" his "compunctions and sympathies" (V.xi.87) has prevented him from achieving success. Monrose confesses his "crimes," helps Aurelia recover her fortune, and shows that he is morally superior to the orphan-robbing patriarchs he has exposed.

Monrose subversively uses the term "knave," traditionally applied to male servants and peasants, to describe members of the social elite.[13] To "rouse [Sir Job's and Mr. Taunton's] terrors," he urges them to "acknowledge themselves knaves" (III.viii.52–53). In a passage that was censored by the opening-night audience, he provides cynical definitions of blockhead, men of understanding, knave, honest men, men of wit, and men of fashion:

> What is a blockhead? A blockhead is a poor devil. Who are men of understanding? Every one who has five thousand a year. What is a knave? He that is hanged for cheating. And what an honest man? He that gets an estate by the same means. Who are most courted? Men of wit. And who are they? Those that give good dinners, make their friends drunk with the best wines, and then pick their pockets at hazard and faro. Who are most imitated? Men of fashion. And he is a man of first fashion who associates with stable-boys in the morning, with opera-dancers and demireps after dinner, and with a Babel mixture of bullies, bubbles, and pickpockets from midnight to sunrise. (IV.i.63)

Monrose suggests that language has been perverted to mask vice, enable imposture, and denigrate poverty and integrity. According to society, a man with a substantial income is by definition a man of understanding; all poor devils are blockheads. Cheaters are knaves or honest men depending on whether they are hung or acquire estates. In this decadent, dissimulative world, the most admired and imitated men are imposters: corrupt lawyers "wear the mask of honesty" (IV.i.62), Sir Job steals an orphan's estate and becomes an alderman, city knight, and magistrate; society fawns over "men of wit" who provide excellent dinners and wines while picking their friends' pockets, and the "man of first fashion" is a dissolute vulgarian.

Monrose is, however, also guilty of abusing language. In a scene that recalls Singleton's futile courtship of Eleanor Sapient in *The Imposters*, he ineptly woos Aurelia Roland. After abducting Aurelia, Monrose tells her that she should "[b]lame the depravity which not merely justifies but renders [his behavior] unavoidable." She dismisses his rhetoric as "the vulgar cant of common place vice" and declares that "[t]he blandishments of words can neither disguise nor palliate [his] unworthy actions" (V.ii.76–77). Subsequently, Aurelia's lover

Oliver appears, and Monrose, still playing the part of an aristocrat, challenges his rival to a duel:

> *Monrose.* I have risked my all. This is the crisis of my fate; and either comply, or one of us shall never depart alive.
> *Oliver.* Your threats are impotent.
> *Monrose.* Then my deeds shall be decisive. (*Produces pistols*). Take this.
> *Oliver.* For what purpose?
> *Monrose.* A gentleman need not ask.
> *Oliver.* Pshaw! Jargon! (V.iv.79)

In a desperate attempt to acquire Aurelia and her fortune, Monrose mimics the cant and jargon of the upper-class rogues he loathes. Vanquished by Oliver's Godwinian objections to dueling, he confesses that he has become what he "despise[s], a braggart" (V.iv.80) and undergoes an epiphany in which he asserts his personal agency: he declares that he will never become any "man's automaton" and that he is "the lord of [his] own actions, and will be self-moved" (V.iv.80). But Monrose's epiphany is not followed by a repudiation of performance or a return to his former lowly identity as a curate's son. Rather, he takes on another role, that of vengeful prosecutor, and vows to "rise on the necks of wretches that hope ere this to trample him in the dust" (IV.iv.80). His claim that he is "the *lord* of [his] own actions" suggests that he has not entirely abandoned his belief that he "ought to have been... a lord" and echoes Singleton's hubristic declaration in *The Imposters* that he is a "lord of [his] own ascendant." Monrose repudiates his imposture but not his social ambitions.

To unmask his wealthy upper-class antagonists, Monrose stages a mock trial in which he plays the parts of defendant, witness, prosecutor, and judge. He prevents the upper-class "harpies" (II.xix.41) who robbed Aurelia from fleeing, informs them that their "presence is necessary in court," characterizes himself as "a bold faced knave that appear[s] without a summons," and calls on Sir Job and his accomplice, Mr. Taunton, to be his "accusers." It is, he explains, "no uncommon case for the least criminal to be condemned by his accomplices" (V.viii.83). Unlike Cumberland's Singleton, whose imaginary trial is improvised and directed by the squirearchy, Monrose is rhetorically and legally in control of the action. Before beginning his prosecution, he has the embezzlers' attorney arrested, and Bow-street runners wait in the wings to take the miscreants into custody. The larcenous plutocrats have nothing to say in their defense: as Monrose observes, "Their silence is their assent" (V.ix.85) to his charges.

Whereas the mock trial in *Knave, or Not?* exposes the corruption of a London alderman and judge, the corresponding scene in *The Box-Lobby Challenge* celebrates patrician benevolence and broad-mindedness. In *The Box-Lobby Challenge*, the court's "Counsel," which includes Lady Jane Danvers, Sir Toby Grampus, and 'Squire Robert, and the judge, who is the defendant's wealthy fiancée, forgive rather than acquit Jack Crotchet, and the play closes with a reconciliation scene in which the imposter is welcomed into the upper class. By contrast, in *Knave, or Not?* the imposter's mock trial arraigns patrician culprits. The opening-night audience hissed at a speech in which Monrose mocks Sir Job Ferment and satirizes fashionable hypocrisy:

> *Monrose.* "Ha, ha, ha!...Why, man, you and I are petty knaves! Console yourself: crimes of a much deeper dye no longer are a nine days wonder. Some friendly scandal, with 'Bless me, who would have thought it!' and a little gross abuse, which you'll not hear, is the utmost penalty. Meanwhile bows, salutations, and grinning courtesy will be current as ever. 'Tis only the needy villain that is shunned." (V.x.86)[14]

According to Monrose, London's financial district tolerates knavery unless the knave is penniless. As Moody explains, "The entire [imaginary court] scene, framed as a legal judgment, challenges the spectators (both on stage and in the theatre), to act as a jury: the trope of the juridical audience has been turned on its head. For even as he convenes a court to condemn his own knavish actions,...Monrose demonstrates that the presumed judges of eighteenth-century society are in fact its greatest criminals" ("Censorship of Jacobin Theatre" 208). In the expurgated script, however, Holcroft removed the passage in which Monrose ironically asks his "jury" to compare his "crimes" to the actions of "these honest, these magisterial men" (V.viii.84) who have stolen an orphan's inheritance. Besides paring down Monrose's prosecutorial rhetoric, Holcroft excised speeches in which his protagonist explains that he resorted to imposture because the world spurns genius, virtue, and talents. In a deleted passage, Monrose declares that his "crime" is "sovereign contempt for the selfishness to which genius and virtue are the daily sacrifice" (V.viii.84). When another character asks him if talents and genius rather than knavery may serve as a "recommendation," he replies that "[t]alents and genius are the admiration of a day: so is a calf with two heads, or any other monster" (V.xi.87). The comedy's late-eighteenth-century London audience refused to tolerate an imposter with such a jaundiced view of English society.

At the conclusion of the play Monrose is forgiven and befriended by the comedy's ethical characters: his sister and Sir Guy Taunton profess their love for him, and the orphan whose fortune he restored calls him her "saviour" and says that he has "proved the dignity of [his] mind" (V.xi.87). Monrose's imposture has positioned him to expose the more execrable imposture of a judge, City knight, and alderman who "has been in masquerade a great part of his life" (II.x.35). Unlike Cumberland's Singleton, he escapes arrest; like Cumberland's Jack Crotchet, he "gain[s] friends that will never forsake [him]" (*Knave, or Not?*, V.xi.87). But in spite of Monrose's apparent reformation, he remains "a disciple of the world and its maxims; [he] can persecute vice in others and practise it [him]self like any potent Don in Christendom" (V.xi.86). He portrays himself as a Janus-faced and self-thwarting contradiction: a knave with a conscience.

Audiences and reviewers found the expurgated version of *Knave, or Not?* less objectionable than the original play because Holcroft removed passages that lambaste the entire aristocracy and judiciary. He also cut the provocative line in which Sir Guy declares that "[s]ystemic vice of all others is the most dangerous" (V.viii.84) and Monrose's even more inflammatory reply. In the licensing manuscript and presumably the play's first performance, Monrose informs Sir Guy that systemic vice "is the very Mechanism of society" (Rosenblum, Notes on *Knave; or Not* cxx). During the revolutionary period, the term "system" was associated with Jacobin political philosophy, and Monrose's critique was so politically charged that Holcroft kept it out of the published text.[15] Holcroft's deletions did not, however, satisfy the government newspaper the *True Briton*. In a review of the comedy's second performance, the *True Briton* conceded that "[t]he Play has been cleared of some of its offensive matter" but insisted that "it is offensive throughout in its structure and tendency" (January 27, 1798). Despite Holcroft's revisions, his cynical imposter continued to raise loyalist hackles.

THE "HARMLESS" CHAMELEON

Holcroft's comedy *He's Much to Blame* opened at Covent Garden on February 13, 1798, less than three weeks after the tumultuous début of *Knave, or Not?* at Drury Lane. On the day before the premiere, newspaper squibs spread rumors about the play's author. According to the *Morning Post and Gazetteer*, "The new Comedy of '*Much to*

Blame' [*sic*], is the production of a young Lady not unknown to the *literary world*, though unknown to the stage" (February 12, 1798). The conservative *True Briton* suspected that Godwin had written the play: "Mr. GODWIN, the Political Philosopher, is said to be the real Author of the approaching Comedy of *He's Much to Blame.* Mr. FENWICK, who superintends the rehearsals, is understood to be a *friendly screen* to avert public prejudices. But if the Play is a good one, and contains nothing in itself offensive, the Public, we trust, are too liberal to harbour any prejudices against dramatic merit, however adverse they may be to the Author in other respects" (February 12, 1798). Presented as Fenwick's work, *He's Much to Blame* ran for 22 nights and received rave reviews. The *Express and Evening Chronicle* was unstinting in its praise: "[*He's Much to Blame*] is certainly one of the best comedies which we have witnessed for some time. The plan is simple and natural; the incidents interesting, and the language polished and easy... This piece has the singular merit of uniting lofty sentiment with great amusement; a quality for which modern comedies have not been distinguished. It was received throughout without the slightest mark of disapprobation, and given out for another performance, amidst warm and unanimous applause" (February 13–15, 1798). Even King George III seems to have approved of the play. In a diary entry dated August 1, 1798, Holcroft recorded that "Mr. *Griffiths, Jun.*,... testified great satisfaction at the shame [the comedy's] success brought on [Holcroft's] persecutors, and that the King, not knowing the author, had commanded it twice" (Holcroft and Hazlitt 2.170).

Not everyone was fooled, however. A reviewer for *The Monthly Mirror* saw through Holcroft's ruse and wondered why the playwright had not claimed authorship: "[*He's Much to Blame*] bears very strong resemblance, in our opinion, to the *Deserted Daughter*, in style, sentiment, interest, and structure, and Mr. Holcroft will probably turn out to be the author: yet, why he should avow a comedy *(Knave or Not)* composed of very dangerous materials, as the event proved, and refrain from acknowledging this, which is perfectly harmless and secure, we are not enough in the secret to conjecture" (Review of *He's Much to Blame* 5.173). According to the reviewer, Holcroft's acknowledgment of *He's Much to Blame* would not have affected its reception. But while *He's Much to Blame* is not as overtly political as *Knave, or Not?*, both comedies satirize the pretensions, selfishness, and fatuity of the social elites.[16] Whereas Monrose excoriates the corrupt aristocracy, in *He's Much to Blame* Sir George Versatile imitates and unintentionally parodies aristocratic capriciousness. Moreover, in the later comedy, male servants echo the censored speech from *Knave, or Not?* in which Monrose declares that he "ought to have been... a lord":

> *Harry*... I warrant... that we [servants] can game, run in debt, get in drink, and be as proud and domineering as [our masters] for their lives.
> *Williams.* Yes, yes: let them but change places and they would soon find we could rise to their vices, and they could sink to ours, with all the ease imaginable.
> *Harry.* They have no such notion though, Mr. Williams.
> *Williams.* That is their vanity, Mr. Harry. (III.i.35–36)

While Larpent suppressed Monrose's anti-aristocratic soliloquy, he let Harry and Williams's comments stand—the interchangeability of servants and masters had been a common theatrical motif since the success of James Townley's farce, *High Life below Stairs* (1759). Larpent appears, however, to have crossed out two politically controversial passages in the licensing manuscript of *He's Much to Blame*: Sir George Versatile's assertion that money can purchase "lords, and commons" (III.viii.48) and a section in which Sir George and Lord Vibrate denounce "the stupidity of juries, the fictions of law, the chicanery of lawyers" (III.x.53) (Rosenblum, Notes on *He's Much to Blame* cxxviii–cxxix).

In *He's Much to Blame*, the chameleonic male characters are vacillating aristocrats rather than manipulative rogues. Both *Knave, or Not?* and *He's Much to Blame* portray the fashionable world as a masquerade, but the plot of *He's Much to Blame* is driven by compliance rather than imposture. The fawning quack Dr. Gosterman and Sir George Versatile embody the fulsome sycophancy that narcissistic aristocrats encourage and reward. Dr. Gosterman sums up their compliant philosophy: "I shall do all as vat shall make agréable. Dat is my vay" (I.vii.16). The only imposter in *He's Much to Blame* is the virtuous Maria Delaval. Desperate to prevent her inconstant lover and brother from dueling, Maria first disguises herself as a man and then conceals her identity with a mask and domino.

Sir George anticipates the compulsively imitative chameleons of James Kenney's *The World! A Comedy* (1808) and Woody Allen's *Zelig* (1983). Like Keats's chameleon poet, Sir George and Kenney's Jack Echo passively mirror other identities, but unlike the chameleon poet, they possess prosaic imaginations and cannot transcend morality: their chameleonism is portrayed as a moral failing that must be overcome if they are to achieve personhood and become responsible members of society. Before becoming a baronet, George Versatile is a poor law student engaged to Maria Delaval, but after inheriting "a title and large estate" (V.iv.84), he succumbs to the influence of "proud and selfish relations" (V.iv.87) and jilts her. When in the company of aristocrats, he has "one infallible rule[:] to please all tempers" (III.vii.46). He obsequiously echoes Lady Vibrate's frivolous opinions:

> *Lady Vibrate.* Are you not of my opinion?
> *Sir George.* To be sure I am! What is it?
> *Lady Vibrate.* That pleasure is the business of life.
> *Sir George.* Oh, beyond all doubt!
> *Lady Vibrate.* That inspecting accounts—
> *Sir George.* Is vulgar drudgery!
> *Lady Vibrate.* And looking after our affairs—
> *Sir George.* A vile loss of time!
> *Lady Vibrate.* That care in the face denotes—
> *Sir George.* The owner is a fool!
> *Lady Vibrate.* And that sorrow is a very ridiculous thing!
> *Sir George.* Fit only to excite laughter!
> *Lady Vibrate.* Why then, Sir George, I am your friend. (III.vii.42–43)

By endorsing, amplifying, and completing Lady Vibrate's hedonistic assertions, Sir George inadvertently parodies a parody of the dissipated woman of fashion. He imagines Lady Vibrate and himself rattling away until "the whole world" becomes "a Galanty show" (III.vii.44), which is "A play or pantomime produced by throwing shadows of puppets on to a wall or screen" (*OED*). As Lady Vibrate observes, he expresses her "ideas...even better than [she herself] can" (III.vii.45).

While conversing with Lady Vibrate, Sir George is "Only a copy of [her] charming self" (III.vii.46), the shadow of a fashionable puppet. However, when the anxious, indecisive, and melancholy Lord Vibrate enters the room, Sir George metamorphoses into the Lord's copy:

> *Lord Vibrate...* (*Sees Sir George. They look full at each other till Sir George catches the same dismal kind of countenance*) Ah, Sir George! Here am I, brim full of anxiety and turmoil!
> *Sir George.* Alas! Man was born to trouble...
> *Lord Vibrate.* My cares laughed at, my vigilance mocked, my sufferings insulted! And why? Because I am cautious! because I doubt! because I am provident! What is man without money?

Sir George. A fountain without water.
Lord Vibrate. A clock without a dial.
Sir George. *(Warming and becoming rapid as he proceeds)* What is it that buys respect, and honor, and power, and privilege, and houses, and lands, and wit, and beauty, and learning, and lords, and commons, and—
Lord Vibrate. Why money! (III.viii.48)

Compared to Monrose, Sir George seems apolitical: he conforms to rather than critiques aristocratic behavior. But as a chameleon, Sir George not only reflects the aristocrats he wants to please, but also exaggerates their moods and beliefs to the point of absurdity. Carried away by his imitation of a cautious, miserly nobleman, he claims that "lords, and commons" are for sale, and Lord Vibrate thoughtlessly agrees with this politically inflammatory, and apparently censored, assertion.[17]

Lord Vibrate is, however, more difficult to copy than Lady Vibrate because his identity is less stable: "All [his] life [he has] been wavering, uncertain, and indeterminate." He has learned from "the sceptics…that appearances deceive, and that nothing is certain" and that he "may be Lord Vibrate, or…the Grand Turk" (II.i.21). Sir George's imitation of this vacillating aristocrat goes momentarily awry when they discuss the "rational use of money":

Sir George. Should [money] not be applied to relieve the aged, comfort the poor, succour the distressed—
Lord Vibrate. What?
Sir George. Reward merit, encourage industry, and promote the public good?
Lord Vibrate. Promote a farce!
Sir George. Very true: the public good is a farce!
Lord Vibrate. The true use of money is to defend our rights—
Sir George. Revenge our wrongs, purchase for the present, provide for the future, secure power, buy friends, bid defiance to enemies, and lead the world in a string!
Lord Vibrate. Ay! Now you talk sense. (III.viii.51)

In this scene, Sir George's parroting of Lord Vibrate duplicates and magnifies the Lord's disregard for the public good, avarice, thirst for power, and vindictiveness. Sir George further underscores Lord Vibrate's dithering selfishness when the nobleman's longtime servant, Thompson, asks his employer for £240 to discharge a debt.

Thompson has "been bound for his sister's husband," and if the debt is not paid, he "must languish out [his] life in a prison." Reluctant to part with such a "large sum," Lord Vibrate asks for Sir George's advice:

> *Lord Vibrate*... Is it not dangerous for a man to have the character of being charitable?
> *Sir George.* No doubt, my lord! It is the very certain way for his house to be besieged by beggars!
> *Lord Vibrate.* The master who pays the debts of one domestic makes himself the debtor of all the rest.
> *Sir George.* He changes a set of servants into a set of duns! He first encourages them to be extravagant, and then makes it incumbent upon himself to pay for their follies and vices! He not only bribes them to be idle, and insolent, but to waste his property as well as their own! (IV.ix.65–66)

Sir George's hyperbolic exclamations and slippery-slope argument that charity toward one servant will corrupt the entire domestic staff make Lord Vibrate's fear of philanthropy seem paranoid and illogical. Moreover, Sir George belies his cynical rhetoric by secretly giving Thompson a bank draft for £240 and thus proves to be more altruistic than the nobleman he is ostensibly imitating. Although Sir George exemplifies the sycophantic chameleonism that transforms fashionable society into a puppet shadow show, he possesses a vestigial moral sense that conflicts with his compliant behavior.

In *He's Much to Blame*, even the virtuous Maria Delaval feels compelled to join the social masquerade. Her brother, Paul Delaval, has come to England to confront Sir George, her "faithless lover" (I.iv.11), and possibly challenge him to a duel. To prevent the two men she loves from killing each other, Maria comes to London disguised as "a youth of fortune and fashion." Her male attire allows her to travel unchaperoned, but she is an unconvincing male impersonator, and her maid has to remind her to stay in character: "you must remember, madam, you are a man. So dry your eyes, forget your misfortunes, and, there, cock your hat, a that fashion, and try to swagger a little; or you will be found out" (I.v.13). She temporarily fools, however, Dr. Gosterman, who does not realize that she is a woman until she almost faints, and he goes "*to loosen her neckcloth.*" Complaining that her "disguise fits ill upon [her]," Maria reveals her gender to Lady Jane and asks her romantic rival to help prevent "[t]he shedding of blood" (IV.iii.56). As she makes her appeal, Maria hears Sir George's voice outside Lady Jane's apartment and hastily puts on his mask and domino, "copied after some Venetian Cicisbeo" (IV.i.55), which he plans to wear at the masquerade he is hosting that evening. Sir George enters and explains to Lady Jane that his saffron domino represents the god of marriage, "Hymen and his robe," and thus prefigures their union. Maria asks him if he is to be married soon, and he exclaims: "What frolicksome gentleman is this? In masquerade so early, and in my domino!" (IV.iv.58). By appropriating Sir George's costume, Maria literally unmasks him. Her voice, which is "so ingenuous, so affectionate, so fascinating" (IV.iv.59), begins to awaken his conscience and memories, and her refusal to remove the mask that she confiscated from him arouses his curiosity and commands his attention. Like the enterprising heroine of Hannah Cowley's comedy *The Belle's Stratagem*, Maria seeks empowerment through masquerade.[18]

Sir George is perceptually as well as morally obtuse. He fails to recognize the masked Maria and initially perceives her as a "frolicksome gentleman." Informed by Dr. Gosterman that the person conferring with Lady Jane is a woman in male dress, Sir George waits to "interrogate" the transvestite. When Paul Delaval appears, Sir George cannot decide whether Paul is a man or woman:

> *Sir George.* *(Aside)* She really has a very fierce look! A kind of threatening physiognomy; and would make no bad Grenadier.
> *Delaval.* I understand, your name is Sir George Versatile?
> *Sir George.* *(Aside)* A bass voice too!—At your service, sir; or madam; I really cannot tell which.
> *Delaval.* Cannot!
> *Sir George.* No, I cannot upon my soul! *(Aside)* A devilish black chin!
> *Delaval.* I have an account to settle with you, sir...
> *Sir George.* Must this account then be privately settled, madam?
> *Delaval.* Madam!...
> *Sir George.* *(Aside)* What a Joan of Arc it is! There is a danger she could knock me down. (IV.xii.68–70)

Sir George's chameleonism begins to dissipate when Delaval sternly warns him that he "should think of things very different from masquerading...and make [his] will" (IV.xii.71). At the masquerade, the unmasked Sir George can no longer imitate Lady Vibrate's lightheartedness and describes himself as "a wild unaccountable non descript [who is] any thing, every thing" (IV.xiii.72). According to him, "A mask is an excellent utensil" (IV.xiii.72–73), and he is lost without one. As Rousseau writes in *Emile* (1762), "The man of the world is whole in his mask. Almost never being in himself, he is always alien and ill at ease when forced to go back there. What he is, is nothing; what he appears to be is everything for him" (230).[19] Maria approaches Sir George, still using his mask and domino to conceal her identity. To make him "better acquainted with [him]self" (IV.xiv.74–75), she reminds him of his disloyalty toward Colonel Delaval and desertion of "Poor Maria." She then "*sinks into Sir George's arms, and her mask falls off*" (IV.xiv.76, italics in original). Her masquerade reveals as well as disguises her identity and prompts moral reflection rather than frivolity.

Both Maria and Lady Jane consider Sir George's chameleonism a moral failing. Maria "fear[s]" that Sir George's imitative compliance "is a vice" (I.vi.15), and Lady Jane explains that "[h]is character is too pliant. If others are merry, so is he: if they are sad, he is the same. Their joys and sorrows play upon his countenance: but, though they may slightly graze, they do not penetrate his heart. Even while he relieves, he scarcely feels them" (III.vi.40). At his masquerade, Sir George admits that compliance is his "worst virtue" and perhaps his worst vice (IV.xiii.73). It has led him to model himself after selfish and fatuous aristocrats and abandon his benefactor and fiancée. To be cured of this character flaw, he must develop a stable personal identity founded on moral commitments rather than social expediency. The morally upright Paul Delaval confronts Sir George and requires him either to sign a confession that Sir George has "basely and most dishonourably injured, insulted and betrayed Maria Delaval" or fight Paul in a duel (V.iv.85). Panic-stricken, Sir George envisions himself as a "reptile" about to be crushed by an inflexible "rock" (V.iv.86). He composes his confession, and Paul reads it, tears up the paper, and forgives him. However, although Sir George repents his former conduct, his behavior remains chameleonic. He echoes and amplifies Paul's emotional outburst as he previously imitated the Vibrates' more superficial sentiments:

Sir George. Mr. Delaval?
Delaval. My brother!
Sir George. *(Falls on his neck)* Can it be? My friend!
Delaval. This stubborn temper—always in extremes! The tiger, or the child.
Sir George. Oh no! 'Twas not to be forgiven! Best of men!
Delaval. Well, well: we are friends.
Sir George. Everlastingly! Brothers!
Delaval. Yes; brothers. (V.iv.88–89)

Unlike the Vibrates, Paul does not encourage Sir George's sycophancy. As Sir George's fraternal enthusiasm increases, his seems to diminish: he begins the reconciliation exclaiming "My brother!" and ends it with the matter-of-fact "Yes; brothers." As a compliant chameleon, Sir George lacks the ability to reform himself—he must be rehabilitated by others, whose principles he will adopt. He is redeemable because he has a "heart" that prompts him to pay a debt that "relieve[s] [the servant Thompson] from the disgrace and horrors of a prison" (V.viii.92). Sir George gives the Delavals credit for his moral reclamation: "if ever again I should recover my own self respect," he gushes, "I shall be indebted for it to this best of men, and to this most incomparable and affectionate of women!" (V.ix.94). If they had not intervened, he probably would have continued his career as a fashionable puppet.

The actor who played Sir George, William Thomas Lewis (nicknamed "Gentleman Lewis"), was considered "the unrivalled favourite of the comic muse, in all that was frolic, gay, humorous, whimsical, eccentric and at the same time elegant" (Dunlap 1:178). A review in the *Oracle and Public Advertiser* suggests that his performance effectively conveyed Sir George's vulnerability and remorse as well as his silliness: "Mr. LEWIS exhibited his usual gaiety; and, what he is not always called upon to exhibit, feeling and judgment" (February 14, 1798). In contrast to Monrose, Sir George does not engage in cross-class passing and refrains from Jacobinical rhetoric. Whereas conservative spectators and reviewers objected to Monrose, they considered Sir George a harmless chameleon because he does not challenge the social status quo. His chameleonism is morally reprehensible but not subversive, and rather than sneering at aristocratic corruption, he unwittingly parodies two feckless aristocrats. The satire in *He's Much to Blame* is Horatian instead of Juvenalian. However, like *Knave, or Not?*, *He's Much to Blame* portrays upper-class society as irresponsible, decadent, and in need of reformation.

Both Holcroft and his friend Godwin believed "in the perfectibility of man" (Holcroft and Hazlitt 2.195). In *An Enquiry Concerning Political Justice* (1793), Godwin argues that because human nature is malleable it can be perfected. He contends in the second edition of *Political Justice* (1796) that "ideas are to the mind nearly what atoms are to the body. The whole mass is in a perpetual flux; nothing is stable and permanent; after the lapse of a given period not a single particle probably remains the same. Who knows not that in the course of a human life the character of an individual frequently undergoes two or three revolutions of its fundamental stamina? The turbulent man will frequently become contemplative, the generous be changed into selfish, and the frank and good-humoured into peevish and morose" (*Political Justice Variants* 4.20). While Sir George's malleability devastates Maria and encourages the selfish propensities of Lord and Lady Vibrate, it also allows the Delavals to rehabilitate him. In contrast, individuals with fixed identities are less amenable to positive change. As Paul declares in the play's final speech, extreme intractability is "dangerous" and creates "misery" (V.ix.94). Writing 40 years after the publication of *Political Justice*, Godwin criticized it for "not bear[ing] in front that man is a fluctuating and variable animal, and that we need every assistance to hold us to the sticking place" (*Political Justice Variants* 4.419). In *He's Much to Blame*, the Delavals hold Sir George "to the sticking place" by forcing him to confront the moral consequences of his compliant behavior.

Holcroft also shared Godwin's commitment to truth and sincerity. In his self-exculpatory *A Narrative of Facts, Relating to a Persecution for High Treason* (1795), he presents himself as "a determined friend to the publication of truth; since by that alone the well-being of man can be promoted" and emphasizes "[t]he virtue of habitual sincerity" (4, 13).[20] Garnai notes that Holcroft railed against "benevolent lies" in his review of Elizabeth Inchbald's play *Every One Has His Fault* (1793), in which Mr. Harmony reconciles "a discordant group of friends . . . through a series of well-meaning falsehoods" (481).[21] On November 14, 1798 the embattled playwright wrote in his diary that he still "supposed [his] principles to be founded on truth" (Holcroft and Hazlitt 2.195). But despite Holcroft's advocacy of truth and sincerity, some of the most sympathetic characters in his plays resort to dissimulation. Mr. Osborne, the hero of *Duplicity: A Comedy* (1781), pretends to be a predatory gambler to prevent sharpers from fleecing his friend. In *Seduction: A Comedy* (1787), Harriet adopts the alias Charles Phelim O'Fireaway and masquerades as an Irish rake in Croatian dress to expose the libertinism of Sir Frederic Fashion (played by the ubiquitous Palmer); Mr. Wilmot, a "rich nabob" (II.iv.28), poses as a rustic servant to thwart Sir Frederic's seduction of a married woman and elopement with an heiress; and Lady Morden plays the role of a dissipated woman of fashion to reclaim her misguided husband. Moreover, as we have seen, Monrose's imposture in *Knave, or Not?* positions him to recover Aurelia's inheritance, and Maria's transvestitism and masquerade in *He's Much to Blame* enable her to appeal to her errant lover's conscience. Holcroft's comedies reflect a conflicted attitude toward deception, which, in a decadent, hypocritical society, may prove more effective than sincerity in counteracting immoral behavior.[22] Dissimulation allows socially marginalized characters like Harriet, Monrose, and Maria to "turn the weapons of oppression against itself." As Sir George Versatile ruefully observes, "A mask is an excellent utensil; and may be worn with a naked face" (IV.xiii.72–73).

Chapter 4

Fluid Identities in Hannah Cowley's Universal Masquerade

The Universal Masquerade

In Hannah Cowley's comedy *The Belle's Stratagem* (1780 premiere), Letitia Hardy plays the part of a vulgar country bumpkin to disgust Doricourt, her already reluctant fiancé, and then performs a very different role at a masquerade: concealing her identity behind a mask, she creates a chameleonic and cosmopolitan persona that enthralls him. She tells Doricourt that she would become "any thing—and all" for the man she loves: "Grave, gay, capricious—the soul of whim, the spirit of variety…[I would] change my country, my sex,—feast with him in an Esquimaux hut, or a Persian pavilion—join him in a victorious war-dance on the borders of Lake Ontario…or enter the dangerous precincts of the Mogul's Seraglio [*sic*]" (IV.i.59).[1] Letitia's willingness to adopt multiple identities to captivate her beloved recalls the exploits of the chameleonic female protagonist of Eliza Haywood's *Fantomina: Or Love in a Maze* (1725), who poses as a prostitute (Fantomina), a chambermaid (Celia), the widow Bloomer, and a masked mystery woman (Incognita) to serially seduce the rakish Beauplaisir. But whereas the chameleonism of Haywood's "young Lady of distinguished Birth, Beauty, Wit, and Spirit" (3.257) leads to her pregnancy and exile to a French monastery, Letitia's masquerade secures Doricourt's "whole soul" (V.v.81) without sacrificing her virtue. Her chameleonic performance is liberating and empowering.[2] In her comedy *A Bold Stroke for a Husband* (1783 premiere), Cowley presents two female characters who, like Letitia, play roles to assert their will: Olivia repels unwelcome suitors by acting the parts of a shrew, a felinophile, and a musical ignoramus, and the cross-dressing Victoria poses as "an accomplished cavalier" (IV.i.53) to romance and foil her husband's mistress.[3] Victoria uses performance to empower herself and reform her spouse.

But while Letitia's cosmopolitan masquerade, Olivia's role-playing, and Victoria's transvestitism temporarily emancipate them and challenge stereotypical notions of feminine behavior, the performances of many other characters in Cowley's comedies are exploitative or misguided. Although Cowley celebrates the agency that female characters achieve through theatrical self-fashioning, her comedies also reveal that male libertines and tricksters, along with their accomplices, frequently use performances to harm others. Because Letitia believes that "[m]en are all dissemblers! flatterers! deceivers!" (I.iv.15), she does not hesitate to invent false identities that mislead her prospective husband. In this chapter, I will examine Cowley's diverse portrayals of chameleonism in her comedies *The World as It Goes; or a Party at Montpelier* (1781) and *The Town before You* (1794 premiere). I will argue that *The World as It Goes* is Cowley's most daring and socially subversive drama and that its catastrophic theatrical failure profoundly influenced the manner in which she handled controversial issues in her subsequent dramas. The widespread condemnation of *The World as It Goes* also sheds light on late-eighteenth-century anxieties and mores. Cowley was mortified by the negative response to her comedy, which she did not include in her posthumous *Works* (1813), but she reworked some of its themes, situations, and characters in her final play, *The Town before You*. This comedy reflects a shift in her attitude toward chameleonism and female agency. In contrast to the chameleonic Letitia, Lady Horatia Horton, the heroine of *The Town before You*, has no desire to reinvent herself.[4] An aristocratic sculptor modeled after Anne Seymour Damer, Horton is an arbiter of fashion who presides over a "school" (II.iii.28) of upper-class women.[5] Unlike Letitia, she is a formative rather than a performative heroine. The most chameleonic and deracinated figure in *The Town before You* is male: Tippy passes himself off on various occasions as a cosmopolitan art connoisseur, an English Lord, an extremely robust woman, and a priest. Whereas Letitia's masquerade detaches "performance from its traditional associations with licentiousness and libertinism" (Arons 255), Tippy's machinations reaffirm the link between chameleonism and skullduggery.

In both *The Belle's Stratagem* and *The Town before You*, conservative male characters lament the fact that London society has turned into a masquerade in which social rank can be simulated and appearances are deceptive. According to Sir George Touchwood, society is "a meer [*sic*] chaos, in which all distinction of rank is lost…'tis one universal masquerade, all disguised in the same habits and manners" (*Stratagem*, II.i.27). As Sir Robert Floyer laments in *The Town before You*, "Whether the people one associates with [in London], are what they appear to be, or whether it may not be all one universal masquerade, there is no guessing" (V.vi.95).[6] For these two bewildered patriarchal figures, performance subverts social order and engenders anarchy. The sinister side of chameleonism is personified in *The Belle's Stratagem* by Courtall, an unscrupulous "Man of Gallantry" (I.i.2). To trick the naive Lady Frances Touchwood into becoming his mistress, Courtall poses as her husband, Sir George. He attends Lady Brilliant's masquerade in the same pink domino, or hooded cloak, that masks Sir George, and Lady Frances is deceived by his performance. She agrees to leave with the faux Sir George, but when Courtall goes to order his carriage, his disapproving friend Saville thwarts the abduction by substituting Kitty Willis, a courtesan "*habited like Lady* Frances" (IV.i.53, italics in original), for the intended victim. Kitty fears that "a Woman of Virtue" is "a difficult character" (IV.i.53–4) to assume, but Courtall cannot tell the difference between the disguised demimondaine and Lady Frances: at the masquerade, identities are interchangeable and virtue is easily simulated. While Courtall's predatory subterfuge threatens to destroy Lady Frances's reputation, marriage, and life, Kitty's impersonation is prompted by money rather than her own beneficence, and she clearly enjoys tormenting the libertine when her identity is revealed.[7] Along with these sordid masqueraders, the comedy features shabbily dressed auction room performers who circulate among customers to promote sales: Mrs. Fagg, who pretends to be "a Gentlewoman" (II.ii.30), and Silvertongue, who misrepresents himself as an "Antiquary" (II. ii.31).

Unsustainable performances often result in a humiliating exposure, as Tippy and his accomplice Mr. Fancourt discover in *The Town before You*. In *The Belle's Stratagem*, Letitia's cosmopolitan masquerade cannot be prolonged indefinitely. To demonstrate to Doricourt that the woman he is obliged marry is not "An Ideot" (IV.i.54), Letitia must reveal that she is both Doricourt's fiancée and the witty masquerader with whom he has fallen in love. Her self-confidence wavers as she prepares to unveil herself: she tells Doricourt that "[t]his is the most awful moment of my life...the slight action of taking off my Mask, stamps me the most blest or miserable of Women!" (V.v.81). If Doricourt is offended or repelled by her unmasking—if he objects to being duped or if Letitia's unveiling breaks the seductive spell her witty, unconventional persona has cast on him—her performance will result in her humiliation and despair. Fortunately for the heroine, Doricourt responds joyfully to her revelation, but in *A Bold Stroke for a Husband*, Don Julio is repulsed by a veiled woman whom he takes to be a beautiful 15-year-old but who turns out to be much older: "when she unveil'd her Gothic countenance," he complains, "to render the thing compleatly ridiculous, she began moralizing" (III.i.36). The play's errant husband, Don Carlos, flirts with a veiled incognita, and after she reveals that she is his wife Victoria, he responds guiltily and angrily: "by heav'n," he exclaims to her, "'tis a surprize fatal to every hope with which you may have flattered yourself.—...am I to be followed, haunted, watched?" (III.ii.45). Victoria's unveiling, unlike Letitia's, results in rejection and mortification. Despite their chameleonic abilities, Letitia and Victoria cannot fully emancipate themselves from the power of the male gaze.

CHAMELEONS ABROAD: *THE WORLD AS IT GOES*

Impostures are ubiquitous in Cowley's unpublished farce, *The World as It Goes; or a Party at Montpelier* (performed on February 24, 1781), which satirizes English tourists visiting a southern French resort and the scoundrels who prey on them. Reviews of the play condemned its indecency and improbability, and its sole performance was disrupted by audience members who loudly objected to a ribald bedchamber episode and repeatedly interrupted the actress Elizabeth Younge as she attempted to recite the epilogue, which included a risqué reference to the transgendering Chevalier D'Eon.[8] In Cowley's revision of *The World as It Goes*, she cut out the controversial and incongruous scene in which a monk attempts to rape Lady Danvers in the garden of a convent and excised some of the bawdy language, but the drama's second incarnation as *Second Thoughts Are Best* (performed on March 24, 1781) was also a failure.[9] According to the *Morning Chronicle and London Advertiser*, "every attempt to ornament and embellish, served...(like white silk stockings worn by a bandy-legged chimney-sweeper,) rather to expose than to conceal the deformity of the whole" ("Theatrical Intelligence," March 26, 1781). This twice-damned comedy, which survives as a Larpent licensing manuscript in the Huntington Library, depicts Montpelier as a place where class and nationality can be easily simulated and affectation is rampant. In the first act, the caustic Colonel Sparwell, pretending to read from a newspaper, declares that Montpelier has "all the Rogues upon Earth Epitomiz'd;—It is over-run with a kind of vermin in the shape of Italian Counts, French Marquises, [and] German Barons" (I.ii.6).[10] The play features the most nefarious female chameleon in Cowley's dramas, a fake French countess who, according to her Irish servant, has performed as "a Bride at Paris, a Maid at Avignon! a Widow at Spa! & here [at Montpelier]...all three at once" (IV.iv.83). Other continental imposters include Von Irkin, a spurious German baron in pursuit of a brash and uncouth English heiress named Molly Grubb, and his accomplice Le Rouge, who poses as the countess's lover and then as her husband to extort money from Molly's father.

The English tourists whom these parasites target also play roles. To establish his reputation as a "Man of Fashion" (II.ii.28), Sir Charles Danvers decides to seduce Mrs. Sparwell and pretends that he is a photosensitive antiquarian who needs to converse with her in darkness. But before he can implement his scheme, he is surprised by Mrs. Sparwell's husband, who confiscates Sir Charles's outfit and masquerades as a specialist in ancient lore to play a joke on his spouse. Sir Charles also affects to be a spendthrift and indifferent to his wife, whom he adores, and Mr. Grubb, a crass "Citizen," boasts of his performance as a French gentleman to his skeptical daughter:

> I behaves for all the world like a French Marquiss [*sic*],—the Countess says any one might think I had been born and bred in Paris, I hits them off so well;—when I first enters the Room, I makes a profound bow with a Borce, and a Pas Grave. Then in the middle I gives them another with a Grin all round,—then I goes up to Madame and gives her a Salute, first on one Cheek, and then on t'other, and when I goes away, then comes the finish,—when I goes away, I wriggles out backward like a Master in Chancery on the Floor of the House of Commons. (I.iii.13)

George Fairfax's impersonation of a French aristocrat is more persuasive: he has both Molly Grubb and her suitor Von Irkin convinced that he is the Marquis D'Arville until a vengeful Mrs. Sparwell unmasks him.

The most socially subversive English poseurs in *The World as It Goes* are Mrs. Sparwell, an unmaternal bluestocking, and Bronze, an opportunistic valet who convincingly masquerades as his master. Cowley portrays each character ambivalently. She satirizes Mrs.

Sparwell's antiquarianism and connoisseurship but has the comedy's protagonist, Fairfax, praise her "understanding" and "excellent heart" (I.ii.8). Bronze, Fairfax's servant, is a manipulative rogue, but he considers himself the mental and moral equal of his upper-class master, who is also guilty of imposture. He foils a French sharper, attracts an heiress, and envisions a parliamentary career for himself. Spectators and reviewers found both characters vulgar and morally offensive, and the chastened playwright took care to make the female aesthete and aristocratic impersonator in *The Town before You* less provocative.

Angela Escott argues that "Cowley refers obliquely to lesbianism in... *The World*, when the satirized female connoisseur, Mrs Sparwell, bids a wistful farewell to her fantasy of a 'Bath Weston' [V.v.93]. The reference is to Bath-Easton, where Sarah Scott lived with Lady Barbara Montagu, following the breakdown of her marriage amidst gossip about her lesbianism. The failure of this play gave Cowley a clear indication of what was acceptable on stage from a female pen—and any mention of unorthodox relationships was not" (28). Colonel Sparwell's mocking allusions to a jug, poetry-writing, and myrtle indicate, however, that "Bath Weston" refers not to Scott and Montagu but to the controversial bluestocking Lady Anna Miller (1741–1781), who founded a salon in Batheaston. Elizabeth Lee explains that Lady Miller "invited all persons of wit and fashion in Bath to meet once a fortnight at her house. An antique vase that had been purchased in Italy—it was dug up at Frascati in 1759—was placed on a modern altar decorated with laurel, and each guest was invited to place in the urn an original composition in verse. A committee was appointed to determine the best three productions, and their authors were then crowned by Lady Miller with wreaths of myrtle. The practice was continued until Lady Miller's death...The society became famous, and was much laughed at" (Lee 405). In *The World as It Goes*, Lady Miller is dubbed Mrs. Myrtle, and Mrs. Sparwell's "Ambition is to be a second Mrs. Myrtle whilst she is travelling." According to Colonel Sparwell, "at Naples [his wife crept] into an old Oven, and c[a]me out like a Chimney Sweeper because Mrs. Myrtle, in the depth of her Researches tumbled into a Cinder-hole, & was almost suffocated with Ashes; to compleat her Character, She designs at her Return to have a little Bath Weston down in Cumberland" (II.i.19).

Proclaiming herself "a woman of science," Mrs. Sparwell refuses to behave like a proper lady.[11] Her passionate desire to purchase a "urinal found in the last Excavation at Pompeia" startles Fairfax, and she "examine[s] a Gallery of naked [statues] with the accuracy of an

Anatomist" (II.i.19). She attempts to mold her seven-year-old daughter into "a woman of science" by testing her knowledge of ancient culture, but when the girl identifies Robinson Crusoe as "the most heroic and Fortunate amongst the Romans," Mrs. Sparwell calls her a "little wretch" and "monster" and sends her away to "live on bread & water [for] three days" (II.i.22). In one of the play's most controversial scenes, Colonel Sparwell and Fairfax play a trick on Mrs. Sparwell by having a man pretend to be a sculpture of Hercules. The Colonel asks his wife to critique the fake statue, and she objects to the drapery that covers Hercules's anatomy: "knock off his Stone Doublet, and then one can judge of his proportions" (IV.iv.65). As Escott notes, Cowley "highlights the taboo on women taking a critical interest in artistic representations of the naked human (male) body" (198). Mrs. Sparwell asserts that the statue's "Thorax is so monstrously narrow, that it could [not] Contain the vital parts," that "there could be no Lungs in that Chest," and "the Muscles of the [right] leg are absolutely in Contortion;...—If it were possible to make a Man from that Model he could never move" (IV.iv.65–66). Much to her chagrin, the man posing as the sculpture "*leaps down, dances, & runs Out*" (IV.iv.66).[12] Thus Mrs. Sparwell is portrayed as immodest, unfeminine, and ignorant about anatomy. The *London Courant* was, however, more offended by Colonel Sparwell's characterizations of Mrs. Sparwell than by her transgressive behavior and grumbled that his "observations on [his wife], were almost always coarse, and sometimes indecent" (February, 26 1781). For example, the Colonel jests that she would prostitute herself to acquire "curiosities":

> *Sparwell*... I believe there's only One Man in the World could Tempt her Virtue! and that's the little old Ciceroni of the Florentine Gallery! He's fourscore, and has a Dromedary back; but if he was to bribe her with a Picture,—a Medallion,—or a Satyr, I wou'dn't answer but She'd make me an Acteon! (II.i.18)[13]

However, while Mrs. Sparwell flouts conventions and lacks feminine modesty, she is oblivious to Sir Charles Danvers's attempt to seduce her and disdains subterfuge. When her husband disguises himself as an antiquarian to play a joke on her, she tells him that she "despise[s] the Principle that could induce him to Stand...in the dark in a feign'd Character, in hopes of finding something in his Wife's Conduct to be displeas'd at" (III.i.43). At the end of the play, she abandons her ambition to set up a "Cumberland Bath Weston" and vows to "improve [her]self in the accomplishments suited to [her]

Sex, & leave Criticism & the arts to those to whom they belong" (V.v.93–94). Fairfax pronounces her "A Woman of...merit," and her husband asks him to "write the first Poem for [his] Wife's Jug" (V.v.93). Although Mrs. Sparwell ultimately forswears connoisseurship, for most of the play she is an empowered, protofeminist woman who advocates female education, repudiates false modesty, dismisses her husband as a person "to whom nature has been niggard in respect to Taste" (I.i.20), and plans to establish a literary salon in Cumberland.

Mrs. Sparwell is the precursor of two disparate characters in *The Town before You*: the play's heroine, Lady Horatia Horton, and Tippy, a bogus connoisseur. Both Mrs. Sparwell and Lady Horatia are strong-minded and unconventional women who dedicate themselves to art and classical culture. Unlike the indecorous Mrs. Sparwell, however, Lady Horatia is concerned about her reputation and hyperfeminine: even her chiseling is described as refined and ladylike. Whereas Mrs. Sparwell unblushingly analyzes the body of a man posing as a statue, Lady Horatia, "with an enchanting modesty[,]...seeks for models only in the graces of her own sex" (I.iv.17). Cowley's portrayal of Lady Horatia rehabilitates the figure of the female aesthete.[14] Moreover, in *The Town before You*, Cowley reconfigures the provocative statue scene from *The World as It Goes* to ridicule a male rather than a female connoisseur. The positive reception of *The Town before You* suggests that a man examining a woman's body was more palatable to Cowley's contemporaries than a woman critiquing a man's seminude physique.

Bronze, Fairfax's ambitious servant, explores both the opportunities and perils of chameleonism. Sensing Bronze's nascent egalitarianism, Fairfax advises him to "keep [his wit] clear of sauciness, or [he]'ll find it the most dangerous quality a valet can possess" (I.i.2). After Fairfax departs, Bronze observes that servants "are sometimes forc'd to carry wit for [them]selves and [their] Masters too" (I.i.3). In a subsequent scene, he masquerades in his employer's clothes:

> Damn fortune! (*looking at himself*) I am as tall, as well made, and have as much Impudence as my Master, and why the devil should he be gone abroad in Embroidery, whilst I am brushing his Cloaths in a Scurvy Livery!...You go there (*flinging away the brush*) And you there. (*throwing off his Coat & Waistcoat*) I'll be a Gentleman one half hour if I swing the Next (*dressing himself*) There, now let me See (*looking in the Glass*) now who would find out that I wasn't Swaddled in Lace, or hadn't an Earl for my Godfather! Ha! a good morning, my Lord!...We sate late last night; a confounded head ache. These Nasty

> Petitions from the Manufacturing Towns always affect my Nerves.—they smell of Ram's Wool, and Oil; Is not that Lady Ball Lustre? (*looking thro' his hand*) A Pretty Girl faith . . . Complection [*sic*] true Italian! hang it, it won't do, there must be something in birth after all, spite of affectation and Silk, I look no more like a Gentleman than Peter Pelican, who drives his Whiskey, and hops Cotillions at Country balls, whilst honest Kate, his Mother, dispenses drams to the Nymphs of Covent Garden. (III.iii.51–52)

Although Bronze momentarily doubts that he can pass for a member of the upper class, after the countess surprises him in his master's clothes and mistakes him for Fairfax, he decides that he "may as well use [Fairfax's] Name as his Coat" and play "the Gentleman at a French Countess's" (III.iii.53–54). At the sham aristocrat's house he flirts with her, antagonizes Grubb, and enlists the aid of his former associate, an Irish ex-convict named Murtagh, who promises him access to the countess's bedchamber. The bedchamber is locked, however, and while waiting for Murtagh to return with the key, Bronze sees Grubb coming down the hallway. To avoid detection, he hides behind a curtain and overhears the countess meeting Grubb for an assignation. Le Rouge interrupts the tryst, claims to be the countess's husband, puts a pistol to Grubb's head, and orders him to write him a draft for £5,000. Still posing as Fairfax, Bronze disarms Le Rouge and commands Grubb to promise Molly to "a dev'lish handsome fellow" (he means himself, not Fairfax) "with a portion of Twenty thousand pounds" (V.v.88).

Bronze's scheme unravels when his master enters the room and refuses to "favor the frolic" that would force Grubb to marry his daughters to them and provide enormous dowries: "What, Rascal," Fairfax exclaims to his servant, "in my Cloaths, & [you] expect me to become a Party in the deceit[?]" (V.iv.89). But even though Bronze's imposture backfires and costs him his job, he refuses to repent:

> what have I done but like my betters made a bold Stroke for a Wife? but I see my Spirit has lost me my place,—So I'll e'en try my Chances with the dice box; if I have Luck, I don't despair of rolling my own Wheels yet; aye, & getting a Seat at Westminster too,—like some other's of my Cloth, and when I am once warm in it, and 'tis proved that the Money I left behind me in the Borough was not Bribery; I'll oppose, be call'd to Order, & abuse the Minister with the best of them. (V.v.92)

At the play's conclusion, Sir Charles has renounced his fashionable affectations, and Mrs. Sparwell promises to "leave Criticism & the arts to those to whom they belong." In contrast, Bronze remains unrepentantly subversive and claims that there is no essential difference between servants and masters or successful gamblers and members of Parliament. Armed with impudence and fashionable clothes, he makes "a bold Stroke for a Wife" that nearly succeeds.[15] The phrase "a bold Stroke for a Wife" alludes to Susanna Centlivre's comedy *A Bold Stroke for a Wife* (1718) and underscores Bronze's self-conscious theatricality. Like Colonel Fainwell, the protagonist of Centlivre's play, both Bronze and Fairfax resort to imposture to obtain a wife. Fairfax's denunciation of his servant rings hollow because he, like Bronze, has practiced dissimulation.[16] Refusing to allow his master to define him as a "Rascal," Bronze insists on his right to behave like his "betters." If he cannot rise in the world through performance, he will try gambling and politics, and he may yet marry an heiress. Molly Grubb expresses disappointment that "the pretty smart looking fellow" has fled and says: "Gad I'll find him out tho'...I like the dog for his Spirit" (V.v.93). Her father suspects, however, that the renegade servant will eventually be hung: "Aye run," he says after Bronze departs, "or Tyburn will Catch you in your way to Westminster" (V.v.92).

Bronze prefigures the presumptuous French servant A la Greque in Cowley's comic opera *A Day in Turkey; or, The Russian Slaves* (1791 premiere) and the opportunistic Tippy in *The Town before You*. After A la Greque and his Russian master Orloff are enslaved by the Turks in *A Day in Turkey*, A la Greque declares that he "feel[s]...as great a man as [his] master" (I.i.3) and boasts that he came to Russia "to polish the brutes a little, and to give them some ideas of the general equality of man" (II.i.18). At the end of the comic opera, confronted with the prospect of being demoted to the position of Orloff's "duteous servant," A la Greque begs the Turkish Bassa to appoint him "principal slave driver" (V.iv.83). Conservative spectators and reviewers objected to A la Greque because his ethnicity and egalitarian rhetoric linked him to the unpopular French Revolution. A reviewer for the *Morning Post* commented that in *A Day in Turkey* Cowley "has hazarded the introduction of numberless political allusions, many of which were violently resisted by the audience" (December 5, 1791). Cowley found it necessary to dissociate herself from A la Greque's political views in the advertisement prefacing the printed version of the comic opera: "It is A LA GREQUE who speaks, not *I*; nor can I be accountable for *his* sentiments" (n. pag.). Whereas in 1781 theatergoers objected to Bronze's ribaldry, ten years later audiences hissed at A la Greque's egalitarianism.

In *The Town before You*, Tippy, like Bronze, poses as an aristocrat and attempts to marry an heiress. Both Bronze and Tippy are transgressive figures, but unlike Tippy, who is a professional swindler, Bronze is an overtly lascivious valet posing as his master: he makes arrangements with an Irish "Pimp" (IV.iv.84) to fornicate with a counterfeit French countess. As an "oversexed liveried manservant" (Straub 45) who pursues a courtesan and attracts an heiress, Bronze is a more problematic figure for Cowley's contemporaries than Tippy, whose awkward attempt to woo a Welsh knight's daughter while dressed as a woman is ludicrous rather than provocative. Whereas in his final speech Bronze defiantly resolves to win a fortune gambling and buy a seat at Westminster, at end of *The Town before You* the unmasked Tippy seems demoralized. The negative response to *The World as It Goes* taught Cowley that the public would not tolerate a bawdy aristocratic impersonator.

THE POLYGRAPH AND THE FEMALE AESTHETE

As the pseudonymous author of amatory verse published in the newspaper *The World* from 1787 to 1789, Cowley became well aware of the opportunities and pitfalls of persona creation and self-masking. Erin Isikoff observes that *The Belle's Stratagem* "insists on the link between Cowley and Letitia": "Letitia's various identities rely not only on facial disguise, but also on the mask of language. It is precisely Letitia's varied conversational personas (like Cowley's comic talent) than earn our notice and our interest. Through vulgar, witty, and proper language, Letitia also writes a comedy for herself... Cowley presents herself anonymously, veils herself, and her mask too is a sort of emancipation from the perils of public performance" (100). Cowley donned another mask in 1787 when she assumed the penname Anna Matilda and began a flirtatious poetic dialogue in the pages of *The World* with Robert Merry, who wrote under the pseudonym Della Crusca. Although in one of her verse epistles addressed "To Della Crusca" (August 4, 1787) Cowley hinted that she was middle-aged and married, for many of her readers the name Anna Matilda became synonymous with untrammeled romantic passion.[17] Unaware that the poets writing as Della Crusca and Anna Matilda had met each other many months previously, in December 1789 *The Morning Post* breathlessly speculated that their first encounter would be rapturous: "The interview between DELLA CRUSCA and ANNA MATILDA, after so much eager expectation and fanciful enthusiasm on both sides, would be a good subject for the pencil, or poetic celebration. Even the ardent loves of ABELARD and ELOIZA [*sic*] would yield to the raptures of such a meeting, if painted by the vivid energy of the Muse" (December 4, 1789).

The actual interview seems to have been a disappointment. According to Frederick Reynolds, the 34-year-old Merry had envisioned Anna Matilda as an "ideal goddess" and when he met a 46-year-old, married, "plain respectable matronly lady—simply poetical and platonic, he walked away in sad dudgeon, and endeavoured to conceal his disappointment, by concealing her name—in vain—for Anna Matilda was soon discovered to be no other than Mrs. Cowley" (2.187–188).[18] James Boaden provides a less histrionic account of the meeting: "the parties became known personally by an accidental rencontre at an inn. Merry was an enthusiast in beauty as well as verse; and the proportion of the former to the latter in the lady was less than might be desired: with a rhapsodical farewell, the correspondence closed" (217).[19] After her unmasking, Cowley was satirized, along with Merry and the other Della Cruscan poets, in William Gifford's *The Baviad* (1791). Mocking Cowley for writing amorous verse to a man who was not her husband, Gifford accused her of "weekly cuckhold[ing] her poor spouse in rhyme" (24). *The World*, which had benefited greatly from the Della Crusca-Anna Matilda correspondence, advised Cowley to end her poetic career: "Mrs. COWLEY, the ANNA MATILDA of this Paper, will do well to write Poetry no more—To keep a good reputation is no such easy matter" (October 11, 1791). Charlotte Smith based her satirical portrait of the unattractive, flirtatious, and delusional Mrs. Manby in *The Old Manor House* (1793) on Cowley:

> Though no longer young, [Mrs. Manby] believed herself still an object of affection and admiration; and that the beauties of her mind were irresistible to all men of taste...As she was by no means insensible to perfection, if it appeared in the form of a young man, she was immediately struck with the figure and address of Orlando [the novel's protagonist]; and...she addressed herself particularly to him[,]...besought him to favour her with some of his productions, and seemed disposed to elect him to emulate, if not to rival, the Florios and Philanders with whom she held a tender correspondence in the news-papers. (499)

Cowley's Anna Matilda persona fascinated contemporary readers, but the poet's unveiling proved embarrassing and tarnished her public image.

Following the revelation that she was Anna Matilda, Cowley sought to rehabilitate her reputation, damaged not only by her association with

Della Cruscanism, but also by the damnation of *The World as It Goes* and the controversy over *A School for Greybeards; or, The Mourning Bride* (1786), which contained expressions that some theater-goers and reviewers found indecent. She presents herself in the preface to *The Town before You* as a serious, moralistic writer who believes that plays should provide instruction rather than cheap laughs. A comparison of Cowley's buoyant advertisement for her farce *Who's the Dupe?* (1779) and her disillusioned preface to *The Town before You*, published 15 years later, reveals that during her playwriting career her attitude toward comic performances and the contemporary stage radically changed. In the advertisement for *Who's the Dupe?*, she dismisses "the common clamour on the declension of the Stage" and declares that "there has been no [other] period in which performances in the Comic line have been represented in such uniform strength" (3–4). She notes that the extralinguistic cues provided by actors' performances are often more effective than the playwright's words in conveying her ideas: "Actors of skill and ability, acquainted with the ideas of the Writer, and assisted by all the advantages of Stage-representation, give impressions of character and situation with more expedition and certainty than can be done by Words alone" (3). In contrast, Cowley's preface to *The Town before You* offers a gloomy assessment of the "state" of the English "Stage." She deplores the decline of contemporary theatrical taste, which has "no relish" for "The patient developement [*sic*] of character, the repeated touches which colour it up to Nature, and swell it into identity and existence," and declares that brilliant playwrights and actors are no longer necessary: "a great Actor, holding a sword in his left hand, and making aukward [*sic*] pushes with it, charms the audience infinitely more than he could do, by all the wit and observation which the ingenious Author might have given him; and brings down such applauses, as the bewitching dialogue of Cibber, and of Farquhar pants for in vain!" (x). According to Cowley, obtuse late-eighteenth-century audiences would rather witness Tippy's antics than listen to clever or enlightening dialogue. She also complains that the most applauded scenes in the stage productions of *The Town before You* featured Tippy's mistreatment of his landlady and hoodwinking of the bailiff and were only added because Mrs. Pope, who played Lady Horatia Horton, fell ill. The popular comic actor William Thomas Lewis, who would later play the chameleon Sir George Versatile in Holcroft's *He's Much to Blame*, performed the part of Tippy. To Cowley's dismay, and the delight of the comedy's audiences, the chameleonic scamp upstaged the protofeminist female artist. Cowley never wrote another drama.[20]

Tippy, who informs his associate Fancourt that he has "been in a thousand shapes, and a thousand places" (II.ii.21) in the last year, is a mercenary, parasitic, male parody of Letitia. Both characters profess extraordinary self-transformative powers, but whereas Letitia's playacting ensures her happy marriage to her fiancé and meets with general approval, Tippy's illicit performances enable him to cheat, steal, and exploit. As I noted in chapter 1, a review from the *Morning Chronicle* claimed that Tippy "is obviously drawn from the Duke of Ormond, whose feats, as the counterfeit of different men of rank, are on record" (December 8, 1794). Tippy may be a composite of the fake Duke of Ormond (also known as Hobart), and an unidentified imposter who passed as a "northern Duke." A writer for *The Monthly Review* observed that "Tippy's great resemblance to Lord Beachgrove [*sic*] seems to be copied from a *nameless* person, who is said to be so strong a resemblance of a *northern Duke*, as to have imposed on his friends and servants" (Art. XIX. *The Town before You* 331). A report in the *Oracle and Public Advertiser* provides further information regarding this mysterious figure: "The man who last winter made so much laugh in town, by his astonishing resemblance to a certain *Northern Duke*, has been lately at Bath. The *vrai-semblance* [representation] is so strong, that there is hardly a shade of difference. It is reported that he was on the point of marriage with a young woman of beauty and fortune, before he was discovered to be only the *Duke's Double*. It must be remembered, that last year he was accosted in Hyde-Park by [Daniel] Mendoza [a famous pugilist], who left him at last, without discovering his mistake" (November 24, 1794). In *The Town before You*, the villainous Fancourt echoes a phrase in the newspaper story when he observes that Tippy's "resemblance" to Lord Beechgrove "is astonishing" (II.i.22).

Tippy, like Hobart, is an identity thief who preys on those who trust appearances, but whereas Hobart reportedly kept his composure even in the most nerve-racking situations, Tippy occasionally panics. And like the northern Duke's double, he exploits his physical resemblance to a nobleman to further his schemes. Tippy boasts that his "strong likeness to Lord Beechgrove" enables him to eat for free, win money gambling, race recklessly through London in a chaise and four, and drink champagne at the Turkish ambassador's former apartments at the Royal Hotel. Fancourt calls him Lord Beechgrove's polygraph, or duplicate, and Tippy haughtily replies: "They call his Lordship *my* polygraph" (II.ii.22). As Hobart's escapades demonstrated, nobility could be convincingly performed by an enterprising commoner to dupe members of the mercantile class. Fancourt suggests a more ambitious scheme to Tippy: he speculates that if the impersonator can somehow prove that Lord Beechgrove is "an imposter" he "may then *enjoy* [the Lord's] Cumberland estate" (II.ii.23). Rather than savoring just a few of the aristocrat's privileges, Tippy might be able to make the identity theft permanent by replacing him. But although Tippy decides against becoming Lord Beechgrove and pursues other schemes, his interchangeability with a politically powerful and wealthy aristocrat enables Fancourt and him to defraud a Welsh knight, Sir Robert Floyer, of £1,000 and threatens to undermine social and economic stability. Perhaps recalling the sensationalist accounts of Hobart's impersonations by John Collard and others, the disabused Sir Robert asks to be put "down as a subscriber" when Tippy publishes a memoir: "Your life," he tells Tippy, "must be an amusing one" (V.vi.97).

As Cowley's preface to the play indicates, her revisions of *The Town before You* focused primarily on Tippy. In the comedy's first performance, "the acute Bumpkin *Tippy*" was a sharper, and another character named Acid was a connoisseur (*Oracle and Public Advertiser*, December 18, 1794; Escott 207–208). Cowley subsequently eliminated Acid, and Tippy became a bombastic art critic as well as aristocratic impersonator and cross-dresser. The *General Evening Post* applauded this change: "Mrs. Cowley has considerably improved her Comedy of *The Town before You* by judicious alteration: Acid is entirely cut out, and Tippy made a Connoisseur. The compression of its parts gives more vigour to the whole; and it is now received with very general approbation" (December 20–23, 1794, italics added). In the revised play, Tippy brags to Fancourt that he learned in Italy how to "talk of statues and intaglios—of busts and medallions," "find fault where ever [he goes]," satirize, and judge. But although he pronounces confidently "on Paintings and Tokay—on Statues and Old Hock" and concludes that "there requires little to be a connoisseur, but impudence" (II.ii.22), Tippy discovers that it is much easier to impersonate his aristocratic double than to pass as an art critic. To fool her admirer, Conway, Georgina poses as a veiled sculpture in Lady Horatia Horton's studio and inadvertently demolishes Tippy's credibility as an art expert. Looking at Georgina through his glass, Tippy declares that she is "a mere wax doll" and insists that "a human figure made on this principle, could never move" (II.iv.34). When he reaches toward the muscle of her foot, Georgina shrieks, leaps down, and dances around him to demonstrate her mobility. Completely deflated, Tippy exclaims that he is "done up as a connoisseur" and flees from the room (II.iv.35). His counterfeit connoisseurship contrasts with Lady Horatia's expertise in and commitment to the art of sculpture. Along with posing as an aristocrat and art critic, Tippy is an enthusiastic cross-dresser who compares his transvestitism to the exploits of Greek heroes. He describes his "scheme" to Fancourt: "A plan . . . sometimes forces me to take shelter, like Hercules, under the disguise of a petticoat . . . Yes, like him, I exchange my club for a distaff, or like Achilles transform my surtout to a gauze robe, and my waistcoat to a lace tucker" (II.ii.23).[21] But his performance as Sally Martin is unconvincing: he looks like a "robust damsel" (V.iii.87), bows rather than curtseys, and swears. Georgina describes him as "A very odd lady" (V.iii.84), and he is soon unmasked.[22]

According to John Genest, "Mrs. Cowley would probably have been better pleased, if the applause, which was deservedly bestowed on Tippy, had been given to [Sidney] Asgill, for his romantic conduct and ostentatious display of patriotism" (VII. 206). Asgill is presented as everything that the chameleonic Tippy is not: sincere, ethical, transparent, and somewhat dull. In the posthumously published 1813 edition of *The Town before You*, which incorporates Cowley's final revisions, Tippy is renamed "Brisk" and many of his lines are altered or deleted.[23] The name change is significant. The *OED* defines "the tippy" as "the height of fashion; the 'swell' or fashionable thing," and the song "Tippy Bob," featuring a self-congratulatory young fop, was popular during the 1790s. Whereas Tippy suggests instability and immaturity, the surname Brisk connotes efficiency and sharpness. Cowley's revisions were clearly intended to make the Tippy-Brisk character more menacing and less personable. In the altered first scene of the 1813 version, Mrs. Fancourt tells her husband that she has heard "with grief" that the ruthless "Mr. Brisk," who, along with Fancourt, is "capable of almost any action that will not endanger" his life, has returned to London (*Works* II.331). Cowley excised the two audience-pleasing scenes that she repudiated in her preface to the 1795 edition: a scene in which Tippy teases his landlady, Mrs. Bullrush, who is trying to evict him from her lodgings, and another in which he cross-dresses as her and pretends to be suffering from a toothache to elude the bailiff (II.i and V.i in the 1795 edition). While playing the part of connoisseur, Brisk is more pompous and verbose than Tippy, and Cowley deleted Tippy's cheeky quip, "They call his Lordship *my* polygraph." More important, whereas Tippy is crestfallen when his schemes are exposed, Brisk remains defiant, denouncing his sister Jenny as a "Traitress" and sneering at Fancourt's "moralizing" (*Works* II.414–415). In the 1813 edition, Fancourt's parting threat is transferred to an unrepentant Brisk, who warns Sir Robert that he and his accomplice "*will* turn out on the wide World—and let the World beware!" (*Works* II.417, italics in original). Both Fancourt and Brisk claim that society's lack of moral discernment has allowed rogues like themselves to prosper. Fancourt explains that "[t]he mark is not very distinctly defined,...in the present day, where the manners of a man called a dashing fellow about Town end, and what...is an approach towards being a Sharper begins" (*Works* II.331). Similarly, Brisk declares that "[t]he world is not so alive to a sense of right and wrong as it was—a mixed character succeeds best in it" (*Works* II.417). Brisk's chameleonism leads, however, to his arrest and public exposure: whereas Sir Robert allows the two culprits to escape justice in the 1795 edition, in the later version he hands them over to the bailiff and vows to publicize their criminal "characters." "[T]he history [Sir Robert has] published" probably would not, however, prevent such a slippery pair from eluding surveillance by reinventing themselves (*Works* II.417).

The Oxford-educated Fancourt is more sociopathic and treacherous than his confederate. While he wooed Mrs. Fancourt to acquire her small fortune, "The sweetness of [his] manners disguised the emptiness of [his] heart" (I.i.4), and their sham marriage was presided over by Tippy disguised as a priest. Fancourt abhors the wealthy and praises Sir Robert's quarrelsome servants: "I like those children of nature; I am fond of natural characters; no disguise—all open honesty—what their hearts prompt, their tongues utter" (III. iii.47).[24] In December 1794, only months after the Reign of Terror had ended, Fancourt's hatred for the rich and ostensible egalitarianism would have reminded the play's audiences of the anti-wealth, anti-property agendas of the French *enragés*, *sans-cullottes*, and radical Jacobins. Moreover, Mrs. Fancourt's evaluation of her spouse's morality in the 1813 edition of the comedy recalls Edmund Burke's indictment of "the new philosophy" of Jean-Jacques Rousseau and his French revolutionary disciples in *A Letter to a Member of the National Assembly* (1791). Burke condemns Rousseau, who had notoriously consigned his children to a foundling hospital, for "exhaust[ing] the stores of his powerful rhetoric in the expression of universal benevolence; whilst his heart was incapable of habouring one spark of common parental affection" (271). Mrs. Fancourt mounts a similar critique of her husband, declaring that his "good-will has distended itself into a mere *Theory* of Benevolence to mankind at large, without being practically displayed to a single individual, not...even to [his] Sister" (*Works* II.331). The cries of Fancourt's hungry children annoy rather than distress him, and he threatens to "slit" his wife's "pretty tongue...and make it chatter double, like a starling's" (III.i.40) if she exposes his and Tippy's scheme to abduct Sir Robert's daughter. Although Fancourt, like Tippy, seems more opportunistic than ideological, his detestation of "rich people" (I.i.2) aligns him with the revolutionaries who sought to rid France of "*riches égoïstes*" and wealthy "blood-suckers" (Schama 755). He pledges to use his theatrical talents to "wage [economic] war" against "the world." "Be of good heart," he urges Tippy, "The foe is numerous, but weak. Conquest and pillage are our own!" (V.vi.99).

Posing as a Welsh antiquarian and political influence peddler, Fancourt takes advantage of Tippy's resemblance to Lord Beechgrove to cheat Sir Robert. Tippy dresses as Lord Beechgrove and pretends to offer Sir Robert "a place at the Board of Controul [*sic*] for Indian affairs" (IV.ii.62) in exchange for a £1,000 loan, which their victim is happy to provide. But although Fancourt had agreed to split the amount with his accomplice, he is incapable of loyalty even to "a brother rascal" (IV.v.70) and gives Tippy only £100. Outraged by Fancourt's treachery, Tippy poses as Lord Beechgrove and truthfully informs Sir Robert that the Welshman has been duped by the Lord's polygraph and Fancourt. Fancourt is, however, a skillful improviser, and, after he promises Tippy the other £400, Tippy again impersonates the aristocrat and the two of them persuade Sir Robert that Lord Beechgrove's warnings about the cheating polygraph were made in jest. The swindlers also conspire to carry off Sir Robert's daughter and force her to marry Tippy, "a plot laid," Mrs. Fancourt declares, "for the bitter anguish of a father, [and] for the ruin of a child" (III.i.40). This scheme, which turns out to be unsuccessful, demonstrates the tricksters' willingness to cause serious harm. They are chameleonic monsters who have absolutely no scruples about plunging women into domestic misery. As Georgina's husband, Tippy might have gained access to Sir Robert's fortune, supplanting a Welsh knight rather than an English aristocrat and furthering Fancourt's project of redistributing money from the wealthy to destitute sharpers.

Fancourt subscribes to a morally subversive theory of comic performance: he argues that "as long as you can get the world to laugh *with* you, you may carry any point you please. Only make wickedness pleasant, and they'll heartily forgive you" (III.i.39, italics in original). According to him, if a man is cheated, his neighbor will laugh at the victim and admire the clever swindler. People "always . . . laugh at wickednesses . . . when they do not suffer by [them]" (III.i.39)—their sense of humor is invariably sadistic and amoral. Fancourt's misanthropic pronouncements may reflect Cowley's disillusionment with comedy as a vehicle for ethical instruction. Audiences "wait[ing] for the next tumble from a chair, or a tripping up of the heels" (preface to *The Town before You* xi) are more inclined to guffaw at Tippy's and Fancourt's predatory performances than appreciate Asgill's patriotism or Lady Horatia's defense of female artistry. Entertaining theatrical villains make wickedness seem pleasant and the sufferings of their victims inconsequential or even humorous.

The Town before You features two female performers, both of whom fail to stay in character. Whereas Tippy and Fancourt use their performances for personal gain, the flighty Georgina plays roles to entertain herself. When Sir Robert doubts that Georgina would be able to pass herself off "as a duke's daughter," she tries to prove him wrong by speaking and acting like "a countess from the Opera" (I.iii.12). To play a trick on Conway, she poses as a statue, which fools Tippy but not her prank's target. More mischievously, she impersonates Lady Horatia Horton, and her flippant behavior in that role convinces Sir Simon Asgill that Horton is not worthy of his nephew Sidney. While pretending to be Lady Horatia, Georgina makes no attempt to behave like her more serious-minded prototype, who loves Sidney, and twice forgets that she is playing her friend rather than herself. Her performance is not only inept, it also mortifies Lady Horatia, who fears that her beloved will consider her "mean, sordid, detestable" (III.ii.45). When Horton attempts to plead her case before the infuriated Sir Simon, he does not realize who she is and unwittingly insults her by denouncing the counterfeit Lady Horatia as a "gill-flirt" and "stone-cutter" (V.ii.79). Georgina is, like Tippy, an identity thief, but she is a practical joker rather than a swindler.

Mrs. Fancourt's masquerade is beneficial, altruistic, and designed to thwart Tippy and Fancourt's malign performances. She decides to risk retaliation from her counterfeit husband and disguise herself as a Savoyard musician and fortune-teller to warn Georgina about the villains' plot. Speaking with a Savoyard accent, she implores the naive young woman to beware two wicked men. But after Georgina refuses to take her seriously and turns away, Mrs. Fancourt becomes desperate, and her performance breaks down. She forgets that she is supposed to be Savoyard and begins to "speak good English." Conceding that Georgina has "detected" her, Mrs. Fancourt explains that "when the heart feels it is hard to dissemble" (IV.iv.65). Her failure to stay in character is an indicator of sincerity—she cannot sustain a duplicitous performance. Unlike Letitia Hardy, Georgina and Mrs. Fancourt are not proficient actresses, but in a drama that associates chameleonism with predation, their amateurishness seems like a positive trait.

Lady Horatia Horton is Georgina's unchameleonic role model, an accomplished artist who disdains subterfuge and the theatrical world of fashion. When Sir Simon Asgill reveals that he has pretended to be poor to test his nephew's virtue, Horton angrily informs him that she despises his "pitiful plot," which has made her confess her love for his nephew (V.iv.92). To her, a female gamester's "labours" and a society belle's "toils" are far more exhausting than marble chipping (II.iv.30). In contrast to the ridiculously affected Mrs. Sparwell, Lady Horatia is a genuine sculpture aficionada. Georgina idolizes Horton and "long[s] to be a sculptor" like her heroine. She explains her infatuation to her father: "Lady Horatia does look so charmingly whilst at her labours; her sweet white hands appear like the very marble she is at work upon...I wish she wou'd teach me her art; I could spend my life amidst fine statues" (I.iii.11). In the scene in which Georgina pretends to be a sculpture, Conway wishes that he, "like Pygmalion," had "the power to warm [his] statue [i.e., Georgina] into love" (II.iv.34). He envisions Horton as a female Pygmalion animating marble forms like herself. "[I]t must be charming," he says, "to see a fine woman sit with a chissel [*sic*], and bring out of a block of marble, a form as graceful as her own; every feature glowing with animation beneath her eye, and every stroke of the mallet warming the cold mass into mind and expression" (I.iv.16–17). Given the strenuous labor that sculpting often requires, Georgina's and Conway's worshipful accounts of Lady Horatia's graceful, feminine chiseling make it almost seem staged: they downplay the physicality of her work. Conway's praise of Lady Horatia recalls Erasmus Darwin's poetic description in *The Economy of Vegetation* (1791) of Anne Damer's delicate craftswomanship and her enchanting busts of two aristocratic women, Lady Elizabeth Foster and Lady Melbourne:

> Long with soft touch shall Damer's chissel [*sic*] charm,
> With grace delight us, and with beauty warm;
> Foster's fine form shall hearts unborn engage,
> And Melbourn's [*sic*] smile enchant another age. (II.111–114)[25]

Sidney Asgill, who loves Horton, is entranced by her artistry and sits for hours "patiently watching the strokes of [her] chissel" (V.ii.80). He emphasizes that she never sculpts the male body: "with an enchanting modesty she seeks for models only in the graces of her own sex, the daughters of Britain, and the matrons of Greece" (I.iv.17). Thus Horton engenders both female disciples and female forms "as graceful as her own" without compromising her sexual reputation. Rather than imitating others, she is imitated by them, and she looks for models to shape her art, not her behavior. Wealthy, aristocratic, and beautiful, she does not need to play roles to achieve empowerment. Whereas Tippy's comparison of himself to a cross-dressing Hercules and Achilles reflects his performative conception of gender, Asgill claims that Lady Horatia's recreation of "the daughters of Britain, and the matrons of Greece" underscores her femininity.

An article in *The Monthly Review* (1795) reasonably assumes that Horton is based on England's sole female sculptor: "*Lady Horatia Horton* seems to be a drawing from *Mrs. Damer*, whose high birth, beauty, and talents, have sufficiently rendered her an object of observation. This lady's passion for sculpture has not always escaped ridicule: but through the organs of *Conway*, a sensible young man of fashion,...Mrs. Cowley has made no feeble defence of it" (Art. XIX. *The Town before You* 330–331). Cowley admired sculptors and imagined herself as a literary Michelangelo, using pen and paper rather than chisel and marble. The preface to *The Works of Mrs. Cowley* reveals that she compared her method of composition to Michelangelo's sculpting: "She was always much pleased with the description of Michael Angelo making the marble fly around him, as he was chiseling with the utmost swiftness, that he might shape, however roughly, his whole design in unity with one clear conception. If she found she could not proceed swiftly, she gave up what she had undertaken" (I.xv). Conway's rapt description of Horton's inspired chiseling reflects Cowley's regard for both Damer and "the sublime art" (*The Town before You* V.ii.80) of Michelangelo.[26]

Andrew Elfenbein argues that Cowley's positive depiction of "Damer/Horton" in the play "defend[s] the figure of the female artist" and "find[s] a new, exemplary role for aristocratic women" ("Lesbian Aestheticism" 6). Lady Horatia is, however, much more conformist in her behavior and attitudes than her prototype. Whereas Damer was criticized for wearing men's clothes and behaving in unfeminine ways, characters in *The Town before You* describe Horton as the epitome of femininity, even when she is wielding a mallet and chisel. Unlike Damer, whose performances in private theatricals and friendship with the actress Elizabeth Farren sparked controversy, Horton eschews role-playing of any sort. Whereas Damer was rumored to have engaged in "Sapphic" relationships after her unhappy marriage was terminated by her husband's suicide (Elfenbein, *Romantic Genius* 97–103), Lady Horatia is portrayed as heterosexual and eventually makes Sidney Asgill the "master of [her] fate" (V.vii.102). Moreover, Horton's concern for her reputation, which she commands Conway to "preserve" as he would his "own life and honour" (IV.i.59) contrasts with Damer's willingness to flout societal expectations.[27]

When at the play's end Lady Horatia's future father-in-law Sir Simon tells her "throw away [her] chisel and [her] marble blocks, and set about making a good wife" (V.vii.102), she does not contradict him. Cowley presents the female sculptor not as a controversial figure but as a feminine, untheatrical, heteronormative, and respectable member of fashionable society.

As Angela Escott points out, "Lady Horatia represents Cowley's vision of a woman practising her art in the face of prejudices and obstacles" (203). Sir Simon antagonizes Horton by dismissing her sculpting as plebeian stonecutting that takes place in "a work-shop" and "a mason's saw-yard." Singling out her statue of Medusa, he says that "she chissels out womens' [*sic*] faces with young serpents hanging in drop curls, by way of a new fashion'd tete." Outraged, Lady Horatia informs Sir Simon that his "more than gothic ignorance . . . is a disgrace to the age in which [they] live, and to [his] own situation" (V.ii.79).[28] She defends not only her creations but also sculpture as a whole. According to her, "The head of the beautiful MEDUSA is amongst the *wonders* of the art," and she asks Sir Simon whether "the touching NIOBE, mourning over her children;—the light ATALANTA flying from her lover—the graceful GANYMEDE caught up to Olympus for his beauty" awakened his "adoration for the sublime art,—for SCULPTURE!" (V.ii.80). In the play's final scene Horton continues to protest against Sir Simon's philistinism. She wonders how she can reconcile herself to a man who "hates the arts; . . . thinks there is nothing dignified in sculpture; [and] hears, without veneration, the names of Phidias, and Michael Angelo" (V.vii.102). Cowley also responded forcefully to criticisms of her works. After *A School for Greybeards* was disrupted by audiences and attacked by reviewers for "indecency" and "indelicacy," she prefaced the printed version of the comedy with "An Address" that accused her critics of having dirty minds and argued that her vulgar, low-bred, coarse, and foolish characters must speak in their proper language (iii–v). In the "Address" she defiantly claims "that the Comedy, as now printed, contains EVERY WORD which was opposed the first night [of the play's performance], from the suspicion of indelicacy" (iv). Although Horton promotes a neoclassical aesthetic while Cowley advocates theatrical realism, they both assert their creative freedom and the value and integrity of their works.

Cowley's sympathetic portrayal of Horton in *The Town before You* reflects her progressive attitude toward female cultural producers.[29] While Cowley claimed to be politically conservative, she was committed to supporting actresses and "claiming freedom of expression for the female playwright" (Spencer 230).[30] As Stuart Curran notes,

Cowley's major plays "are all vehicles for actresses, starting with an unknown Sarah Siddons who debuted in her first play, *The Runaway*, in 1776" ("Women Readers" 174).[31] Moreover, three of her comedies were inspired by women playwrights: *Who's the Dupe?* is an adaptation of Susanna Centlivre's *The Stolen Heiress* (1702), *A Bold Stroke for a Husband* owes a debt to Centlivre's *A Bold Stroke for a Wife*, and *A School for Greybeards* is a reworking of Aphra Behn's *The Lucky Chance* (1686).[32] Melinda C. Finberg notes that "Cowley was the first professional female dramatist to draw directly from the works of other professional female playwrights" (Introduction xxxix).

In the 1813 edition of *The Town before You*, Cowley deleted Sir Simon's patronizing speech in which he advises Horton to abandon sculpture and seek to become a model wife. There seems to be no question that Horton will continue to sculpt in the later version of the play, particularly while Asgill is away pursuing a naval career. Through her portrayal of Horton, Cowley reinvents her conception of female agency. Whereas Letitia, Olivia, Victoria, and Seraphina (in *A School for Greybeards*) are witty, self-assertive heroines who achieve their goals through performance, Horton's empowerment is derived from wealth, position, and artistic achievement.[33] To be truly emancipated, an eighteenth-century Englishwoman needs a fortune of her own or a wealthy and complaisant husband or father. *The Town before You* also suggests that virtuous women can circumvent predatory male chameleons by banding together. Mrs. Fancourt warns Georgina of the danger posed by Tippy and Fancourt, and Georgina reciprocates by rescuing her from poverty and domestic bondage and adopting her as a "mother, sister, friend" (V.vi.99). Their loyalty to each other contrasts with Tippy and Fancourt's mutual distrust, and female solidarity triumphs over antisocial male chameleonism.

Chapter 5

Mary Robinson's Polygraphs

Analyzing Chameleons

The memoirist Laetitia-Matilda Hawkins, who had been Mary Robinson's neighbor in London during Robinson's celebrity years, remembered her as a theatrical, sartorial, and cosmetic chameleon:

> She was unquestionably very beautiful, but more so in face than figure; and as she proceeded in her course, she acquired a remarkable facility in adapting her deportment to her dress. When she was to be seen daily in St. James's Street and Pall Mall, even in her chariot this variation was striking. To-day she was a *paysanne*, with her straw hat tied at the back of her head, looking as if too new to what she passed, to know what she looked at. Yesterday she, perhaps, had been the dressed *belle* of Hyde Park, trimmed, powdered, patched, painted to the utmost power of rouge and white lead; to morrow, she would be the cravatted Amazon of the riding horse: but be she what she might, the hats of the fashionable promenaders swept the ground as she passed. (2.24)[1]

Following a short but successful career as a Drury Lane actress (1776–1780), Robinson achieved notoriety as the mistress of the Prince of Wales. On stage, her performances in cross-dressing breeches roles won plaudits, and after her retirement from acting she established herself as a fashion icon. She posed for the leading portraitists of the late eighteenth century: Joshua Reynolds, Thomas Gainsborough, John Hoppner, and George Romney. Gainsborough portrayed her as melancholy shepherdess sitting next to a Pomeranian dog and holding a miniature, presumably of her estranged lover, the Prince of Wales; Romney depicted her "as a demure Quaker" (Byrne 168). Following a serious illness in 1783—most likely acute rheumatic fever—Robinson suffered from progressive lower limb paralysis and eventually had to be carried around by servants.[2] Despite her disability, however, she continued to reinvent herself. She became a pro-Foxite political campaigner, a proponent of French revolutionary ideals, a Godwinian reformist, a Wollstonecraftian feminist, an anti-Jacobin, a Della Cruscan poet, a Romantic poet, a novelist, a newspaper essayist and editor, and a social satirist. She published many of her poems under pseudonyms, creating a range of distinctive poetic personae: Laura, Laura Maria, Lesbia, Oberon, Sappho, Julia, Tabitha Bramble, Horace Juvenal, Humanitas, M. R., Titania, Portia, and Bridget.[3] Judith Pascoe characterizes "The Robinson of the 1790s" as "a cultural chameleon, adopting every literary fashion,...a staged self" (1).

Robinson was an analyst as well as a practitioner of chameleonism and explored its advantages and drawbacks throughout her literary career. In her works, she presents a diverse array of chameleons: a natural actress, a moralistic Sylphid, protean Fashion, sartorial chameleons, a conflicted male impersonator, opportunistic self-fashioners, and polygraphs. She also depicts female characters who can only play one role: that of Ovid's brokenhearted Sappho. Robinson's poetic chameleonism and her portrayal of a spontaneous actress in her novel *The Natural Daughter* (1799) suggest that it is possible for a chameleon to be both performative and authentic. As Pascoe and Daniel Robinson have demonstrated, Robinson's poetic personae represent different facets of herself. Pascoe contends that Robinson's poetic "'disguises' contribute to a presentation of self that is no less 'authentic' than Wordsworth's...institution of an authorial voice so stable that the poet is conflated with the narrator of the poem...Robinson's multiple poetic voices represent a form of truth concerning a fragmented self; her pseudonyms also allowed her to speak a truth that could not be conveyed by 'Mary Robinson,' the fallen woman" (178). In his foundational study of Robinson's poetry, Daniel Robinson persuasively argues that "[h]er avatars are not disguises—they are all testaments, artifacts of her literary and cultural authority. She continues to use a pseudonym even after everyone knows it belongs to her. An avatar thus is all about being that version of oneself...This is how she manifests and proliferates herself through form" (22). Rather than serving as masks, Robinson's personae reflect her multiple selves. Her poetic chameleonism enables her to be more rather than less authentic.

Robinson believed that great actors could be both chameleonic and genuine. Her acting mentor was the legendary actor David

Garrick, who was famous for losing himself in his roles and popularized the natural style of acting (Angus 31). Frances Burney marveled at Garrick's "natural" metamorphoses: "Mr. Garrick altered the expression of his features, and almost his features themselves, by apparent transformations—which, however less poetical, were at least more natural than those of Ovid. Mr. Garrick possessed not only every possible inflexion of voice,...but also of countenance; varying his looks into young, old, sick, vigorous, downcast, or frolicsome, at his personal volition; as if his face, and even his form, had been put into his own hands to be worked upon like Man a Machine" (1.170). As Shearer West observes, the great tragic actress Sarah Siddons (1755–1831) "carried Garrick's 'natural' style of performing to a deeper level, making actors of his generation appear stilted and bland by comparison" (192). In an October 13, 1794 letter, Robinson pays tribute to Siddons's dramatic verisimilitude: "we shall wait long—very long—before we see anything like that *inspiration* that characterises a Siddons—the soul beaming through every veil of fiction, and making out more lovely than nature in all its fairest adornment...Mrs Siddons...is the most perfect mistress of the character she undertakes to represent of any performer I ever beheld" ("Letters" 304, emphasis in original). Robinson also admired Dorothy Jordan's natural acting and writes in her newspaper series *The Sylphid* (1799–1800) that Jordan was "animated with the fascinating unsophisticated smiles of all attractive nature" (186).[4] In *The Natural Daughter*, the protagonist Martha Morley adopts the alias Mrs. Denison and joins a theatrical troupe. As an actress, she combines "[t]he easy elegance of [Elizabeth] Farren [*c.* 1759–1829]" and the "genuine playful graces of the queen of smiles—the attractive Jordan" (84). Her performances are natural, spontaneous, and unaffected:

> She was the pupil of Nature; her feelings were spontaneous, her ideas expanded, and her judgment correct. She scorned to avail herself of that factitious mummery, that artificial, disgusting trick, which deludes the senses by exciting laughter at the expence of the understanding. She was lively and unaffected: her smiles were exhilarating; her sighs were pathetic; her voice was either delicately animating or persuasively soothing; she neither giggled convulsively nor wept methodically: she was the thing she seemed, while even the perfection of her art was Nature. (83)

Simultaneously chameleonic and natural, Mrs. Morley eschews artificial tricks and becomes what she seems. She somehow manages to blend Farren's elegance and Jordan's genuineness. Because she is an actress, however, she is "deemed an unfit associate for the wives and daughters of the proud, the opulent, and the unenlightened" (85), and the social elites compel Mrs. Morley's manager to discharge the pupil of nature.

Robinson's editorial series *The Sylphid* comments on life and fashions "in the metropolis of England" (169) and reflects her mixed assessment of chameleonism. In the series, Robinson assumes a shape-shifting persona that has "the power of changing [her] form, as suits the observation of the moment" and "can assume the minute exterior of the smallest insect, or *personate*... the most inanimate objects" (165, italics in original). Like Keats's chameleon poet, the Sylphid "has no self" and "is every thing and nothing" (Keats *Letters* 1.386), but unlike the chameleon poet, the Sylphid is moralistic. While she boasts about her chameleonic abilities, she denounces the frivolous changeability of degenerate "Fashion," who is "gaudy, varying, transient, and insubstantial" and whose "nurse [is] the Camelion; air-nourished, and perpetually changing its appearance" (172). In the Sylphid's second editorial, she lists her reformative goals: "I will draw forth merit; protect unfriended genius; unveil *pretended* chastity; goad with the thorn of conscious reproof the ostentatious bosom; and expose the specious violator of domestic joy, the oppressor of the unhappy" (169, italics in original). In contrast, polymorphic Fashion metamorphoses "a celebrated beauty" into a heavily made-up chameleon "bending before a flattering mirror": "In a moment she was grave and gay; prudish and coquettish; volatile and reserved: while she performed each character with an evident facility, which was scarcely credible." As she preens herself and rehearses social performances, the beauty's lackey callously drives away "an ingenious artificer, a neglected poet, a half-starved historian, and a poor country curate" (174).[5] *The Sylphid* both celebrates and deplores chameleonism: whereas the Sylphid's revelatory chameleonism allows her to expose human corruption, injustice, and folly, Fashion's mindless chameleonism engenders dissipation.

This chapter will focus on Robinson's diverse portrayals of chameleons in her novels *Walsingham; or The Pupil of Nature* (1797) and *The False Friend: A Domestic Story* (1799). In her fiction, Robinson anticipates the postmodern theory that identity and gender are performative (Ty 31, 43; Mellor 253–254) but also portrays characters with fixed and innate selves and moral orientations.[6] Her flexible conception of identity encompasses both "the *ancien régime*" conception of identity as mutable, relational, and theatrical, and "the modern regime of selfhood," which envisions the self as stable, interiorized, and essential (Wahrman 167–168, 265–311).[7] Although several of Robinson's heroines and the eponymous protagonist of her unfinished novel "Jasper" (1801) appear to possess a relatively stable core self consisting of "innate qualities, which depend not on the perishable basis of worldly splendour" (*The Natural Daughter* 100), their attempts to behave ethically and altruistically are consistently misinterpreted in a society that judges by appearances and is easily manipulated by skillful role-players.[8] As an actress, fashion icon, pseudonymous poet, and public figure, Robinson embodied chameleonism, yet many of her chameleonic characters are dysfunctional, depersonalized, or villainous.

The Lucky Escape, Pseudonymous Chameleons, and Polygraphs

On April 30, 1778, Robinson's afterpiece *The Lucky Escape* premiered at Drury Lane Theatre. In this early work, composed by Robinson when she was either 20 or 21, clothes are the preeminent signifiers of identity.[9] *The Lucky Escape* features an imposter, a female character who proposes to cross-dress and fight a duel, and a sartorial chameleon. The imposter is "A Sharper and great Beau" (1) named Charles Venture, who poses as "a man of great property" and "dresse[s] fantastically" (I.ii.5) to convince Sir Toby Stedfast that he is an excellent match for Sir Toby's daughter Maria, an heiress worth £10,000. Sir Toby wants Maria to marry Venture, but she loves Edwin. To rescue Maria from her predicament, her enterprising friend Letitia resorts to subterfuge. She tells Venture that Maria plans to elope with an unworthy man and suggests that he challenge his rival to a duel. Terrified, Venture exclaims that he "see[s] no sense in standing like a Crow to be shot at," and Letitia offers to dress in his clothes and fight Maria's lover in his place. In response to Venture's comment that she does not "look masculine enough for a Man," Letitia points out that none "of our Beaux look Masculine" (I.ii.10): fops and women are interchangeable. She boasts that she is "impatient to meet [her] Antagonist, and hope[s] to prove that in a just cause a Woman may dare any thing" (I.ii.11).

In the final scene of *The Lucky Escape*, Maria's lover Edwin assumes Venture's identity by wearing his clothes. For the impercipient Sir Toby, apparel confers identity: he does not notice that Edwin's features, voice, and manner are different from Venture's and offers the sartorial chameleon a marriage deed. They are interrupted by

Venture, who is no longer "fantastically dressed" and forces his way past the servants. Sir Toby fails to recognize him, and Venture misidentifies Edwin as Letitia masquerading as himself. When Letitia arrives, Venture "starts and walks around her surpriz'd" and asks her if she can "assume what shape [she] please[s]" (II.iii.18). Letitia then unmasks the imposter by producing an incriminating letter from him to his accomplice, Lawyer Trickwell, and Venture flees. In *The Lucky Escape*, Robinson touches on many of the themes that she explores more extensively in her novels: imposture, paternal tyranny, the fluidity of identity, transgendering, female dueling, and sartorial chameleonism. While Venture is a precursor of the fortune hunters in Cumberland's *The Imposters*, Letitia prefigures the playful chameleon Letitia Hardy in Cowley's *The Belle's Stratagem*.

Along with clothes, names are important markers of identity in Robinson's novels, and for various reasons many of her characters become pseudonymous chameleons. In *Vancenza; or, The Dangers of Credulity* (1792), Philip Alberoni, a lowborn Spanish youth, becomes the servant of an Italian aristocrat. He rises from his lowly station by murdering his patron, stealing money and jewels, assuming the alias Marquis Petrozi, and joining Madrid society as an aristocratic gambler. In *The Widow; or, A Picture of Modern Times* (1794), Lord Allford courts and marries the novel's female protagonist in America under a false name; in England, his wife takes on the alias Julia St. Lawrence and, because she does not know her husband's true identity, has a difficult time reuniting with him. The title-character of *Angelina; A Novel* (1796) begins life as Angelina Jones, becomes Angelina Wantworth when she marries, subsequently lives in Gothic isolation as Angelina Sydenham and then Angelina Arundel, and ultimately becomes Lady Acreland. Monsieur Ravillon, a social arriviste in *Hubert de Sevrac, A Romance* (1796), impersonates the Marquis de Sevrac during a sea voyage and, as a result, one of the Marquis's enemies fatally stabs him. The eponymous protagonist of *Walsingham* disguises himself in a woman's masquerade costume to escape from debtor's prison and subsequently adopts the alias Mr. Montagu to avoid the consequences of his "rash conduct" (212). In *The False Friend*, the villainous Mr. Treville becomes Somerton, the racist nabob Sir Hector Upas becomes Lord Arcot, and the novel's heroine, Gertrude St. Leger, temporarily identifies herself as Miss Beauclerk. And as I have already noted, the heroine of *The Natural Daughter* refashions herself as Mrs. Denison, "a strolling actress" (86).[10] The name changes of these characters alter their social facades but not their subjectivities. For some of them, aliases further villainous schemes or provide temporary refuge from harassment; in the case of Monsieur Ravillon, his decision to adopt the Marquis de Sevrac's identity proves lethal.

In *Walsingham*, Robinson portrays a society swarming with opportunistic chameleons. The title-character learns to consider "the world as a vast and varying theatre, where every individual [is] destined to play his part, and to receive the applause or disapprobation of his surrounding contemporaries" (74). Even minor characters are chameleons. For example, a sanctimonious Methodist uses the £300 his wife stole from Walsingham to transform himself into an elegantly dressed rake. When Walsingham prevents the former "saint of the rostrum" from entering a coach with a prostitute, "[t]he affrighted Camelion" curses and attacks him with a bludgeon. Walsingham retaliates, and he and "the metamorphosed preacher" fight each other "with scientific precision" until the imposter drops Walsingham's pocketbook and runs away. Because the hypocritical Methodist plays his part so badly, he earns the "disapprobation of his surrounding contemporaries": the mob who witnesses his unmasking indignantly "shouts and hisses" at him (280).

Among the performers in this play-acting society are the "polygraphs" or impersonators who dedicate themselves to imitating others.[11] In Hellenistic Greek, polygraph means writing much, and by the eighteenth century the word could signify a copying device, an individual who writes on many subjects, and a person who imitates or looks identical to another.[12] A Polygraphic Society was established in 1787 to promote the "Art of Multiplying or Copying Pictures in Oil Colours, by Means of a Chymical and Mechanical Process." The society hoped to convince the public that "the Copies possess the Effect of the Original, so as scarcely to be distinguished therefrom" (*Public Advertiser*, 10 May 1787). Like Tippy, Lord Beechgrove's polygraph in Cowley's *The Town before You*, Robinson's polygraphs are chameleons who plagiarize the lifestyles, activities, and personal appearances of their prototypes, but unlike Tippy, the polygraphs in *Walsingham* are voiceless—their activities are reported by Lord Kencarth—thus the reader is offered little insight into their subjectivities.

The polygraphs who impersonate the frivolous Lord Kencarth suppress their identities completely in order to assume his. According to Kencarth,

> a true polygraph would break an arm, fracture a leg, knock out an eye, or starve himself into a decline, rather than lose a single trait of

> his noble original... [L]ast year... I wore deep mourning four times, on purpose to dish my shadows in sables... [M]y phantoms were taken in:—one of them was nabbed by his tailor, for the bill which he contracted;—the knowing one smoked the sham, and my shadow was nicked and locked up, for being my representative one hour every day in Pall Mall and Bond-street.

The aristocrat good-naturedly rescues his shadow by paying the debt and promising "to wear a drab frock for the next twelve months," and when Kencarth breaks his arm in a riding accident and has to recover for three weeks in his room, his "polygraph regularly appear[s] in Fops-alley and Bond-street during the whole time, with his arm in a sling, and with a phiz as sharp as a hatchet" (374). As Sharon Setzer points out, "Kencarth's... admission that he has worn 'deep mourning' four times in the last year for the express purpose of 'dishing' his polygraphs... underscores the irony that they are copying a copy rather than an original" ("The Dying Game" 319).

One of Kencarth's polygraphs becomes completely deracinated. Before taking on the role of Lord Kencarth he has acted as "the polygraph of three different deep ones":

> First he was the walking shadow of an unpopular character; and personified his prototype... to a miracle. But in his perambulations, his ears were so often affronted by sarcastic remarks... that... he shifted his shape, and... approached one degree nearer to insignificance. He next became the phantom of a noble Viscount; but it would not do; three fêtes and a court equipage dished his fortune,... while all the world laughed at him, and nobody respected either his taste or his prodigality... [E]ven his original was ashamed of his folly... The third person that poor Proteus undertook to personify, was a young Baronet. With a month's starvation, a crop, and four flannel waistcoats, he contrived to pass current among Jews, jockies, low women of all characters, and high women of no characters at all; till having outrun the constable, and not knowing a flat that would give him tick for a shiner,... he was nabbed six times in one week;... so, not having either the fortune or the honesty of his prototype, he dabbled in trade, popped into the Gazette, and three months after started again with a new face, as [Lord Kencarth's] representative. (460–461)

The polygraph's unexplained ability to acquire "a new face" allows him to elude constables and bailiffs and "disrupt[s] the physiognomic assumption that details of subjective depth could be read in an individual's face and body" (Mole 199). His impostures and disguises lead, however, to humiliation, financial disaster, and death. It is unclear what he expects to gain by impersonating "an unpopular character" or by becoming "the phantom of a noble Viscount" and squandering a fortune: he may be foolish, a compulsive exhibitionist, or simply self-destructive. Kencarth sadly recounts his pathologically dedicated polygraph's sudden demise:

> News arrived from Bath that I was down of a fever with little hopes of getting about again. Queer my sconce, if my polygraph didn't get drunk five nights following, till his pulse was up to a physician. Quiz me, but old stiff-wig came a day after the fair; poor graphy was taken in, kept his bed three days, and hopped the twig on the fourth, queer my nobility!... Dash me, I was obliged to bury my ghost, lest he should continue to frighten the Dowagers, and set me down as a dead letter on the list of knowing ones. (460)

Whereas Cowley's polygraph is a calculating opportunist, Robinson's graphy loses the capacity to distinguish himself from his model and is so dedicated to his role that he continues to play it even when his impersonation endangers his health. Although this serial impostor presumably begins his career in order to benefit socially and financially from his assumed selves, in the end he drinks himself to death and, since his model outlives him, fails as a polygraph. He can imitate a man's personal appearance and habits, but he cannot simulate his wealth or ability to survive. The uncanny ability of this chameleon to impersonate members of the ruling class poses, however, a potential threat to social stability that remains implicit rather than explicit in the novel. Emily Allen argues that polygraphs are economically as well as socially subversive: "they are mostly in the business of stealing other people's credit, and Kencarth's description of perfect copies circulating through the metropolis sounds suspiciously like the progress of paper money, here indistinguishable from counterfeit" (88). Graphy is a transgressive figure who elides differences in class, credit, and personal identity. Even after dying, he threatens to become interchangeable with his prototype, to haunt "the Dowagers" who preside over high society and reduce Kencarth to "a dead letter." As Cowley's Tippy points out, the "noble original" is always in danger of becoming his copy's duplicate.

Walsingham moralizes that while his "ancestors delighted in displaying a proud originality," the decadent "present generation" imitates "even the deformities of nature" (374). The novel implies that in late-eighteenth-century England, polygraphs are everywhere and individuality is rare. Identities are fluid and contingent: commoners pass as aristocrats; a pious Methodist turns into an elegant rake, and

Mr. Hedge, an itinerant tinker born in an oyster-cellar, becomes a wealthy duelist and gambler dubbed "*comme il faut* in the circles of dissipation" (397). Walsingham pauses briefly in his narration to pity "the wretched imitators of Proteus . . . who, to gratify the false ambition of a moment, ensure eternal disgrace, while they make it the labour of their lives to copy those follies, of which the dullest among them would blush to be the originals" (462). Kencarth's impersonators obviously choose their prototype for his social rank rather than his personal attributes—they are willing to copy "even the deformities of nature." For them, the identity of a foolish, eccentric, vain, superficial, and spendthrift aristocrat is preferable over that of the most admirable and intelligent commoner. In imitating an aristocrat, Kencarth's polygraphs subvert the social hierarchy; by copying aristocratic follies, they unintentionally satirize the vices and follies of English high society.

Like Jean-Jacques Rousseau in *Confessions*, Walsingham presents himself as having been made unlike anyone else in existence.[13] According to him, he is an original in a society filled with polygraphs. His identity is, however, far from fixed, and he possesses the polygraph's ambition to rise socially. He grows up in South Wales on an estate owned by Sir and Lady Aubrey, his aunt and uncle. As a "child of nature" raised apart from "the artificial scenes of life" (108), he seems to be the antithesis of the inauthentic polygraph. After the death of Sir Aubrey and the announcement that Lady Aubrey has given birth to Sir Sidney, the dispossessed Walsingham is abandoned to wander "like a wild inhabitant of the mountains" (64). When he later visits Lady Aubrey and Sir Sidney in the south of France, he is labeled a "vulgar brat" (96) and accused of impersonating the real Walsingham. Desperate to establish himself as an original rather than a polygraph, he asks his tutor: "Am I not Walsingham?" (97).

Walsingham's Rousseauistic individualism leads him to behave impulsively and irrationally, as Rousseau does in *Confessions*.[14] He fails to control his obsessional passion for Isabella Hanbury, despite her repeated rejections of him. In his attempt to explain why "indifference or scorn" only serves to increase "the enthusiastic fondness of [his] heart," he invokes nature. He admits that his emotional perversity "may be folly; it may be weakness bordering on idiotism; it may be a mean and despicable want of pride and fortitude," but he nevertheless "pronounce[s] it Nature" (348). His theory that his actions are preordained by nature seems, however, self-serving when he applies it to his treatment of Amelia Woodford. Amelia desperately loves him, but he does not return her affection even though she "fatally, strikingly resemble[s] Isabella" (261). At a masquerade he encounters a masked woman whom he mistakenly identifies as Isabella but who turns out to be Amelia impersonating Isabella. He takes the unfortunate polygraph to his lodgings, and there, "The time, the place, the potency of the fatal draughts which [he has] swallowed,... madden [him]! all the claims of unprotected innocence, all the laws of honour [are] violated" (290). Rather than marrying the woman he has dishonored, Walsingham persuades himself that their "mutual misery would have been the inevitable consequence" of their union and argues that she is "the victim of her own fatal curiosity" (296).[15] He becomes increasingly irrational. As soon as Amelia becomes resigned to losing him, he feels "a wish, which owe[s] its origin to [his] perverse nature" (370), to marry her. Defending himself before Isabella, he declares that Amelia "was her own destroyer" and that he "was an involuntary seducer," but when Isabella smiles at him "insultingly" he "violate[s] the laws of propriety" by forcing her against himself (394–395).

However, although Walsingham treats women terribly, he is not completely selfish. In fact, he seems to be trying to become the polygraph of Harley, the naive and benevolent hero of Henry Mackenzie's *The Man of Feeling* (1771). Although poor, he gives £10 to a "forlorn stranger" (175), and, in a scene that recalls Harley's emotional reunion with old Edwards in *The Man of Feeling*, he is deeply moved by the story of a disabled beggar who, like Edwards, has been the victim of a press gang (Mackenzie 59–66; *Walsingham* 382–390). Like Harley, who writes a pastoral after hearing a rumor that Miss Walton is to be married, Walsingham composes verse to vent his feelings. As G. J. Barker-Benfield points out, however, in eighteenth-century literature "the man of feeling [is] shown to respect women and make common ground with them" (249). In contrast to Harley, whose reverence for Miss Walton prevents him from revealing his love for her until he is on his deathbed, Walsingham stalks Isabella and refuses to marry the woman he has dishonored. Angry at Isabella's "trifling coquetry" (429) he punishes her by "coldly, deliberately" (467) pursuing Lady Arabella, whom he does not love. Whereas Mackenzie contrasts the man of feeling to a misanthropist who applies "his talents to the vilifying of his species" (25), in *Walsingham* the protagonist takes on both of these identities: despite his poetic sensibility, he begins "to hate [his] species" (486) and torments women.

During Robinson's acting career she frequently played women posing as men, and her success in these roles inspired her lover, the Prince of Wales, to ask her to meet him at Buckingham House in male disguise. She "decidedly objected," however, to the plan because of

"The indelicacy of such a step, as well as the danger of detection" ("Memoirs" 257). Although in this instance Robinson professes to have had little confidence in her ability to pass as a man, in *Walsingham* she explores the consequences of prolonged transvestitism (Sidney Aubrey poses as a man for 18 years) as practiced by an upper-class woman who is not a professional actress. Unlike Kencarth's polygraphs, Sir Sidney does not impersonate a specific individual. Like them, however, she adopts a false identity in order to enhance her social and economic position. Her performance as a male baronet is impeccable: she "fenced like a professor of the science; painted with the correctness of an artist; was expert at all *manly* exercises; a delightful poet; and a fascinating companion" (129, my emphasis).[16] As Julie Shaffer observes, Sidney "suggest[s] through her convincing masquerade that gender is a learned rather than natural affair that can be signified and interpreted solely by the externals of behaviors and clothing" (71). The "established law" of primogeniture, which dictates that "the heir male" (490) must be the exclusive beneficiary of an inheritance, shapes her destiny. According to her father's will, a male heir inherits all of Glenowen and a sum of £60,000. Rather than accept this sexist will, Sidney's avaricious mother and her diabolical waiting woman conceal "the sex of the infant Sidney" (492) at the time of her birth. Years later, they make her agree to hide her sexual identity until her mother's death.

Sidney presents herself to Walsingham and Isabella as a witty, vivacious, and flirtatious Grand Tourist fresh from "beholding all the *belles* of France, the mountain nymphs of Switzerland, and the love-inspiring dames of luxurious Italy" (131). When Lady Aubrey selfishly refuses to grant £3,000 to Colonel Aubrey, the rightful heir to Sir Edward's estate, Sidney quixotically pledges to join the army rather than "live the slave of avarice" (143). Her mother takes her threat seriously and supplies the money. Sidney's attempts to come between Walsingham and Isabella are misread by the protagonist as signs of his cousin's passion for Isabella rather than for himself. He observes Sidney and Isabella walking with their arms around each other and overhears Isabella agree to "return to Switzerland" with his cousin and "be [Sidney's] dear and inseparable associate" (161). Concluding that Sidney is a libertine, Walsingham challenges her to a duel. His cousin accepts a pistol with a "placid smile of defiance" and, after Walsingham's shot misses, instantly "discharge[s] his[/her] pistol in the air" (164). With the possible exception of her suicide attempt, Sidney plays the role of gentleman much more successfully than her hyperemotional, obsessively jealous, and surly cousin.

Lady Aubrey finally reveals her daughter's lifelong transvestitism at the end of the novel, and Sidney's transformation into a woman begins immediately thereafter. Although "Sidney has been educated in masculine habits," Walsingham's tutor is confident that in time she will be able to "fashion her manners to the graces of her sex" (492). She completes this behavioral training in Switzerland and becomes, in the protagonist's opinion, the ideal combination of feminine and masculine qualities: although she is "feminine in manners[,]...her mind still retains the energy of that richly-treasured dignity of feeling which are the effects of a masculine education" (495). *Walsingham* presents gender roles as arbitrary social constructions that one can adopt or discard as one wishes. Sidney convincingly plays a number of male roles, including fop, Grand Tourist, man of feeling, libertine, duelist, and prospective soldier; the sentimental Amelia professes herself ready to "bear the fatigues of a soldier's wandering life [and] even disguise [her] sex, to be the partaker of [Walsingham's] peril" (298), and Lady Arabella speculates that in the future "affairs will be monstrously changed: men will make caps and puff ribbands; and women forget their sex, to box and ride races" (339). *Walsingham* suggests that since women can function effectively in male roles, they should have the same freedoms, rights, and opportunities as men. Although Sidney's passion for her cousin eventually makes her transvestitism unbearable to her, it also enables her to receive a "masculine education" and temporarily enjoy the prerogatives of an upper-class male.

But this play-acting and self-fashioning eventually take their toll. Sidney must suppress her individuality and play a role scripted by her greedy mother and her vindictive governess. After Walsingham prevents her from committing suicide, she laments "To adore one object—to deceive another—It were better that I should expire." Far from feeling liberated, she comes to despise herself: "What am I," she exclaims, "amidst the profusion of wealth which chance has heaped around me? A...vile, degraded, infamous, and sordid hypocrite!" (151). Although her position as a rich male baronet gives her freedoms denied to late-eighteenth-century women, her closeted sexual orientation becomes a burden that nearly destroys her. While transvestitism emotionally devastates Sidney, Amelia loses her virginity, reputation, and self-respect after becoming Isabella's polygraph, and Kencarth's favorite polygraph destroys himself. Although polygraphing can be temporarily liberating and empowering, it is also a dangerous and somewhat disreputable activity. A blurb published in the *Oracle and Public Advertiser* facetiously suggested that Robinson's novel embarrassed the real polygraphs and drove them into seclusion: "Since the

Publication of *Walsingham*, not a single *Polygraph* is to be seen in the promenade of Pall Mall or Bond-street" (February 8, 1798). However, while Walsingham deplores the fatuity and dysfunctionality of polygraphs, he insists that Sidney's transgender chameleonism has molded her into an ideal androgyne, a combination of feminine manners and a masculine education. In her feminist polemic *Letter to the Women of England, on the Injustice of Mental Subordination* (1799), Robinson argues that women should be able to duel and praises the military exploits of women like Hannah Snell, who disguised herself as a man and "brave[d] the very heat of battle... amidst the smoak and din of a naval engagement" (137–138, 144 and n). In *Walsingham*, Sidney participates in a duel, and both she and Amelia are willing to join the army. Although Sidney is tormented by her chameleonism, she can be regarded as a progressive figure who anticipates a future in which women possess the education and rights afforded to men.[17]

OPPORTUNISTIC CHAMELEONS IN *THE FALSE FRIEND*

In *Conjectures on Original Composition* (1759), the poet, playwright, and essayist Edward Young blurs the distinction between personal and literary originality.[18] According to him, "Imitation is inferiority confessed" (36):

> [B]y a spirit of *Imitation* we counteract Nature, and thwart her design. She brings us into the world all *Originals:* No two faces, no two minds, are just alike; but all bear Nature's evident mark of Separation on them. Born *Originals,* how comes it to pass that we die *Copies?* That medling [*sic*] Ape *Imitation*, as soon as we come to years of *Indiscretion*..., snatches the Pen, and blots out nature's mark of Separation, cancels her kind intention, destroys all mental Individuality; the letter'd world no longer consists of Singulars, it is a Medly [*sic*], a Mass; and a hundred books, at bottom, are but One. Why are monkies such masters of mimickry [*sic*]? Why receive they such a talent at imitation? Is it not as the Spartan slaves received a licence for ebriety; that their betters might be ashamed of it? (24, italics in original)

For Young, apelike imitation circumvents our natural development both as individuals and as writers. The loss of "mental Individuality" reduces most of us to copies and our writings to mechanically produced duplications of a hundred other compositions. Using the word "genius" to refer to a person's characteristic inclination or leaning, Young declares that "nothing *Original* can rise... in any other Sun

[but] the beams of [one's] own Genius" (13). In his account of Joseph Addison's death, he asserts that the essayist's originality can be found in his life as well as in his literary productions. Young writes that Addison sent for a young relative, told the young man to "See in what peace a Christian can die" (54–55), and calmly expired: "His compositions are but a noble preface; the grand work is his death" (56). The originality of one's self or genius determines the originality of one's writing: the imitative self can only compose slight variants of the same book. In Addison's case, his singular death is his greatest achievement and the moving epilogue to his literary productions.

Young's notion that people can be identified as originals or copies informs a comic scene in Robinson's *The Natural Daughter* that features the uncouth, uneducated, and nouveau riche Leadenhead family, who seek to ennoble themselves by buying "honours, dignities, titles, precedence, and connections" (86). When Miss Bridget Leadenhead cannot decide which dress would be appropriate for the reception of "a lady of fashion" (87), her brother Gregory advises her to "bribe . . . her grace's or her ladyship's woman . . . for the sight of one of her lady's new dresses." Their mother objects, however, "to the idea of permitting the opulent family of Plummet Castle to demean themselves by copying any body. 'I like to be the original,' said she, with an air of self-importance." "'[O]riginals we are all likely to be,'" her son replies, "'for nobody will take the pains to imitate us, unless we learn something of people of fashion'" (88). Whereas Mrs. Leadenhead is too ignorant to recognize her parvenu family's complete lack of originality, Gregory Leadenhead illogically maintains that their "originality" will only be imitated if they learn how to copy the social elite. In addition to the comically unoriginal Leadenheads, the novel features a denatured copyist who behaves immorally and pathologically.[19] The heroine's polymorphic sister Julia Bradford achieves popularity in fashionable society by knowing "the art of being all things to all people" (28) but subsequently incarcerates her mother in a madhouse, murders her baby, and commits suicide on the bed of her final lover, "the homicide Robespierre" (185).

Two types of imitative selves appear in Robinson's epistolary novel *The False Friend*: chameleons who play roles that at least temporarily empower them and a hapless copy, the heroine Gertrude St. Leger, who appears predestined by her melancholic temperament and cloistered education to relive her mother's tragic life and fall prey to Lord Denmore, her mother's nemesis and Gertrude's guardian. The novel's villain, Mr. Treville, is a "Proteus [who] change[s] his conduct with every circumstance that favour[s] his design" (155).[20] According to this corrupt clergyman, "Every man may be what he will, by seeming what he is not" (74). Naive and morally circumspect, Gertrude lacks Treville's adaptability and duplicity. "Educated in total seclusion from the world," she is "the pupil of precept...and the slave of sensibility" (367). Like Young's imitative writers, who inadvertently lose their "mental Individuality" during their "years of *Indiscretion*," she is self-consciously literary and, rather than fashioning a distinctive identity, she becomes an eighteenth-century version of the lovelorn Sappho of Ovid's *Heroides* and unwittingly reenacts her mother's tragic life. In fact, Gertrude has the name and appearance of her dead mother, who was also a "VICTIM OF SENSIBILITY" (408). The two Gertrudes and another depressive female figure in the novel, Mary Ashgrove, are static, vulnerable members of a society in which "every man of sense seems flying from himself; assuming a character foreign to his nature; and, as if ashamed of being a rational creature, aping the excentricities [*sic*] of those sophisticated mortals, whom his sober reason cannot fail to execrate" (89).

Treville and the novel's other chameleons are, like the fatuously arrogant Leadenheads, occasionally targets of satire: Gertrude's chiastic description of Treville as "a fashionable divine, divinely fashionable!" (15) mocks social-climbing clergymen who pretend to be devout in order to enhance their social standing. However, like the two Gertrudes and Mary Ashgrove, the male chameleons live conflicted and sometimes tragic lives. Treville, Sir Hector Upas, and Lord Denmore become consumed by the parts they perform, and during moments of crisis they are forced to confront their inner emptiness and lack of authenticity. All of them, like Julia Bradford, die prematurely, Sir Hector by his own hand. In *The False Friend*, opportunistic chameleonism and Gertrude's obsessional imitation of Sappho and other victims of sensibility are both destructive and pathological behaviors. Copies are not fully or even partially realized human beings. They contrast with the more authentic protagonist of *The Natural Daughter*, who even when performing as an actress is "the pupil of Nature; her feelings [are] spontaneous, her ideas expanded, and her judgment correct."[21] Although employed in an imitative profession, Martha Morley is somehow able to avoid the "spirit of *Imitation*" that Young claims "counteract[s] Nature, and thwart[s] her design." She is persecuted for her unconventional behavior, but "neither insult nor oppression [can] contaminate" her "sublimity of soul" (185), and at the novel's end she marries a benevolent aristocrat. While complete originality is unattainable in Robinson's novels, she suggests that in order for individuals to retain at least some control over their lives and avert despair, they must develop selfhoods strong enough to resist the pressure of social conformity and the machinations of protean tricksters. In *The False Friend*, the most viably authentic female character is Miss Stanley, who sees through and ultimately rejects two protean false friends, Sir Hector Upas and Lord Denmore, without succumbing to Sappho's fate.

While Robinson's previous novel, *Walsingham*, challenges essentialist conceptions of gender, *The False Friend* associates chameleonism almost exclusively with men. In *The False Friend*, life scripts are much more limited for women than they are for men, particularly for women who become enslaved by their literary sensibilities and obsessional passions. Like the polygraphs in *The Town before You* and *Walsingham*, many of the characters in *The False Friend* possess fluid identities that enable them to be what they will by seeming what they are not. An effeminate "male coquette" named Lord Daffodil paints his face brown and thus "assume[s] that healthful hue, which dissipation has stolen from the attributes of Nature" (272). The double agent Mrs. Ferret poses as a patriotic English counterintelligence operative but is actually a spy for the French; the exploitative nabob Sir Hector Upas becomes Lord Arcot and then poses as a magistrate to trick Gertrude. But when the novel's heroine reluctantly pretends to be "a Miss Beauclerk, the daughter of a deceased clergyman" (219), her masquerade backfires. As an "artificial character" (226) she feels inauthentic and dishonest, and her deception leads to a nearly fatal duel between one of her new friends and Lord Denmore. Unlike the protean Treville, she can only fill one role convincingly: that of a victim of obsessional and unrequited love. As her pseudonym suggests, she is a beautiful (beau) clerk or copyist, incapable of scripting a nonderivative life for herself.

Gertrude describes the urbane Reverend Treville as "a finished model for the whole school of clerical nondescripts. Too polite to be religious; too witty to be learned; too youthful to be serious; and too handsome to be discreet: in four words, a fashionable divine, divinely fashionable!" (15). According to her, his manners and appearance prevent him from being virtuous, and as "a fashionable divine" he has become the prototype for numerous "clerical nondescripts." A consummate actor and social parasite, Treville is one of Lady Denmore's seductive "danglers," "a bear-leader [traveling tutor], a sycophant, and a toad-eater" (15, 335). As Robinson's eponymous persona explains in *The Sylphid*, the "toad-eater" possesses "astonishing . . . pliability," and "suits his looks, manners, voice, and opinions, to those of the patron on whom he depends for *the day's enjoyment*" (33, italics in original).

Unlike Tippy and Lord Kencarth's graphy, Treville does not impersonate individuals; rather, he plays the generic role of a high-minded, genteel clergyman ready, at a moment's notice, to recommend volumes of devotional literature to any woman entrusted to his care. After behaving like a libertine in front of Gertrude, he quickly shifts back to his clerical guise when Lord Denmore appears. Although Treville is actually writing a letter to Lady Denmore, he informs her husband that he is "making a list of books, the only sources of mental improvement, for [his] fair charge." He recommends "Fordyce's Sermons, Hervey's Meditations, Beveridge on Prayer, Campbell on Moral Virtue, Mason on Self-Knowledge, Sherlock on Death, and Wollaston's Religion of Nature." When Denmore mentions Samuel Richardson's *Clarissa* as a suitable novel for his ward to read, Gertrude obliquely suggests that "the character of Lovelace" (149), a rake and rapist, is the fictional prototype for Treville. Dazzled by Treville's performance, Denmore is incapable of taking her hint.

Eleanor Ty characterizes Treville's nature as "unstable" (71), but Gertrude suspects that he is consistent in one respect: "he seems to act as a perpetual shadow on his own imagined splendour" (16). His constant role-playing is motivated by vanity and self-interest. Gertrude marvels at Treville's ability to "perpetually assume[e] a character the opposite of that which Nature had given him, and which habits of profligacy had confirmed unequivocally" (143). His adaptability allows him to victimize women and manipulate powerful men like Lord Denmore: he is at "one moment the slave of Lady Denmore; the next the subtle betrayer of her credulous husband" (155). After changing his name to Somerton, Treville becomes one "of those household reptiles" who is "at once *l'ami de la maison* [the friend of the house], and the abuser of its hospitality" (311). Whereas Gertrude remains a passive victim for much of the novel, the mobility of the two-faced "clerical Janus" (112) is temporarily empowering. Posing as a virtuous Anglican clergyman, he befriends the powerful, seduces their wives, and schemes to enrich himself. He also becomes the model for "nondescript" polygraphs eager to emulate such "a fashionable divine." But while his ability to seem "what he is not" enhances his maneuverability in Georgian society, it also renders him completely inauthentic, the "perpetual shadow," of his devious and egotistical imagination. When he believes that he is dying, "his eyes [seem to be] looking inward on his soul" and assume "an expression at once vacant and ghastly" (345). Shorn of his multifarious facades, he is "a coward, a superficial, arrogant imposter" (344) with an empty inner self.

Although Sir Hector Upas/Lord Arcot impersonates a magistrate, he is more transparent and less of a role-player than Treville/Somerton. Like Treville, however, he is amoral, motivated primarily by avarice and sexual desire, and determined to reinvent himself. His surname, Upas, alludes to a poisonous southeastern Asian tree that was thought to destroy everything around it, and Sir Hector has risen from the "lowly sphere of a scavenger" to the rank of lord by victimizing others. He begins his social ascent as "the pliant deputy" (21) of a dissipated nobleman, and, after learning his master's secrets, acquires a small fortune through blackmail. As a nabob in India, "he soar[s] like a pestilential cloud, and amidst the reiterated groans of desolation, triumph[s] with impunity" (22). Back in England, he joins high society and boasts about his experiences abroad:

> When I was in India, I used to have fifty little black wenches every day to sing me asleep after dinner; and I used to make them fan me with heron's feathers, and sprinkle my couch with otta [attar] of roses: 'twas prodigiously delightful!...[W]e send a dozen black vagabonds up to Persia for our essences [perfumes], and it is bad luck indeed, if out of twelve four does [*sic*] not return with his commission...[T]he climate sometimes kills them,...But they were created for our use, therefore we never care what becomes of them: there's plenty to be found; they overrun the country as thick as blackberries. (37–38)

A corpulent megalomaniac, he considers himself one of the "props of the eastern world" (38), and, when Sir William St. Leger entrusts him with Gertrude's inheritance, he does not hesitate to embezzle it. With his stolen wealth he becomes a landed aristocrat, Lord Arcot (Arcot is a city in India), but when Sir William returns and is on the verge of unmasking his false friend, Arcot commits suicide rather than lose the wealth and rank he has spent his life acquiring.

If Sir Hector/Lord Arcot is a polygraph, a lowly "scavenger" posing as an imperious nabob and nobleman, he is an incompetent one: he trumpets his illiteracy, racism, sexism, and boorishness to anyone who listens to him and seldom understands their sarcastic replies. Even his performance as a justice is "a contrivance of Somerton's" (328). Arcot's performance as an Asian potentate puffing at his "hooka[h]" on "a superb chintz sofa" with a vase of "aromatic gums" at his feet elicits contempt rather than admiration from Gertrude:

> The Oriental magnificence which marked every thing around me, only served to contrast the prominent object, and to render him more than disgusting. The saffron-tinted complexion and uncouth form,

> acquired no graces from the tasteful back-ground which the scene presented; but as deformed persons generally adopt those ornaments which render their defects more strikingly conspicuous, so did Lord Arcot decorate his unwieldy figure with the most delicately-chosen habiliments; while he, like the destructive poppy, displayed his gaudy trappings, a loathsome weed amidst the profusion of nature. (311)

The nabob's *tableau vivant*, carefully staged on a chintz sofa, ironically prefigures his last appearance in the novel: he is discovered by Gertrude on a sofa in Lord Denmore's saloon, a suicide "bathed in his own blood" (395).

Lord Denmore, like Treville and Arcot, attempts to seem what he is not. He presents himself as Gertrude's honorable, sanctimonious, and austere guardian, but he is actually her father, guilty of seducing and impregnating his best friend's wife when Sir William St. Leger was in India. A moralistic hypocrite, he is the forerunner of Mr. Morley, the arch-villain of Robinson's *The Natural Daughter*. Terrified of being unmasked as a "*False Friend*" (400, italics in original) and the destroyer of the original Gertrude St. Leger, he hints at but does not unequivocally reveal his illegitimate daughter's relationship to him. As a result, Gertrude consistently misinterprets his motivation and behavior as romantic rather than dysfunctionally paternal. Denmore bewilders her by denouncing her father (himself) in the third person, dissociating his present identity from his past self. He informs her that her "father was a villain!" (28) and later declares: "Your father, Gertrude, was a monster of deceit, a false friend, and an enemy to virtue" (115). His use of the past tense suggests that he believes, or wants to believe, that he is no longer the "monster" he once was.

Assuming that Gertrude shares her mother's vulnerability to seduction, Denmore repeatedly accuses her of sexual misconduct. When Treville and Lady Denmore elope with Gertrude's inadvertent assistance, Denmore denounces his naive ward as "a practised pander" and suspects her of having had an affair with Sir Hector Upas: "My soul shudders at your depravity," he writes in a letter to her, "Such a refinement of vice would astonish, even in the mind of experienced age" (161). Bursting into a room containing Gertrude and the seriously wounded Treville/Somerton, he immediately suspects the worst: "Perdition! Somerton here! rash girl! lost, lost Gertrude!" (345). Everyone in the novel except for Denmore himself regards him as either Gertrude's stern, morally circumspect guardian or her besotted lover, and she becomes infatuated with him, unaware that their union would be incestuous. The charade ends, however, when

Denmore's betrayed friend returns from India and looks "earnestly" in his face. Denmore swoons and is subsequently "led to his chamber in a state of mental stupor" (395). No longer able to sustain his impersonation of a moral exemplar and man of honor, he temporarily loses his reason. What his disenchanted fiancée Miss Stanley says of him is also applicable to the novel's other male role-players: "Men are rarely what they seem" (405). The men who torment Gertrude and shape her destiny become indistinguishable from their facades; when unmasked, as Treville/Somerton is by the prospect of death and Denmore is by the appearance of Sir William St. Leger, they look inward and behold vacancy. Whereas lower- or middle-class polygraphs like Tippy and graphy use their chameleonic abilities to impersonate aristocrats, in *The False Friend* Lord Denmore creates a false self in order to create the illusion that he is morally fit to *be* an aristocrat.

COPYING SAPPHO

A number of Romantic-era women writers, including Robinson, Anna Seward, Felicia Hemans, and Letitia Elizabeth Landon (L. E. L.), considered the Greek poet Sappho as an important poetic precursor.[22] When reviewers of Robinson's 1791 *Poems* dubbed her the English Sappho, she was flattered to be identified with the "TENTH MUSE" (*Poems* 1.325) and adopted "Sappho" as one of her pseudonyms (Curran, "Robinson's *Lyrical Tales*" 20–21).[23] In the "Account of Sappho" that precedes Robinson's *Sappho and Phaon* (1796), she confidently declares that "the precious fragments of the immortal Sappho, will be admired, when the voluminous productions of inferior poets are mouldered into dust" (*Poems* 1.326). Her sonnet sequence pays tribute to Sappho and her literary descendents, Robinson's "illustrious countrywomen; who...persevere in the paths of literature, and ennoble themselves by the imperishable lustre of MENTAL PRE-EMINENCE!" (*Poems* 1.324).[24]

Robinson's knowledge of her literary foremother was, however, severely limited by her ignorance of ancient Greek and by the fact that only a few translations of Sappho's fragments were available to her.[25] Yopie Prins notes that "Sappho entered into the tradition of English verse through the Ovidian myth of her suicide, and until the early nineteenth century she was primarily known by English imitations of her two most famous poems, the 'Ode to Aphrodite' and 'Ode to Anactoria'" (3). Robinson derived her conception of the "tenth muse" from male writers such as Ovid, Longinus, Joseph Addison,

Ambrose Philips, Alexander Pope, William Mason, and Jean-Jacques Barthélemy. Her *Sappho and Phaon* contains references to Ovid's *Sappho to Phaon* and quotations from Pope's 1712 translation of Ovid's poem (Sonnets XXI.9; XXIII.1, 10; XXXV.9, 11; XLII.14). Thus the Sappho she knew was largely the invention of male authors, some of whom ventriloquize the Greek poet's voice in epistolary poems, imitations, or translations that purport to express her thoughts and feelings. Moreover, Sappho's association with sexual license made her a risky choice as a role model for an eighteenth-century woman writer (Daniel Robinson 115–117).[26] Robinson's reputation had been destroyed by her well-publicized affairs with the Prince of Wales and other men during the 1780s, and her identification with a sexually voracious Sappho might have undermined her efforts to rehabilitate herself in the late 1790s.

It is not surprising, therefore, that Robinson felt protective of her precursor's reputation.[27] She argues in her "Account of Sappho" that because the poet wrote "for future ages," she would not have "produce[d] any composition which might tend to tarnish her reputation, or to lessen that celebrity which it was the labour of her life to consecrate." Thus any objectionable verses attributed to Sappho must have been "erroneously given to posterity, either by ignorance or design," by "innumerable translators" who were incompetent or envious of her "merit" (*Poems* 1.326). In the address to the reader prefacing *Sappho and Phaon*, Robinson writes that Ovid's and Pope's "*portraits*" of Sappho are "*replete with shades, tending rather to depreciate than to adorn the Grecian poetess*" (1.324, italics in original). Although she does not specify what these "shades" are, she may have objected to Ovid's and Pope's allusions to Sappho's homoeroticism.[28] She quotes approvingly from Barthélemy, who contends that Sappho uses "the impassioned language of love" in her lyrics to depict "the most innocent connections" (1.327) between her and her female disciples, and in Sonnet XXXII of *Sappho and Phaon* Robinson recasts a line from one of Sappho's homoerotic lyrics (fragment 31) to make it refer to her heterosexual love for Phaon.[29] As an adoring mother dedicated to the welfare of her daughter, Maria Elizabeth, Robinson probably would also have deplored Ovid's and Pope's unmaternal portrayals of Sappho: they have the Greek poet summarily reject the notion that her daughter could console her for her loss of Phaon.[30] Although Ovid's tale of Sappho's unrequited love and suicide moved and inspired Robinson, she resented what she regarded as his and Pope's disparagement of a poet whom she considered her poetic forebear.

Sappho does not, however, provide a positive role model for the female characters in *The False Friend*, who tend to be either victims or instruments of male tyranny. Like Ovid's "Sappho to Phaon" and Pope's translation, *The False Friend* is epistolary, but whereas Ovid's Sappho addresses her complaints to the unresponsive boatman who has abandoned her, Gertrude writes to a sympathetic woman, Frances Montgomery. Gertrude's education, unlike the instruction of Sappho's female disciples and Robinson's training by the brilliant alcoholic Meribah Lorrington, is guided by a man, Lord Denmore.[31] Gertrude explains to her correspondent that Denmore's "features" seem "imprinted on [her] brain" (7), and she believes that he has the ability to trace her "torturing thought through all the labyrinths of [her] brain, and [find] that it [leads] to his image indelibly impressed upon its fibres" (117). Her brain passively mirrors her obsession. She writes that under her guardian's tutelage, she has been "wrapt [*sic*] in pleasing dreams" from which she "awake[s] a new-created being" (45), a Galatea to his Pygmalion. Without knowing it, she echoes a passage from a letter her mother wrote to Denmore after being seduced by him: "I AM a new-created being! I live, I breathe only for your happiness!" (26).

Denmore's "recreation" of both Gertrudes ultimately reduces them to copies of Ovid's Sappho and reflections of each other. In one of the novel's many Gothic scenes, Gertrude fearfully enters the chamber of the apparently dead but soon-to-revive Lady Denmore. She is terrified, however, not by Lady Denmore's inanimate form, but by her own pale reflection in a mirror: "I beheld my own features, to which the light that I carried gave an additional paleness; I stood as though my feet were rooted to the ground; the house was as silent as the grave, and my blood seemed to freeze with the terrors which assailed me." Her face mirrors Lady Denmore's "ghastly . . . pale . . . countenance" (82) and the features of Sappho's bust in Denmore's library, which possess "the paleness of a corpse" (377). Lady Denmore's passion for Treville ultimately destroys her; Gertrude exists in a hall of mirrors reflecting and multiplying the cadaverous faces of specular women who are or will be the victims of male false friends.

According to Gertrude, Denmore teaches her "to analyze the human heart; to separate the dross of folly from the pure and solid ore of truth." "[G]uided by his classic taste, and enlightened by the power of his intellectual pre-eminence," she explores "the paths of virtue and philosophy" and traces the progress of humankind from ignorance to knowledge (45). Denmore refuses, however, to reveal that he is her biological father. Gertrude's mother is partly to blame for his reticence; on her deathbed, she commands him "never to disclose [her daughter's] origin or prospects" until she is 18, "and not even *then*, if by any action of her life she ... prove[s] unworthy" (406). Accordingly, he does not tell his ward that she is his daughter, the product of an adulterous affair, and she falls in love with him.

Denmore profoundly influences his daughter's conception of Sappho. His sternly patriarchal bust stands in the library, the room in which her mother died, haunting Gertrude when he is away and even discouraging her from entering the room. According to Gertrude, it "seems to possess the powers of the basilisk," a mythical creature that can kill with a look, and she feels "as if it ha[s] something destructive in its influence over [her] senses" (46). She has the bust removed, planning to replace it with the less intimidating and more inspirational head of Sir Isaac Newton, which she believes will enable her to "traverse ... the paths of unknown worlds." Accompanying Denmore's bust is the head of Sappho, which fascinates Gertrude: "it has softness, blended with strong intellectual traits, and, though not regularly beautiful, is irresistibly pleasing." Her guardian explains to her that "[t]he Grecian poetess ... was not famed for personal attractions; she was, like many children of genius, equally distinguished for the gifts of mental pre-eminence and the persecutions of misfortune; she was ... the most favoured and the most unhappy of women" (50).[32]

Robinson's representation of Sappho as a sculptural fragment recalls Addison's description of one of Sappho's fragments (fragment 31) as "the Trunc [*sic*] of a Statue which has lost the Arms, Legs and Head" (2.390).[33] But whereas Addison compares Sappho's poem to a decapitated, maimed torso, in *The False Friend* the poet is represented by a bust, a fragment with a head. In *A Letter to the Women of England*, Robinson bitterly alludes to a headless statue, "the *good woman* of St. Giles" (158). According to her, this decapitated figure is "*almost* the only female in the kingdom *universally* allowed to be a *good woman*" (158n, italics in orginal). In contrast, a woman with a head can think and express her opinions and therefore poses a threat to the status quo. Robinson suggests that in spite of the obliteration of most of Sappho's poetic legacy, her voice has not been completely silenced, and thus she has not been transformed into a decapitated figure like Addison's trunk or "the good woman of St. Giles."

After "reading some anecdotes of ... Sappho," possibly by Addison, Gertrude learns that the poet "loved—she was deserted—she was the victim of an [*sic*] hopeless passion." Like many eighteenth-century readers, she is more familiar with the poet's legend than with her poetry.[34] Remembering that Sappho "buried her burning bosom in the deep wave," she imagines that she hears "the harp of the unhappy Lesbian" in a "wild cascade" of water (51). Earlier in the novel, heartbroken over Denmore's cold treatment of her, Gertrude rushes after his departing carriage, falls in a stream, and is saved by him from drowning. Thus the story of Sappho's fatal leap from the Leucadian Rock reminds her of her own unrequited love. Convinced that she is "borne, in defiance of every effort, towards that abyss where [she] is inevitably doomed to perish" (128), Gertrude accepts Ovid's apocryphal tale of Sappho's heterosexual passion and suicide and, like several of the novel's other female characters, believes herself destined to replicate it in her own life. Robinson writes in her "Account of Sappho" that "Addison was of [the] opinion, that the writings of Sappho were replete with such fascinating beauties, and adorned with such a vivid glow of sensibility, that, probably, had they been preserved entire, it would have been dangerous to have perused them" (*Poems* 1.326).[35] In *The False Friend*, however, it is the influence of the male-authored *Sappho to Phaon* that proves dangerous. Like Ovid's Sappho, Gertrude becomes a "VICTIM OF SENSIBILITY,"[36] although in her case she loves an older rather than a younger man.

Gertrude conceives of herself as a writer, prefacing her description of Lord Denmore's guests with the statement that "it is the duty of impartial writers to place merit in the full lustre of its own brilliancy; and to shew the deformity of vice, in the clear, but faithful mirror of reflection" (16). Her precursor Sappho was regarded as a mental anatomist; commenting on Philips's version of fragment 31, Addison notes that as "*Longinus* has observed,... this Description of Love in *Sappho* is an exact Copy of Nature" (2.393). In her "Account of Sappho," Robinson provides evidence of Sappho's psychological acuity:

> The story of Antiochus has been related as an unequivocal proof of Sappho's skill in discovering, and powers of describing the passions of the human mind. That prince is said to have entertained a fatal affection for his mother-in-law Stratonice; which, though he endeavoured to subdue its influence, preyed upon his frame, and after many ineffectual struggles, at length reduced him to extreme danger. His physicians marked the symptoms attending his malady, and found them to exactly correspond with Sappho's delineation of the tender passion, that they did not hesitate to form a decisive opinion on the case, which had produced so perilous an effect. (*Poems* 1.325)

Whereas Sappho's poetry enables Antiochus's physicians to discover their patient's transgressive love for his mother-in-law, Denmore's readings of "the Grecian poetess" apparently do not provide him with any insight into Gertrude's symptoms, and he fails to diagnose her incestuous passion for him. According to Robinson, Sappho fell victim to the malady she so brilliantly described. Like her forebear, Gertrude is "*a lively example of the human mind, enlightened by the most exquisite talents, yet yielding to the destructive controul* [*sic*] *of ungovernable passions*" (*Poems* 1.324, italics in original). But unlike Sappho, Gertrude regards writing as her avocation rather than her vocation, and her ability "to analyze the human heart" does not extend to Denmore, whose behavior she consistently and fatally misinterprets. According to her, men idolize women in order to enslave them: "Created to protect us, they expose us to every danger; endowed with strength to sustain our erring judgment, they are ever eager to mislead us" (127). Gertrude, Gertrude's mother, Lady Denmore, and Mary Ashgrove, who is the "victim" of Treville/Somerton's "falsehood" (322), become obsessed with capricious and self-absorbed men, and their emotional dependence on these late-eighteenth-century Phaons condemns them to short and unproductive existences.

Haunted by her guardian's glowering bust, which, along with Sappho's head, has been transferred from the library to her chamber, Gertrude decides to move it again. However, as she lifts it up, the "weight nearly overpower[s] [her] strength," and she knocks over "the head of Sappho, which . . . shatter[s] into a thousand pieces," like the poet's fragmented poetic corpus. Symbolically, Gertrude's patriarchal burden has obliterated any positive influence Sappho might have had on her (Cross, "He-She Philosophers" 61). Sighing "with sorrow and vexation," she tries to collect "the fragments which [lie] scattered round [her]" (360). Her task, like that of scholars who attempt to reassemble Sappho's works from scattered fragments, cannot succeed, but, typically, her main concern is that Denmore will be distressed by the accident. The destruction of this artwork is followed by the erasure of another. A servant discovers a red leather case with a portrait of a woman who looks like Gertrude, and it turns out to be a picture of Gertrude's mother. Unfortunately, the servant throws the red case into a brook to avoid being accused of stealing, and the portrait's colors are "entirely effaced" (364). Later, Gertrude learns that the model for Sappho's bust was her mother. Finding that the head's "countenance" is intact, she kisses and hugs "the precious fragment." She addresses the face "in the language of filial affection" and "on [her] knees invoke[s] the gentle spirit of [her] angelic parent to sustain [her] soul, and to soothe it into resignation." This association of Sappho with motherhood contradicts Ovid's and Pope's depictions of her as unmaternal. However, while the alabaster face representing Gertrude's parent and Sappho seems "to smile upon [her]," it possesses "the paleness of a corpse" (377). Instead of hope, her mother bequeaths her misery and death.

The novel identifies Sappho not only with Gertrude's parent but also with the protagonist herself, who inherits her mother's name and features. The representation of Sappho is thus a copy of the first Gertrude, whom the second Gertrude strongly resembles. The younger Gertrude does not, however, recognize herself in the alabaster face she kisses: she is a copy without being aware that she is a copy. Adrienne Rich writes that "[m]atrophobia," or the fear "of *becoming one's mother*," "can be seen as a womanly splitting of the self, in the [daughters'] desire to become purged once and for all of [their] mothers' bondage, to become individuated and free" (237–238). Because Gertrude has never known her mother, she cannot engage in this process of individuation, this matrophobic purgation of "the victim . . . the unfree woman, the martyr" (Rich 238) from the self. Ignorant of her parents' identity, Gertrude becomes a victim of sensibility like her mother and an eighteenth-century Ovidian Sappho rather than an original. By withholding her parents' identity from Gertrude, Denmore precipitates her demise. Instead of being nurturing and protective, his relationship to her is psychologically abusive, tyrannical at times, and potentially incestuous. The first and second Gertrude both love a man whom they can never marry and die in despair.

Thus Sappho's fragmentation and the erasure of Gertrude's mother foreshadow Gertrude's fate. Rather than being inspired by Sappho to pursue a literary career, Gertrude abandons her correspondence and is found dead soon after her mother's husband kills Denmore in a duel. As Susan Allen Ford observes, "the destruction of Sappho suggests [that] there can be no discovery of a poetic voice that can transcend and give form to Gertrude's suffering" (66). The virtuous, rational, and worldly-wise Miss Stanley takes over her correspondence with Frances Montgomery, as she did earlier in the novel when Gertrude was seriously ill.[37] Miss Stanley has survived a bad marriage and her own relationship with Lord Denmore, which she breaks off when he proves "unworthy" (405). She exemplifies what Robinson's essay *Present State of the Manners, Society, &c. &c. of the Metropolis of England* (1800) calls "the spirit of emulative contention" (118). Her imitativeness is tempered by an enlightened contrarianism and a refusal to be dominated by others. As Miss Stanley points out to Frances, whereas "a woman of the world, a reasoning, rational, discriminating mortal" finds the charms of unsuitable men easy to resist, Gertrude's education "in total seclusion from the world" (367) has left her vulnerable to the "fascinations" of Lord Denmore's "magic." Far from regarding Gertrude as a potential writer, Miss Stanley compares her to Petrarch's Laura (368), who, as Robinson notes in *A Letter to the Women of England*, is said to have been unable to read or write (151).[38]

To Miss Stanley, Gertrude's downfall is her lack of a comprehensive and practical education rather than her persecution by men. As Robinson knew from her reading of Barthélemy, the concept of an academy for women is one of Sappho's positive legacies (*Poems* 1.326). In *A Letter to the Women of England*, published the month after *The False Friend* appeared, Robinson calls for a "UNIVERSITY FOR WOMEN, where they should be politely, and at the same time classically educated" (159). If Gertrude had received a classical education, she might have been able to read Sappho in the original, unmediated by male translators, Ovid, Pope, or her father. More important, if she had been educated at a university for women rather than by her father, she might have been able to heed "the admonition of Reason" (*A Letter to the Women of England* 159) and overcome her passion for him. Gertrude admires Mary Wollstonecraft, "whose monument is built on the immortal basis which supports the rights of woman," but she fails to apply the feminist's rationalist "precepts" to her life (123). In some ways, she resembles, however, the "female Wert[h]er" portrayed in Godwin's *Memoirs of the Author of a Vindication of the Rights of Woman* (1798) (242).[39] According to Paula Byrne, "*The False Friend* is in many ways more a response to the death of Mary Wollstonecraft than an outpouring of feelings about [Robinson's former lover Banastre] Tarleton" (345). Godwin's controversial account of Wollstonecraft's obsessional relationship with Gilbert Imlay, punctuated by her attempt to commit suicide by drowning, may have reminded Robinson of Ovid's Sappho and influenced her portrayal of Gertrude St. Leger.

Unlike *The False Friend*, *A Letter to the Women of England* looks forward to a positive future for women. In spite of the male appropriation of Sappho's legend, Robinson believed that the Greek poet could inspire women to become "liberally, classically, philosophically, and usefully educated" (*A Letter to the Women of England* 159) and enjoy productive lives rather than throw themselves off cliffs. Morgan Rooney argues that the heroine of Robinson's *The Natural Daughter* develops into "a new, writing, self-authorizing female subject whose intellectual powers, mobility, and independence endow her with a dignity that enables her to assume her rightful position as the equal partner of man" (371). *The False Friend* disputes, however, this uplifting vision of female self-authorization through writing. Instead of achieving mobility, the avatars of Ovid's Sappho in *The False Friend* petrify into pallid corpses or a fragile marble bust. Gertrude St. Leger, her mother, Lady Denmore, and Mary Ashgrove become copies rather than originals, manipulated and victimized by male role-players and false friends.

THE SOCIAL MASQUERADE

Robinson's attitude toward chameleonism was conflicted and constantly evolving. In 1779, her performance as Perdita in *The Winter's Tale* captivated the Prince of Wales and temporarily improved her social position—the infatuated Prince made her his mistress, escorted her into St. James's Palace, and gave a grand ball for her—but her impersonation of the innocent shepherdess backfired when the Prince discarded her and left her with a ruined reputation and an insufficient financial settlement. In *Present State of the Manners, Society, &c. &c. of the Metropolis of England*, published shortly before her death, she reports that London is overrun with sartorial and behavioral chameleons:

> The public promenades, particularly on the sabbath, are thronged with pedestrians of all classes, and the different ranks of people are scarcely distinguishable either by their dress or their manners. The duchess, and her *femme de chambre*, are dressed equally alike; the nobleman and his groom are equally ambitious of displaying the neat boot, the cropped head, and the external decorations, as well as the quaint language, of the stable-boy. The dapper milliner, and the sauntering female of slender reputation, imitate the woman of fashion, in the choice of their cloaths, and the tenour of their conversation; while all ranks of females display a lightness of drapery, which would completely characterise the dimensions of a Grecian statue. (198)

For Robinson, clothes and manners are unreliable markers of class identity. Maidservants can pass as Duchesses, noblemen imitate stableboys, and milliners and prostitutes mimic women of fashion. Robinson claims that many metropolitan chameleons create false selves in order to establish "singularity of character": "Notoriety is...the leading spring of action; and those who are most zealous in acquiring it, frequently mistake its characteristics for those of celebrity. For this important purpose, we behold authors writing in contradiction to their avowed principles; actors caricaturing nature, till they deprive her of every grace; painters presenting to the eye imaginary forms, disproportioned—distorted—and unlike any thing human; men effeminized like women; and women assuming the masculine deportment of the other sex" (202). Desperate to achieve notoriety, these chameleons betray their convictions, distort nature, or cross gender. Rather than becoming singular, they become hypocritical and inauthentic. They are publicity seekers posing as non-conformists. *Present State of the . . . Metropolis of England* envisions London society as a masquerade in which the costumes are "scarcely distinguishable," subjectivities are masked, class passing is endemic, and everyone plays roles.

Although the lives of inauthentic, chameleonic characters generally end in tragedy in *The False Friend*, in an August 24, 1800 letter to William Godwin, Robinson insists that "artificial creature[s]" often thrive in late-eighteenth-century society:

> I never could dissemble . . . In the broad circle of Society it is frequently convenient, some will maintain that it is justifiable, to assume a character, rather than to sustain one. I am a living proof that such artifice is advantageous, and that to be ingenuous, is to ensure a long succession of pains and disappointments! Had I been an artificial creature—I might have been in wealth and vulgar estimation, a creature to be envied! But the impetuosity of my temper; the irritability of my feelings;—the proud, indignant, resentful energy of my soul, placed a barrier betwixt me and Fortune, which has thrown a gloom on every hour of my existence. So much for *Self.* ("Letters" 316–317).

Chronically ill, in debt, and abandoned by her longtime lover Banastre Tarleton, Robinson sees all of the advantages and none of the disadvantages of chameleonism. As Martha Morley discovers in *The Natural Daughter*, "to *seem* and not to *be* [is] the all-powerful clue to private praise and public reputation" (120, italics in original). Both Robinson and her character Walsingham despise polygraphing, the servile copying of noble originals, but in her letter to Godwin, Robinson suggests that her Rousseauistic individualism placed "a barrier between [her] and Fortune." "So much for *Self*," she bitterly writes—in a society that judges by appearances, artificial creatures like the polygraphs in *Walsingham* may have a significant advantage in the competition for "wealth and vulgar estimation."

Chapter 6

James Kenney's Opportunistic, Reformative, and Imitative Chameleons

Raising the Wind

On October 14, 1843, Edgar Allan Poe's "Raising the Wind; or, Diddling Considered as One of the Exact Sciences" appeared in the Philadelphia *Saturday Courier.* In this satirical *jeu d'esprit*, Poe explains that "the verb to diddle" derives from Jeremy Diddler, a theatrical character whose name had become synonymous with petty swindling: "Since the world began there have been two Jeremys. One wrote a Jeremiad about usury, and was called Jeremy Bentham. He...was a great man in a small way. The other gave name to the most important of the Exact Sciences, and was entitled Jeremy Diddler. He was a great man in a *great* way—I may say, indeed, in the very greatest of ways." Poe defines "Man [as] an animal that diddles": "'Man was made to mourn,' says the poet. But not so:—he was made to diddle. This is his aim—his object—his *end.*—And for this reason when a man's diddled we say that he's '*done.*'"[1] The satire concludes with a description of "a very decent, but rather elaborate diddle" featuring "A middle-aged gentleman" who "has the whole air...of your well-to-do, sober-sided, exact, and respectable 'man of business,' *par excellence*—one of the stern and outwardly hard, internally soft, sort of people that we see in the crack high comedies." The middle-aged gentleman advertises for young men of impeccable integrity who possess "the most satisfactory testimonials of morality" and are "piously inclined." Because "the duties to be performed involve high responsibilities, and large amounts of money must necessarily pass through the hands of those engaged, it is deemed advisable to demand a deposit of fifty dollars from each clerk employed" (1). But after "some fifteen or twenty young men piously inclined" have given the respectable man of business their deposits, the diddler absconds with their money. Like the Social Monster, the Northern Imposter, and the fake Duke of Ormond, Poe's middle-aged swindler is an accomplished actor operating in an urban "theatre" (in his case, Philadelphia) who resembles the "sort of people that we see in the crack high comedies."

Poe took the title of his satire from *Raising the Wind, A Farce* (1803) by the Irish-born dramatist James Kenney (*c.* 1780–1849), which was a huge success in both America and Britain. Both of Poe's parents acted in the play: his father performed the roles of Richard (a servant) and Fainwou'd, and his mother played the sentimental Peggy Plainway at least five times (Quinn 710, 712, 721).[2] A line spoken twice in *Raising the Wind*, "I only asked for information" (I.i.5, II.ii.40), became a nineteenth-century catchphrase. At the beginning of farce, Jeremy Diddler is broke and desperate but attempts to maintain his genteel facade. He tries to get a waiter named Sam to give him tenpence, and after Sam refuses to lend it to him, Diddler claims that he "only asked" about the money "for information":

> *Diddler*... Sam,—you haven't got such a thing as ten-pence about you, have you?
> *Sam.* Yes [they look at each other—DIDDLER expecting to receive it.] And I mean to keep it about me, you see.
> *Diddler.* Oh—aye—certainly. I only ask'd for information. (I.i.5)

In a later scene, he has a similar conversation with a servant:

> *Diddler.* Um—you haven't got such a thing as a guinea about you, have you?
> *Servant.* No, sir.
> *Diddler.* Aye—that's all, John, I only asked for information. (II.ii.40)[3]

Diddler's assertion that he only asks for information is funny because it is so transparently insincere. To salvage his "wounded pride" (I.i.7), he pretends that he is idly curious about whether or not a waiter possesses tenpence. Byron used Diddler's signature line twice in his letters. Writing to his publisher John Murray on September 5, 1812, he inquires how much Murray would give "for a poem of 6 Cantos" like the first two cantos of *Childe Harold's*

Pilgrimage (1812) and quotes Diddler's catchphrase in a postscript: "My last question is in the true style of Grub Street, but like *Jeremy Diddler* I only 'ask for information'" (*Letters and Journals* 2.191). In an October 3, 1819 letter discussing his plan to relocate to Venezuela, Byron requests John Cam Hobhouse to "speak to [James] *Perry* of the M[orning] C[hronicle]... about this—and ask like Jeremy Diddler—not for eighteen pence—but information on the subject" (*Letters and Journals* 6.225–226). The chameleonic Diddler, who adroitly shifts identities to manipulate his dupes, was an iconic figure for Byron and many other nineteenth-century writers. References to Kenney's farce may be found in Charles Dickens's *The Life and Adventures of Nicholas Nickleby* (1838–1839), Edward Bulwer-Lytton's comedy *Money* (1840), and in Herman Melville's *The Confidence-Man* (1857), in which a character speculates that a beggar nicknamed Black Guinea may "be some sort of black Jeremy Diddler" (22).[4] "To raise the wind" means "to procure money or the necessary means for some end" (*OED*), and after *Raising the Wind* became a theatrical hit, the verb "diddle," meaning "to cheat or swindle; to victimize; to 'do'" (*OED*), entered the English language.

This chapter focuses on Kenney's diverse and culturally resonant representations of opportunistic, reformative, and imitative chameleons in *Raising the Wind*, *False Alarms; or, My Cousin* (1807), and *The World! A Comedy* (1808). Before becoming a successful playwright, Kenney worked "in the prominent London banking-house of Herries, Farquhar, and Co.," and his comedies explore "the nature of character and identity formation in a world ever more dominated by the marketplace" (Terry Robinson 1083, 1086). As Lieutenant M'Lary observes in *False Alarms*, "It's a maxim now-a-days to attend to no lady or gentleman, but your own sweet self; and upon the reasonable principle, that if we all take care of ourselves, we shall be all taken care of" (I.i.12). Kenney's male chameleons embrace the capitalist ethos of self-interest and alter their identities to enrich themselves and rise in society.[5] However, the opportunistic performances of the chameleons in *Raising the Wind*, *False Alarms*, and *The World!* frequently result in their humiliation. These plays suggest that while assuming a false identity may enhance a chameleon's creditworthiness and eligibility in the marriage market, prolonged chameleonism is morally and psychologically unsustainable. Diddler considers his "vagabond" lifestyle dishonorable (I.i.6), and in *The World!*, fashionable society compels the Zelig-like Jack Echo to engage in "pursuits from which [his] heart and [his] conscience for ever must revolt" (V.iii.79).[6] In *Raising the Wind* and *The World!*, the women who love the chameleonic characters provide them with the opportunity to stabilize their fluid identities and develop moral agency. *False Alarms* features a female chameleon who masquerades as the gallant Captain Bronze to teach her school-friend's errant husband a lesson. Although she is, like Diddler, dissimulative and mischievous, her imposture is intended to help her friend and reform a would-be rake rather than to improve her financial or social position. *False Alarms* indicates that chameleonism can be disinterested as well as acquisitive.

Raising the Wind debuted at Covent Garden on November 5, 1803 with William Thomas Lewis, who had previously played the polygraph Tippy in Cowley's *The Town before You* and the chameleon Sir George Versatile in Holcroft's *He's Much to Blame*, performing the role of Jeremy Diddler. The *Hampshire Telegraph and Sussex Chronicle* reported that Diddler "was represented by Mr. Lewis in his most brilliant *dashing* stile;—the characters as well as incidents are *resemblances*, if not imitations of some already on the stage; Diddler, the *wind-raiser*, is the *Sponge* of Reynold's [*sic*] *Cheap Living*" (November 14, 1803). In Frederick Reynolds's *Cheap Living: A Comedy* (1797), Spunge, played by Jack Bannister, is a convivial opportunist who tricks people into lending him small sums of cash, feeding him dinner, and treating him to iced Burgundy. He engages in petty swindles, rescues a young woman from the sexual advances of the villainous Scatter (acted by "Plausible Jack" Palmer), and helps her brother, Sir Edward Bloomly (played by the cross-dressing Dorothy Jordan), thwart Scatter's fraudulent schemes. At the play's conclusion, Spunge insists to Old Woodland that he has a symbiotic rather than parasitic relationship with his dupes ("flats"):

> *Old Woodland.* Egad!—I believe yours is the best mode of living cheap after all—other people only save by retail——
>
> *Spunge.* And I by wholesale!—what signifies saving and stinting yourself at home?—never have any home at all—live on the flats—they are always glad of your company.
>
> *Old Woodland.* Are they?
>
> *Spunge.* To be sure—man and wife...after the honey-moon, glad when a friend pops in to interrupt the tête-à-tête—"My dear, I am so distrè [distrait]"—"and I so annoyed—aw! aw!"—[*yawning*]—in I come—as I shall often—very—very often.—"Ah, Spunge! glad to see you Spunge!—stay and eat mutton, my honest fellow!"—they devour my discourse—I devour their dinner—all parties are pleased;—and there's the true mode of living cheap. (V.iii.67–68)

Although the comedy's epilogue, written by the editor and poet John Taylor, condemns sponges as "men of prey, / Who live by shuffling arts from day to day" (lines 19–20), Spunge is an engaging character who capitalizes on the fact that entertainment and fellowship are services that the well-to-do will happily pay for with meals and lodgings.[7] He constantly metamorphoses himself in response to the susceptibilities, demands, and probity of his various audiences. In a society swarming with prosperous dupes, affable leeches can secure credit and live cheaply. According to the epilogue, Spunge "represents a num'rous kind— / For ev'ry family its Spunge may find" (lines 7–8).

In *Raising the Wind*, Jeremy Diddler is an ebullient and myopic social parasite who "lives by spunging" (I.i.4). Unlike Spunge, however, he yearns to "earn [his] breakfasts and [his] dinners ... honorably" (I.i.6). Moreover, Diddler is more chameleonic and amorous than his prototype: he performs the roles of a sentimental lover ("the all-accomplished Mortimer" [I.ii.15]), Mr. Plainway's imaginary nephew, a nouveau riche cockney named Fainwou'd, and an epistolary Adonis. Whereas Spunge attaches himself to a baronet to achieve financial security, Diddler sets out to wed a wealthy woman who will "pay [his] debts and heal [his] wounded pride." For Diddler, the alternative to imposture is penury: if he had not "surmounted" his ethical "delicacy," he "must have starved long ago" (I.i.7). As a fortune hunter, he recalls Cumberland's Singleton/Lord Janus, Polycarp, and Jack Crotchet; Holcroft's Harry Monrose; and Cowley's Bronze and Tippy, upwardly mobile chameleons who court wealthy women. His myopia is moral as well as visual; as Plainway observes, "short-sighted is roguery" (II.ii.33).

Kenney portrays Diddler as a disarmingly vulnerable scamp who reveals his hopes and fears to spectators and readers in soliloquies and asides. After he fails to secure enough credit from a waiter to obtain a breakfast, Diddler bemoans his vagabondage and lack of "capital." His melancholy is, however, short-lived. He rallies his spirits with a quotation from Mark Akenside's didactic philosophical poem *The Pleasures of Imagination* (1744): "'awake thee, rouse thy spirit!' honorably earn thy breakfasts and thy dinners too."[8] Since he considers sponging, his "present trade," dishonorable and other trades require apprenticeships, he decides to mend his fortunes by marrying "A rich wife" and becoming what the heroine of Cumberland's *The Fashionable Lover* calls "a legal prostitute" (III.iii.37). Although his "degenerate ... wardrobe is confoundedly again [him]," he composes a "passionate billet" to an heiress "lately come to the house at the foot of the hill" (I.i.6–7). Manipulating "the romantic imagination"

(I.i.9) of an impressionable woman is the most lucrative diddle that Diddler can undertake, and he hopes that it will enable him to live off someone else's wealth for the remainder of his life. He constructs an identity calculated to appeal to readers of sentimental literature, and Peggy Plainway, a devotee of Miss Somerville's *The Victim of Sentiment* (II.ii.16), succumbs to his performance.

Diddler is both self-consciously literary and a master of improvisation. His love letter parodies the amorous, epistolary, and pseudonymous Della Cruscan verse that appeared in London newspapers during the late 1780s. As Angela Esterhammer and Michael Gamer have demonstrated, the Della Cruscan movement was inspired by the Italian improvvisatori, who extemporized poems based on randomly selected themes before enthusiastic audiences. Like the improvvisatori, Della Cruscan poets prided themselves on their ability to generate impromptu verse (Esterhammer, *Romanticism and Improvisation* 32 and Gamer 32). After quickly scribbling his billet-doux, Diddler pauses to admire it: "'To the beautiful maid at the foot of the hill.' The words are so delicate, the arrangement so poetical, and the tout-ensemble reads with such a languishing cadence, that a blue-stocking garden-wench must feel it!...She can't resist it!" (I.i.9). Later in the play, Diddler squirms as Peggy Plainway's father reads his letter aloud:

> Most celestial of terrestrial beings! I have received a wound from your eyes which baffles all surgical skill. The smile of her who gave it, is the only balsam that can save it. Let me therefore supplicate admittance to your presence to-morrow, to know at once if I may live or die.
>
> That if I'm to live, I may live your fond lover;—
> And if I'm to die, I may get it soon over.—
> Adonis. (II.ii.32–33)

Kenney also satirizes Della Cruscanism in *Debtor and Creditor* (1814), in which Bob Gosling, an egotistical "trading citizen" (I.i.10), writes "amatory poetry" to women who fancy themselves his "Rosa or Julia."[9] Gosling carries around an ugly black book that contains his "orders and invitations, amatory sonnets and accounts current, billets-doux and bills of exchange" (I.i.13). For Diddler and Gosling, romance and business are intertwined, and they compose sentimental verse to market themselves to heiresses. To them, lovemaking is both a poetic imposture and a financial strategy. Their cynicism contrasts with Charles Cheviot's sentimental Della Cruscanism in *The World!* The melancholy Cheviot—whose poetic avatar is Fidelio—derives "solace" from the newspaper verse of his "dear poetical correspondent... Rosabella" but deplores her "anti-poetical" line "*Leighton Buzzard, first of May*" (II.ii.22). However, even this *poète maudit* values money. Upon receiving a letter containing a banknote he exclaims: "A hundred pounds! egad, this is a pleasanter correspondent than Rosabella" (III.ii.46).

Diddler's shortsightedness causes him to submit his poetic improvisation to the wrong person. Unable to "distinguish" a single "feature" on the face of a woman who appears at a window in Plainway's house (I.ii.16), he mistakes the middle-aged Miss Laurelia Durable for "the beautiful maid at the foot of the hill" and asks Sam to deliver his love letter to her. After Sam returns, Diddler slips into the house and hides himself in a closet, hoping to obtain an interview with the beautiful maid. A servant ushers Fainwou'd into the adjoining room, and Diddler overhears Fainwou'd saying that his marriage to Peggy Plainway has been agreed to by their fathers and that he has a letter of introduction to Plainway. Having previously won Peggy's affections in Bath under the name of Mortimer, Diddler decides to sabotage his rival. He poses as Plainway's nephew and informs Fainwou'd that Plainway has affianced his daughter to "sir Robert Rental, a baronet, with a thumping estate" and regards Fainwou'd as "quite a vulgar, conceited, foolish fellow" (I.iii.22). Outraged, Fainwou'd inadvertently drops his letter of introduction and leaves. Diddler picks the letter up, presents it to Plainway, and assumes Fainwou'd's identity.

As Plainway observes, Diddler's impudence and frivolity contrast with the "extreme timidity and bashfulness" (I.iii.25) attributed to Fainwou'd in the letter of introduction. Diddler is a pseudonymous chameleon who changes his name but not his extroverted behavior. The man he inaccurately impersonates is also attempting to refashion himself. Fainwou'd's name invites comparisons to Colonel Fainwell, the protagonist of Susanna Centlivre's *A Bold Stroke for a Wife*, who assumes four identities to obtain the permission of four guardians for him to marry Anne Lovely. However, whereas Fainwell is an accomplished chameleon, Fainwou'd would like to feign gentlemanliness but fails miserably: at "a large assembly" he picks "up the tail of a lady's gown, and [is] going to present it to her for her pocket-handkerchief." He believes that his "father's money has made [him] a gentleman" (I.i.3), but his uncouth behavior provokes merriment. Even though he is penniless and shabbily dressed, Diddler plays the role of a gentleman more convincingly than his cockney rival does. Temporarily, performance trumps money.

Diddler's improvisations become more challenging after Peggy recognizes him as "the all-accomplished Mortimer" and Miss Durable identifies him as her epistolary Adonis. He feels compelled to sing the popular song "The Beautiful Maid" from Thomas Dibdin's *The Cabinet; A Comic Opera* (1802) to both women:

> Diddler, [*concluding a song.*]
> Nor retirement nor solitude yield me relief,
> when away from my beautiful maid
> [*to Peggy.*]
> when away from my beautiful maid
> [*to Miss* D.*]*
> when away from my beautiful maid, &c.
> [*addressing himself alternately to the two ladies.*] (II.ii.31)

Diddler plays three roles simultaneously—Mortimer, Adonis, and Fainwou'd—and cannot sustain his triple performance. After leaping to the conclusion that Diddler/Fainwou'd intends to seduce her, the melodramatic Miss Durable "affects to faint." Peggy overhears Diddler's attempt to mollify Miss Durable and realizes that the man she knew as Mortimer composed the love letter signed Adonis:

> *Diddler.* (supporting [Miss Durable]) Upon my soul, madam, I would not interfere with your honor on any account. (aside) I must make an outrageous speech; there's nothing else will make her easy. [falls on his knees, Peggy enters listening.] Paragon of premature divinity! what instrument of death, or torture, can equal the dreadful power of your frowns? poison, pistols, steel-traps, and spring-guns, the thumb-screw, or lead-kettle, the knoot [*sic*], or cat o'nine tails, are impotent, compared to the words of your indignation! cease then to wound with them a heart, whose affection for you, nothing can abate, whose—
> *Peggy.* [interrupting him, and shewing the letter.] So, sir; this is your effusion, and this is the fruit of it—false, infamous man!
> *Diddler.* (aside to miss D.) . . . You'd better retire, and I'll contrive to get off.—My dear miss Plainway——
> *Peggy.* Don't dear me, sir. I've done with you.
> *Diddler.* If you would but hear——
> *Peggy.* I'll hear nothing, sir, you can't clear yourself; this duplicity can only arise from the meanest of motives, Mr. Mortimer.
> *Miss D. Mr. Mortimer!* then I am the dupe after all——
> *Peggy.* You're a mean——
> *Miss D.* Base——
> *Peggy.* Deceitful——
> *Miss D.* Abominable——(II.ii.36–37)

Miss Durable and Peggy, like Diddler, model themselves on stock characters from sentimental novels: while he masquerades as a sentimental lover, the women envision themselves as heroines of sensibility victimized by the gallant Mr. Mortimer, who is either a mercenary or Lovelacean seducer. Even after his two-timing has been exposed, Diddler continues to play the role of ardent suitor with both women. The "false Adonis" (II.ii.45) tells Miss Durable that he will explain everything to her in the garden, and when she leaves, he says in an aside that he hopes she will be "Floating in the fish-pond" (II.ii.37). He then professes his love for Peggy and asks her to elope with him immediately. Despite Diddler's manifest duplicity, Peggy cannot resist the opportunity to enact a scene from countless sentimental novels and agrees to his proposal. She imagines that "the all-accomplished Mortimer" is infinitely superior to "the vulgar, the sordid Fainwou'd" (I.ii.15), whom she has never met.

Bereft of cash and credit, Diddler rapidly improvises. He does not have the money to hire a carriage for the elopement, and the real Fainwou'd arrives "in a terrible rage" (II.ii.38) to demand an explanation from Plainway. Unable to intimidate Fainwou'd "with affected dignity" (II.ii.39), Diddler decides to appropriate the cockney's post chaise, but he needs a guinea to bribe the postboy. Pretending that he has gotten rid of Peggy, he persuades Miss Durable to lend him her purse, and when she objects to his leaving her to pay the postboy, he behaves like a Gothic heroine:

> *Diddler*... oh!—oh dear, oh lord!
> *Miss D.* What's the matter?
> *Diddler.* Your cruelty has so agitated me,—I faint,—a little water—a little water will recover me;—[falls into a chair] pray get me a little water!
> *Miss D.* Bless me, he's going into hysterics! (II.ii.41)

Diddler's gender-bending ruse succeeds. While Miss Durable gets water, he flees with her purse and Peggy in Fainwou'd's post chaise. Subsequently, Fainwou'd, Plainway, and Miss Durable come to the realization that "[t]he other mr. Fainwou'd" (II.ii.43) is an imposter. Much to their amazement, Diddler reappears "*dancing and singing*" (II.ii.44) and informs them that he has received a letter from his uncle's executor bequeathing him £10,000. He confesses that he has "been a sad rogue," blames his transformation into a "shabby dog" on "Idle habits, empty pockets, and the wrath of an offended uncle," and declares that he has reformed: "I've felt too much my past degeneration, not to make the best use of my present good fortune" (II.ii.45–46). Diddler's claim that he has inherited £10,000 convinces Plainway that he is eligible to marry his daughter, but Peggy is disappointed that her fiancé's name is so unglamorous: "What! and I am to have a lover of the name of Diddler?" (II.ii.46). As a reader of sentimental novels, she prefers the surname Mortimer, which Diddler may have stolen from the sensitive lover Lord Mortimer in Regina Maria Roche's best-selling novel *The Children of the Abbey* (1796). Her disillusionment seems to have begun.

A November 6, 1803 review of *Raising the Wind* assumes that Diddler tells the truth about the inheritance: "Diddler just receiving intelligence of the death of an uncle, who has left him a fortune,…resolves to mend his way of life, and is united to Peggy" (*E. Johnson's British Gazette and Sunday Monitor*). Terry Robinson maintains, however, that Diddler "presents a false letter, which states, he claims, that his late uncle has bequeathed him ten thousand pounds" (1089). If Robinson is correct, Diddler defrauds the Plainways, and his advocacy of "honest industry" (II.ii.47) in his closing speech is hypocritical. But while Diddler may misrepresent the letter, he does receive one. In an earlier scene, a messenger hands Sam a letter addressed to "Mr. Jeremiah Diddler," and Sam notices that it has a "fine seal" and "feel[s] like a bank note" (II.i.30–31). He delivers the letter to Diddler, who prevents him from talking about it: Diddler "stop[s] [Sam's] mouth" and says "That's enough Sam—the less we say, the better" (II.ii.46). Thus the evidence regarding the bequest and the efficacy of Diddler's performances is equivocal. He might have been left £10,000, he might have received a lesser sum (perhaps only "a hundred-pound note" [II.ii.45]), or he might have been left nothing. If he has inherited a fortune, his social and financial elevation is due to his uncle's generosity rather than his devious performances, which have tended to backfire; if he has fabricated the bequest, the farce conveys a cynical message: dissimulation may be a more effective means of raising the wind than "honest industry."

When Plainway asks "what claim" Diddler has on Peggy, Diddler replies, "'Not my deserts, but what I will deserve'" (II.ii.45), borrowing a line from a speech in Shakespeare's *Richard III* in which Richard III urges Queen Elizabeth, whose sons he has had murdered, to convince her daughter (his niece) to marry him (*Richard III* IV.iv.415). In the promptbook version of *Richard III* performed on the early nineteenth-century London stage and published in *British Theatre; or, A Collection of Plays, which Are Acted at the Theatres Royal, Drury*

Lane, Covent Garden, and Haymarket (1808), Richard's hypocritical protestations are condensed:

> *Gloster* [*sic*]. Oh, my kind mother! (I must call you so)
> Be thou to her, my love's soft orator;
> Plead what I will be, not what I have been;
> Not my deserts, but what I will deserve.
> And, when this warlike arm, shall have chastis'd
> The audacious rebel, hot-brain'd Buckingham;
> Bound with triumphant garlands, will I come,
> And lead your daughter, to a conqueror's bed. (IV.v.63)[10]

Richard boasts in *The Third Part of Henry the Sixth* that he is the consummate political chameleon: "I can add colors to the chameleon, / Change shapes with Proteus for advantages, / And set the murtherous Machevil to school" (III.ii.191–193). In *Richard III*, he successfully woos Lady Anne with "dissembling looks" (I.ii.236) after having killed her husband and father-in-law; her marriage to him is short and miserable. Diddler's implicit comparison of himself with Shakespeare's misogynistic monster casts doubt on his moral reformation and suggests that he, like Richard, regards women as dupes to be exploited and will forsake Peggy if it suits his purposes. Diddler is, however, a comic rogue rather than a tragic villain. In a soliloquy, he reveals that his goal is not to usurp political power but to transform himself from a sponge into a member of the landed gentry: "I'll visit the country squires upon other terms. I'll only sing when it comes to my turn, and never tell a story or cut a joke but at my own table" (I.ii.18). His morality, like his identity, is fluid and contingent. With Peggy and Miss Durable, Diddler is a romantic chameleon; with Sam, Fainwou'd, and Plainway, he is a credit chameleon whose social status fluctuates according to his apparent creditworthiness. At the play's conclusion, he renounces his "past degradation" (II.ii.46), but it appears unlikely that he will ever engage in "honest industry." Diddler's Falstaffian charm notwithstanding, during the nineteenth century he personified financial parasitism and the triumph of economic self-interest over ethics in Anglo-American culture.

FALSE ALARMS

Kenney's comic opera *False Alarms; or, My Cousin* debuted on January 12, 1807 and had an impressive run of 21 performances. It features a Diddlerian chameleon named Tom Surfeit, played by John

Bannister, whose energetic performance transformed the "notorious lounger" (II.ii.54) into an audience favorite. According to *The Monthly Mirror* reviewer, "Mr. Bannister's *Tom Surfeit* was full of life and spirit. His song…in which he describes a major about to cut his throat for love, but who thinks better of it, and cuts his corns, was a song, from *top to toe*, to the fancy of the galleries, and loudly encored by them" ("Memoranda Dramatica, &c" 69). Like Diddler, Surfeit is a spendthrift opportunist who acquires a letter that enables him to impersonate an heiress's intended husband. The son of a tavern-owner, he has squandered the £5,000 he inherited from his uncle on "[o]ne sailing boat, one curricle, two bits of blood, two dozen of fashionable friends, [his servant] Gabriel, and [his mistress] Kitty Fleecer" (I.i.14). He abandons his legal career because "he despise[s] the slow returns of half-guinea motions; he has a passion for growing rich extempore" (I.ii.16). Whereas Kenney portrays Diddler as a loveable rogue, the opportunistic chameleon in *False Alarms* is a callous coxcomb. Instead of helping Miss Umbrage up when she falls out of a stagecoach into the dirt, he tramples over her, and he casually discards his former lover, Caroline Sedley, and his long-suffering servant, whom he has not paid in two years. "Poor Caroline," he soliloquizes, "I once told her I was dying for her; but she must know, well enough, nobody dies for love now-a-days" (II.i.40). While *False Alarms* satirizes Diddlerian opportunism, it celebrates reformative female chameleonism. Caroline, who poses as a debonair dragoon, tricks Surfeit into revealing his inconstancy and rehabilitates her former schoolmate's wayward husband.

Miss Umbrage and Lieutenant M'Lary, a bluff Irishman, regard Surfeit as the embodiment of "modern manners." After Surfeit "*Intercepts* [Miss Umbrage] *as if unconsciously, and seats himself*" in the chair she attempts to take, she strikes a Burkean note: "So this is modern manners.—How must the contemplative mind sigh over the departed gallantry that distinguished the unsophisticated cavaliers of the middle ages" (I.i.11, italics in original).[11] According to M'Lary, Surfeit is "a buck of the last breed" (I.i.12). The preface of the satirical pseudo-biography *Memoirs of the New Insect* (1792) defines the "buck" as an androgynous species of dandy whose "colours are various, and [who] cast their coats, like the camelion['s], sometimes to ten different shades a day. It is difficult to distinguish the male of these reptiles from the female…Liquor they are peculiarly fond of…They are…chiefly to be found in the boxes of the theatres, public gardens, concerts, &c…Although their first appearance has a terrible aspect, they are as harmless and inoffensive, when sober, as new born babes.

A buckling of this species differs from a buck, much in the same manner as a hornet from a wasp" (n. pag.). To Miss Umbrage and M'Lary, Surfeit is a sartorial chameleon who represents modern incivility, selfishness, and consumerism. In contrast to the buck described by *Memoirs of the New Insect*, he is offensive even when he is sober, but his fatuousness renders him harmless.

In a song, Surfeit laments that when he lost his stylish carriage, he became a friendless nonentity:

> When I came on the world without notice or name,
> 'Twas my curricle bore me to fashion and fame;...
> But when I was knock'd up, and my horses knock'd down,
> Tom Surfeit's disaster soon ran through the town;
> Then seeking my friends, my misfortune to smother,
> When I look'd at them one way, they all look'd another,
> But if rattling, and dashing, and splashing away,
> Again I recover, and blaze into day.
> How their necks will relax, and their mem'ries come home,
> And my ears again ring with their "How d'ye do Tom!" (I.i.15)

Surfeit wants to cut a dashing figure in London society, but he lacks the money to buy curricles, fame, horses, mistresses, and friends. Because Caroline Sedley does not possess the resources to finance his extravagant lifestyle, he decides to pursue Emily, the wealthy ward of "a quandam potatoe [*sic*] merchant" (I.i.10) named Plod. Surfeit does not, however, possess Diddler's ability to play the sentimental lover. Rather than courting Emily with Della Cruscan effusions, he "sport[s] one of [his] decoy lounges in the inn yard" to attract her attention and subsequently "*Struts about*" in front of Peter Plod's house in another "decoy lounge" that he believes will "do the business" of arousing her passion (II.i.40–41, italics in original). Emily does not notice his posturing.[12] She gives a billet-doux to M'Lary to deliver to her lover Edgar Gayland, but Surfeit assumes that the letter is meant for him and takes it. In the letter, Emily asks Edgar to masquerade as Plod's nephew: "If you wish to be convinced of my affection, come as soon as possible, disguised as my guardian's nephew, Peter Plod, whom he has fixed on for my husband... He's the mate of an Indiaman just arrived from a voyage, and his uncle hasn't seen him from his infancy.—Further instructions I'll whisper when we meet.—Your's in a flurry, Emily" (II.i.42). Surfeit follows Emily's instructions, and when he shows up at Plod's house in a naval uniform, she concludes that he must be "the real Peter" and decides that she will "seem to be taken with him" to "put [her] guardian off his guard, and give [her] a better chance of escape" (II.ii.48).

In the conversation that follows, Surfeit overplays his role and delivers asides to Emily that bewilder her:

> *Surfeit.* Ha! young lady! How are you? Shiver my topsails, Plod, as tight a little frigate as I've seen in all my voyage. (*winks at her.*) [*aside to Emily*] I say, true to the touch, you see.—I shall get on here, shan't I?
> *Emily.* (*aside.*) What can he mean by such familiarity?
> *Plod.* What, at your whispers already, you dog, eh?—(*jogs him.*)
> *Surfeit.* (*jogging him.*) Sailor-like, you know,—bring 'em to at once.
> *Plod.* You're right—nothing like it.—Well, I'm devilish glad to see you tho'—why you've come a day before your letter mentioned.
> *Surfeit.* Have I? (*aside to Emily.*) What I've written a letter, then?
> *Emily.* How singular! (II.ii.49)

Surfeit's description of his voyage from India jumbles up geography, and he fancifully boasts that he "should have been honoured with a medal from the [East India] company, expressly for having saved fifty hundred weight of their best lump sugar from the hands of the enemy" (II.ii.50). Emily also playacts, declaring that she likes "Peter" "prodigiously" (II.ii.51) and singing a nautical duet with the sham sailor. When left together, however, she and Surfeit find themselves at cross-purposes: he believes that she wants to elope with him, and she thinks he is insane. Miss Umbrage suddenly enters and immediately exposes Surfeit's imposture: "This is a man I travelled with—an animal called a buck—a notorious lounger—known by the name of Tom Surfeit" (II.ii.54). Surfeit runs away to escape being thrown into a pond by servants.

Whereas the female characters in *Raising the Wind* are dupes, in *False Alarms* Caroline and Emily easily hoodwink conceited male characters. Caroline convinces Sir Damon Gayland that she is a young captain intent on seducing his wife, and Surfeit's delusional vanity allows Emily to trick him into helping her run away with Sir Damon's son Edgar. Imprisoned in Plod's house, Emily sees Surfeit and decides to "impose on his vanity" (III.i.59). She pretends that she wants to elope with him and asks him to fetch a ladder so she can escape. Surfeit happily complies, but when he "*Goes to embrace her, she perceives* Edgar, *and runs to him*" (III.i.61, italics in original). When the vengeful Surfeit attempts to inform Plod and Miss Umbrage of the elopement, M'Lary threatens him with a shillelagh, and he hastily retreats. Surfeit later tries to resume his courtship of

Caroline, but she mocks him and tells him that she has agreed to marry M'Lary. In his final speech, Surfeit slips into his legal persona and impotently threatens Plod and Miss Umbrage with lawsuits: "I'll indict [Plod] for an assault, and [Miss Umbrage] for aiding, comforting, and abetting;—so prepare your defence, sir,—for the whole Inner Temple will be retained in behalf of an injured member of their honorable society" (III.ii.78).

To be effective, imposters must recognize their acting limitations and understand their audiences. Surfeit grossly overestimates his ability to charm and hoodwink others and needlessly antagonizes Miss Umbrage, who avenges herself by exposing him. Moreover, he lacks the capacity to detect imposture in others. When "Caroline *enters completely dressed as a dragoon officer, and struts by him singing*" (II.i.42, italics in original), Surfeit does not recognize her, and she gets him to reveal his inconstancy:

> *Caroline*... Your name's Surfeit.—I've seen you with Caroline Sedley.
> *Surfeit.* (*mantling.*) Oh! you have—why, then, perhaps you know whereabouts I am in that quarter? (*winks.*)
> *Caroline.* (*winks again.*) I do—I do.
> *M'Lary.* What the devil! my little Caroline too—sure, and at that rate you must have had a dip in the Shannon, Mr. Surfeit.
> *Surfeit.* I understand you M'Lary—you've a penchant that way, yourself, I know.—Well, I sha'n't have her, as you may guess—I am otherwise disposed of—So, I say, my little trooper, as you know her, break my affair to her, will you, and recommend M'Lary.
> *Caroline.* Ha! ha! ha! (*aside.*) Was there ever such native effrontery?
> *Surfeit.* What, you're laughing? Ha! ha! ha!—[M'Lary]'s a bit of a quiz;—but he's an honest fellow. (II.i.43)

Rather than diddling others, Surfeit is repeatedly diddled. His "native effrontery" does not compensate for his bungled performances as a lover and sailor. Both Surfeit and Diddler are mercenary lovers who resort to imposture, but Surfeit is an impercipient buck rather than a clever sponge and proves to be no match for an intelligent female imposter.

While male chameleons tend to be opportunistic and deracinated in Kenney's comedies, in *False Alarms* he portrays a reformative female chameleon who recalls Cowley's Letitia Hardy, the seductive masquerader in *The Belle's Stratagem*, and Victoria, the virtuous transvestite in Cowley's *A Bold Stroke for a Husband*. The cross-dressing Caroline Sedley was performed by Maria Duncan (1780?–1858), who was celebrated for her breeches roles and had played Letitia Hardy during her first season at Drury Lane (1804–1805). Caroline masquerades as Rosalinda to flirt with Sir Damon Gayland and then plays the role of Captain Bronze to restore Sir Damon to his wife and to discover whether Surfeit's "good humor... springs from his heart, or disguises the want of one" (I.i.7). Although he is a 50-year-old married man, Sir Damon, like Surfeit, views himself as a gallant buck whom women cannot resist. At a masquerade he meets a "lovely incognita" and imagines that his "conversation, [his] elegant gaiety... [has] riveted her for ever" and that he "alone can make her happy" (I.iii.17–18). He receives letters from the mystery woman and takes sadistic pleasure in "making [his] beautiful young wife jealous—the torment of her life—robbing her of comfort by day, and repose at night" (I.ii.17). From Caroline's point of view, however, Sir Damon's flirtation with her is a casual "frolic": "We met by accident a few months ago, at a private masquerade, given by lady Lavish. He singled me out, haunted me, and made me the most passionate protestations. My old propensity to a frolic induced me to listen to him, and consent we should correspond. On exchanging names, mine of course a feigned one, what was my surprise, to find I had been flirting with the very man who had recently become the husband of my old friend and schoolfellow." Although she knows that her behavior is "wrong," Caroline corresponds with Sir Damon because she is "curious to discover if he could be really unfaithful to so much merit." From the beginning of their acquaintance, she manipulates him, and whereas she knows his name, he only knows her pseudonym, Rosalinda, and has never seen her "figure" (I.iii.23).

In contrast to Diddler and Surfeit, who improvise their impostures, Caroline carefully plans her performance and bases it on an accurate assessment of her dupe's character. She assures Lady Gayland that Sir Damon's infatuation with her masquerade persona Rosalinda stems from vanity rather than passion and unfolds her scheme to reform him: "I have procured a letter of introduction from lady Lavish in favor of captain Bronze, a young officer, joining his regiment in this town, which captain Bronze... I represent.—I make free with [Sir Damon's] house, coquet with his wife, and seduce her affections. He is alarmed, and reproaches you [Lady Gayland]—you retort—disclose his secret attachment, and the lady is found to be my cousin... I demand vengeance—you a separation—the event will be the proof of his affection, and, my life on't, the cure of his folly" (I.iii.24). Lady Gayland initially objects to this "strange" proposal, but her maid, Susan, convinces her that the imposture is an assertion of women's rights: "It's the cause of the whole sex, and, in the name of us all, I demand vengeance" (I.iii.24).

Caroline's performance as Captain Bronze parodies the foppish military gallantry denounced by Wollstonecraft in *A Vindication of the Rights of Woman.* According to Wollstonecraft, "officers are... particularly attentive to their persons, fond of dancing, crowded rooms, adventures, and ridicule. Like the *fair* sex, the business of their lives is gallantry.—They were taught to please, and they only live to please" (26–27). Caroline's Captain Bronze sings, dances, extols Lady Gayland's beauty and grace, and gazes at her "*with languishing tenderness*" (I.iii.31, italics in original). Despite Caroline's diminutiveness and androgyny—she is referred to as a "little fellow" and a "little dragoon," and M'Lary describes her as "neither one thing nor t'other, like a dish of kalechannon"—Sir Damon considers her "a damn'd dangerous" sexual rival, and when Caroline/Captain Bronze challenges him to a duel to defend the honor of Captain Bronze's "cousin, Caroline Sedley," the would-be rake despairs: "he'll murder me beyond all doubt" (II.i.34, 43–44; III.ii.70–72). To further terrify Sir Damon, Lady Gayland shows him his letters to Rosalinda and insists "on a permanent separation" (III.ii.70). Her repentant husband begs for her forgiveness, agrees to his son's marriage to Emily, and promises never to offend his wife again. After Sir Damon kneels and kisses her hand, Lady Gayland reveals Caroline's imposture:

> *Lady Gayland.* My dear Caroline, now I triumph indeed.
> *Sir Damon & M'Lary.* Caroline!
> *Caroline.* Captain Bronze and Rosalinda, in the single person of lady Gayland's old friend and school-fellow, Caroline Sedley...
> *Sir Damon.* Why its [*sic*] all a joke then?
> *Caroline.* It is, sir Damon: but a joke that I hope has taught you never to risk again the solid happiness of a british fire-side affection, for the dangerous and vapid gallantry of vanity or dissipation.
> *Sir Damon.* It has, it has, my dear Rosalinda, and I'm sure I shall always be grateful for the lesson. (III.ii.76)

As in Cowley's *The Town before You*, female solidarity triumphs over male selfishness. In the comic opera's closing speech, Caroline contends that her performance as Captain Bronze was honorable because it helped a friend: "if zealously to serve a friend, be no less the soldier's pride, than bravely to encounter an enemy, captain Bronze may hope, that though his sabre is yet unstained, his regimentals are not dishonored" (III.ii.78). Whereas Diddler and Surfeit act alone to enrich themselves and Sir Damon performs gallantry to torment his wife and gratify his vanity, Caroline allies herself with other women, enlists Surfeit's alienated valet as a fellow conspirator, and uses her theatrical abilities to help her friend and teach Sir Damon a lesson. Although she is mendacious and has a mischievous "propensity to a frolic" (I.iii.23), her loyalty to her friend contrasts with Diddler's and Surfeit's rapacious opportunism. She turns imposture into an instrument of female empowerment and moral instruction.

THE WORLD!

On March 2, 1812, Kenney married Holcroft's widow, Louisa Mercier Holcroft, and through her met Holcroft's friends Charles and Mary Lamb, Henry Crabb Robinson, and William Godwin. Kenney's connection to Holcroft was theatrical as well as personal: his comedy *The World!*, which premiered at Drury Lane on March 31, 1808, was heavily influenced by Holcroft's *He's Much to Blame*. Both plays feature an imitative chameleon who forsakes his true love, unsuccessfully woos an upper-class woman, and, following a confrontation with his true love's brother (in *He's Much to Blame*) or half-brother (in *The World!*), repents and reforms. In contrast to opportunistic chameleons like Diddler, Sir George Versatile and Echo are credulous followers. However, while Sir George is a baronet who imitates aristocrats, Kenney's Jack Echo is a novice businessman who copies anyone who appears to exemplify "the popular style" (I.ii.13). His maladroit courtship of Lady Bloomfield is instigated by his uncle's financial needs rather than Echo's snobbery. Whereas *He's Much to Blame* satirizes England's sclerotic class system, *The World!* targets financial chicanery.

Holcroft's and Kenney's chameleon comedies were both theatrical hits: while *He's Much to Blame* was performed 22 times, *The World!* ran for 23 nights and enjoyed many revivals. Surprisingly, although Byron was fond of borrowing Diddler's signature line from *Raising the Wind*, he did not seem to share his contemporaries' enthusiasm for *The World!* In *English Bards and Scotch Reviewers* (1809), he writes: "KENNEY's 'World', ah! where is Kenney's wit? / Tires the sad gallery, lulls the listless Pit" (570–571).[13] Byron's barb misrepresents the comedy's popular reception and may reflect the fledgling poet and socialite's insecurity. His first verse collection, entitled *Fugitive Pieces*, was published in 1806, and friends who objected to some of the volume's erotic poems persuaded him to suppress and destroy it. In *The World!*, a bookseller named Margin summarily rejects a young woman's "volume of fugitive poetry" and instructs his associate to tell "the little

Sappho, that I have already a plentiful stock of poetry called fugitive, that never stirs out of the shop" (III.ii.44). Struggling to establish himself as a poet and in London society, Byron might not have been able to see the humor in Kenney's satire of poetic poseurs and social chameleons. Of course, it is also possible that his abuse of Kenney and other early-nineteenth-century comic dramatists was indiscriminate and meant to evoke nostalgia for the eighteenth-century playwrights he revered: George Colman the younger, Richard Cumberland, and Richard Brinsley Sheridan (*English Bards* 578, 580).

Reviewers of *The World!* praised Kenney's writing, Bannister's portrayal of Echo, and Robert William Elliston's performance as the hyperemotional poet Charles Cheviot. *The Morning Chronicle* claimed that *The World!* "deserves to take a rank among the classical comedies of our language . . . the writing, as far as it is possible to judge merely by the ear, is natural, forcible, and elegant . . . Mr. ELLISTON and Mr. BANNISTER, in *Cheviot* and *Echo*, did all that the heart of an Author could wish: for Mr. ELLISTON had one of those characters of mixed sentiment and gaiety, in which he is almost always seen only to be admired; and Mr. BANNISTER, whose part was of very various and doubtful effect, contrived, by the perfect chasteness and yet irresistible humour of his whole performance, to obtain admiration at once for the author and the actor" (April 1, 1808). Leigh Hunt penned an enthusiastic review of the comedy:

> The incidents are managed with great mastery of stage effect, and the language is superior to any comic dialogue since the dramatic days of SHERIDAN and CUMBERLAND. It is principally in the satirical observations of *Cheviot* that Mr. Kenney seems to have aimed at the revival of true comedy . . . BANNISTER'S character of *Echo* was perfectly suited to his admirable combination of humour and feeling. Nothing could shew his command of this union to greater advantage, than his sudden touch of the pathetic in the very midst of intoxication. This was the triumph of refined feeling over vulgarity of manner. Mr. ELLISTON however in *Cheviot* was the great interest of the performance . . . In his soliloquy to the bank note, which in the midst of poverty he is about to give away, he exhibited all that natural dryness of humour which I have so often remarked as his peculiar excellence. (*The Examiner*, April 3, 1808, 217–218)

The reviewers marveled at Bannister's and Elliston's abilities to shift suddenly yet naturally from comedy to pathos and to elicit sympathy for their mercurial characters.

The character Bannister played so brilliantly recalls the provincial squire of Prior's "The Chameleon" (Figure 6.1). Echo is "incapable

Figure 6.1 Mr. Bannister as Echo.
"I have a collection of trifles here, but I don't know whether I shall publish them." *The World*. Engraved by Edward Scriven from a painting by Samuel De Wilde (1808). Reproduced courtesy of the Rare Book & Manuscript Library of the University of Illinois at Urbana-Champaign.

of any fixed character whatever": "his every ambition to excel, renders him the timid slave of the world; its ridicule, and its prejudices—his habits, opinions, . . . his very manners, change with the hour; and his last acquaintance, however unworthy of his imitation, generally serves him for an example." His uncle, an insolvent financier named Plutus Subtle, seeks to turn him into "an inveterate man of business" (I.i.5) and plans for Echo to become his partner, marry the wealthy widow Lady Bloomfield, and provide his firm with desperately needed capital. Echo soon falls, however, under the sway of a fop named Loiter, whose frivolous manner he mimics:

> *Loiter.* (*entering*) Ha, ha, ha! well I'm devilish glad to see you among us, Jack.
> *Echo.* (*anxiously adopting his manner*) Thank ye, thank ye! we shall be devilish jolly here, dare say—ha, ha, ha! (*aside*) must relax a little from the man of business, now, or this jockey will smoke me. (I.ii.8)

Echo's simulation of "a man of spirit and fashion" (I.ii.9) is interrupted by a stern lecture from Withers, a "consequential old fellow," who urges him not to "degrade the honest emotions of [his] nature" (I.ii.9, 11). Impressed by Withers's manner, Echo begins to imitate him, but when a servant laughs at his suddenly authoritative bearing, he reverts to "Loiter's...popular style" (I.ii.13). In another scene, Echo parrots Subtle's requests for financial information:

> *Subtle.* Let me see our last letter from New-York.
> *Echo.* And let me see the last letter from the leeward islands.
> *Subtle.* And bring me the journal.
> *Echo.* And bring me the waste-book. (II.i.18)

Echo's next model is Harry Dauntless, who has transformed himself from Echo's "little red-faced" and "stock-headed" (i.e., senseless) "school-fellow" into a swaggering "man of figure" (II.i.19). According to Loiter, Dauntless possesses neither gentility nor talents, but his bravado has enabled him to secure a position in society: "Harry has been shied, cut, and scouted, till he has incurred the full penalty of his audacity;—and his pretensions are admitted at last by virtue of perseverance, where they had no earthly chance of success beside...You see its [*sic*] all owing to the bra—w—w— (*imitating a flourishing, impudent air*)." Dauntless boasts that he has married a "captivating creature" from a "branch of nobility" and will soon recover the "immense fortune [that has been] withheld from her" (II.i.20).

His former schoolmate's apparent success convinces Echo that Dauntless's audacity is "the leading style" (II.iii.31), and he decides to copy it while courting Lady Bloomfield. He never considers acting like himself because he lacks both self-confidence and a self-concept.

But his imitation of Dauntless startles Lady Bloomfield's father, Social, who advises Echo to modify his behavior:

Echo. (*in the manner of* Dauntless) How are you?
Social. (*a little surprised*) Pretty well, I'm much obliged to you—and how is your worthy mother?
Echo. Quite well—quite well.
Social. I'm rejoiced to hear it. And when did you arrive?
Echo. This morning, sir; only this morning. But I wouldn't lose a moment, you see, in paying my respects to you and lady Bloomfield. How is the lovely widow?
Social. Charmingly, charmingly. (*aside*) Bless me, he has a very odd manner with him. The very thing Stella dislikes so much . . . [Y] ou'll excuse me, mr. Echo . . . there is something of assurance and self-sufficiency in your manner that I'm very sure is not accompanied by any correspondent feeling . . . Something of the modern coxcombs . . . my daughter is uncommonly observing—a little more of the air of politeness.

Chastened by Social's admonishment, Echo concludes "that damn'd bra—w—w— is not the leading style after all" and that he should adopt his "father's old-fashioned way" (II.iii.30–31). His new approach backfires, however, when Lady Bloomfield catches him rehearsing compliments:

Echo. (*to himself*) Something I think of this sort——
Lady Bloomfield. Is he talking to himself or to me?
Echo. Madam, after the very high eulogiums I have heard of your beauty, I find myself extremely disappointed; and my disappointment arises from finding you so much *more* beautiful than any description can possibly render you. (*still to himself*)
Lady Bloomfield. Sir, (*he perceives her and becomes much surprised and confused*) I ought to be extremely flattered by your excessive politeness, though it obliges me to say that after the description I had heard of your character, it has occasioned in my mind a disappointment of a very different nature.
Echo. Madam, I——
Lady Bloomfield. You seem alarmed, sir.
Echo. No, madam. Only——(*aside*) heaven be praised, here comes mr. Social. This comes of practicing compliments. (II.iii.33)

Echo does not have Diddler's improvisational skills, and Social and Lady Bloomfield consider his performances gauche and inauthentic. Humiliated, he vows to give up his pursuit of Lady Bloomfield, but Social persuades him to "woo her in her own way": "she's fond of poetry now, you must write her sonnets—of course you [must] become a poet immediately" (III.i.41–42). When Echo objects that he has "never made a rhyme," Subtle tells him to hire a poet to write for him. In Subtle's opinion, "literary fame is of easy purchase" and poets, who are "[a]ny thing, every thing, and nothing," are easy to impersonate: to "become a ready made poet immediately" (I.i.7, III.i.42) and inspire Lady Bloomfield's regard, all Echo has to do is to buy and claim authorship of a volume of poetry.

Thus rather than imitating the poet Cheviot's mercurial behavior, Echo sets out to acquire some of his poems. He goes to the bookseller's shop and overhears Cheviot offering to sell a manuscript for £50. Assuming that the work is a verse collection, Echo buys it, but the manuscript turns out to be a volume of sermons that the altruistic Cheviot bought from Eleanor Barclay, who needs the money to secure her mother's release from debtor's prison. Echo's makeshift attempt to "set up [his] new character" as a poet ends in embarrassment when his friends look over his "collection of trifles" and discover that it consists of "[s]ermons on several occasions—chiefly for the benefit of youth" (III.ii.52–53). He angrily blames Cheviot, the world, and himself for his humiliation: "Damn the poet! he has cheated me-exposed me—all the world exposes me. I expose myself—I am in a high fever! and all for what? to make a figure—and a pretty figure I'm like to make. Instead of being praised for an amateur poet, here have I paid fifty pounds to be quizzed for a methodist" (III.ii.54). Although Echo is adept at imitating others, his misdirected attempts to "make a figure" inspire mockery instead of admiration. At a tavern, he attempts to regale his associates with "comical stories," but they laugh at his maladroitness rather than at his jokes. On the following day he "feel[s] rather the worse for [his] excess" but decides that drinking is "a stylish foible, and even noblemen have cherisht it to a proverb." Social is, however, disgusted by the "terrible rakish libertine kind of roll about [Echo's] eyes" and calls him a "half-finished fool" and an "under-graduate in foppery" (V.iii.75–76). Echo's simulations of "a man of spirit and fashion," an authority figure, a conceited buck, an old-fashioned gentleman, a poet, and a tavern raconteur elicit either laughter or contempt from the people he wants to impress.

Echo's love for Eleanor, which is derided by "the world," eventually inspires him to renounce his imitative chameleonism. But like Sir George in *He's Much to Blame*, he is too fickle and unreflective to reform himself and requires a moral instructor. In Echo's case, the instructor is Cheviot. Desperate to eliminate Cheviot as "a rival admirer of lady Bloomfield" (V.iii.77), Echo adopts Dauntless's manner and challenges the poet to a duel. When Cheviot refuses to fight and suggests that he loves Eleanor rather than Lady Bloomfield, Echo is dumbfounded:

> *Echo.* I don't know what to say or think. You are surely some minister of justice sent to torture and distract me! what do you know of my Eleanor? where is she? don't rack me with suspense, but be merciful, and tell me at once.
>
> *Cheviot.* Our acquaintance is but short, sir. Yesterday we met for the first time. I found her sharing with her mother a condition of the lowest misery. Every friend had left them with their better fortune. (V.iii.78)

Echo quickly realizes that without Eleanor, the world's "praise, its wealth, its honors, have no joy for [him]" and abjures his crawling chameleonism: "I have hitherto crawl'd upon the surface of the earth—crept in the shadow of insignificance! at once, the ape and bye-word of inferior beings. But my fetters are snapped, and my heart pants to assert its freedom" (V.iii.79). He asserts his newfound freedom by refusing to aid Dauntless, whose supposedly aristocratic wife "turns out to be a female sharper—a petticoat adventurer" and has absconded and left her feckless husband to deal with "a couple of writs from her landlord and milliner" (V.iii.79–80). Mrs. Dauntless is a female Diddler, and her disappearance exposes the hollowness of her husband's bravado. After insulting and dismissing Loiter and Dauntless, Echo resolves to "throw [him]self a prostrate penitent at [Eleanor's] feet" (V.iii.81). According to Eleanor's mother, he has been "restored to his native goodness—nothing could resist the flow of his penitence; and having no temptations to dissemble, [Eleanor and she] cannot doubt its honesty" (V.iv.84). However, Echo's apparent reformation, like Sir George Versatile's rehabilitation by the Delavals, could be seen as yet another imitation. Whereas Sir George assumes Paul Delaval's principles, Echo adopts Cheviot's sentimental and grandiloquent manner. Cheviot implores Echo to preserve "the independence of [his] mind" (V.iii.79), but for Echo, mental independence is an unattainable ideal. His imitativeness renders him susceptible to both negative and positive influences. As the errand runner and gossipmonger Christopher Index explains to Subtle, Echo's malleable personality is not "unpromising": "you've neither presumption nor obstinacy to deal with. Only watch him a little steadily, till habit has modelled him to your wishes, and you may make him just what you want" (I.i.6). Echo owes his redemption to Cheviot's intervention, and the continuation of "his native goodness" depends on Eleanor's success in molding him into a stable and ethical person. If the post-reclamation Echo remains a copy—of Cheviot or Eleanor rather than attitudinizing coxcombs—he could at least become a stable and principled copy. But if Eleanor fails to watch and guide him "steadily," he might again degenerate into "the ape and bye-word of inferior beings."

Whereas Echo is a serial imitator, Cheviot represents himself as a melancholic, honorable, and altruistic nonconformist. However, as Terry Robinson has observed, the seemingly authentic "Cheviot, rather than proving to be Echo's opposite, becomes his doppelgänger of sorts, but instead of mimicking multiple people as Echo does, Cheviot mimics only one: Richard Savage" (1094). Cheviot is, like Richard Savage (1697/8–1743), a debt-ridden poet of uncertain parentage. Whereas Savage claimed that he was the illegitimate and disowned son of Anne Brett, formerly the Countess of Macclesfield, and Richard Savage, the fourth Earl Rivers, Cheviot is a foundling: "He was found one fine summer's morning at the foot of one of [the Cheviot hills]—a forlorn—chubby brat, squalling for his breakfast" (I.ii.15). Proclaiming himself Savage's "apostle," Cheviot recites lines from Savage's autobiographical poem "The Bastard" (1728):

> *Born to himself, by no possession led!*
> *In freedom foster'd, and by fortune fed:*
> *Nature's unbounded son, he stood alone,*
> *His heart unbaiss'd, and his mind his own.* (II.ii.23; "The Bastard" 13–14; 19–20)

Cheviot has read Samuel Johnson's *Life of Savage* (1744), which portrays Savage as a tragic victim and emphasizes his compassionate nature: "Born with a legal Claim to Honour and to Affluence, he was in two Months illegitimated by the Parliament, and disowned by his Mother, doomed to Poverty and Obscurity, and launched upon the Ocean of Life, only that he might be swallowed by its Quicksands, or dashed upon its Rocks... Compassion was indeed the distinguishing Quality of *Savage*;... whoever was distressed was certain at least of his Good-Wishes; and when he could give no Assistance, to extricate them from Misfortunes, he endeavoured to sooth them by Sympathy and Tenderness" (5–6, 48). According to Cheviot, Savage "perished in a prison... with proud resignation, that made it a palace to him" (II. ii.23), and Cheviot ostentatiously displays the stoicism, independence, and compassion he attributes to his hero. He declares that "[t]he parents who left [him] unsheltered among the hills of Cheviot assigned [him] the freedom which such a cradle should inspire," claims that he "can banquet on a crust" and "revel in a prison," scorns "affluence" (II.ii.28), and refuses charity. Like Johnson's Savage, Cheviot regards himself as "a forlorn, solitary wretch" (III.ii.48) and sympathizes with the distressed.

Cheviot's destiny is, however, far from tragic. By the comedy's end he is engaged to a wealthy woman and united with his parents and his half sister Eleanor. Whereas in Johnson's *Life of Savage* the ill-fated poet's cruel mother rejects and persecutes him, in *The World!* Cheviot's mother falls into his arms and is "overpowered" (V.iv.86) by her maternal feelings. According to Subtle, Cheviot is a chameleon poet who can be "[a]ny thing, every thing, and nothing" (I.i.7). Besides copying Savage, he emulates the Della Cruscan poets, impersonates Margin the bookseller, and fantasizes about engaging in a "chivalrous enterprize" such as "a voyage of discovery" or "a modern crusade" (V.i.70). As a lover of poetry, Lady Bloomfield finds Cheviot's poetic persona attractive, but his histrionic manner leads her to question his sincerity. Their first meeting occurs in a theater and recalls Captain Waterland's introduction to Laetitia Rayner in Cumberland's *The Box-Lobby Challenge*: in both cases, a young man wins the admiration of an attractive upper-class woman by kicking a lobby lounger who has insulted her. Although Cheviot's chivalrous performance earns Lady Bloomfield's gratitude, he perversely "shun[s] her acquaintance" because she is as "rich as she's enchanting" (II.ii.24). After learning that Cheviot is in danger of being arrested for debt, Lady Bloomfield sends him £100 enclosed with a letter that she signs "Your capricious mother—Fortune." Cheviot welcomes the banknote and letter as "a mighty pleasant harlequinade" (III.ii.46), but when Eleanor approaches him in Margin's bookshop and tells him about her mother's sufferings in King's Bench prison, he pretends to be Margin and gives her £100 for her father's unmarketable book of sermons. His impersonation of "a respectable tradesman" and generosity toward Eleanor arouses Lady Bloomfield's suspicion, and she accuses him of being "a perfect masquerading man of gallantry" rather than "an amatory poet—a seducer only by proxy" (IV.i.59). She subsequently learns, however, that Cheviot's "audacious philanthropy" (IV.i.61) has ensured his own imprisonment for debt.

In the play's final scene, Lady Bloomfield responds to Cheviot's protestations of devotion by mocking his inflated rhetoric:

> *Cheviot.* (*with sudden warmth*)...[E]ncouraged by the firmness of my purpose, to banish myself [from] your presence for ever, let me assure you that it is with impressions of your beauty, grace, and virtues, that never can be effaced; and that I must ever live to bless and to adore you.
> *Lady Bloomfield.* Why, sir, these are the gallantries of a knight-errant at the feet of his mistress.
> *Cheviot.* And yet they were meant but as the passing devotions of a pilgrim at the shrine of a saint.
> *(kneels with fervent respect)*
> *Lady Bloomfield.* Psha, stand up, for shame! I'm afraid you are a foolish, affected young man, disguising a coquettish vanity of conquest, beneath the mask of honorable humility. (V.iv.82–83).

Lady Bloomfield dismisses Cheviot's gallantries and Della Cruscan effusions as inauthentic. She critiques his courtship of her as she previously ridiculed Echo's performance of "excessive politeness," and when Cheviot proposes to her, she teasingly accuses him of hypocrisy:

> *Cheviot*... [A]t this dear shrine, successful or rejected in my suit, I must remain a fixed and constant votary.
> *Lady Bloomfield.* Now, sir, when you would seem to distrust your success, you know it's hypocrisy; and you may thank the indolence rather than the mercy of your saint, that she does not punish it as you deserve. (V.iv.87).

Lady Bloomfield, like Caroline Sedley, is a playful, intelligent, and benignly manipulative woman who stage-manages the reformation of a dysfunctional male poseur. Whereas Eleanor seeks to return Echo to his "native goodness"—his unspoiled rusticity—Lady Bloomfield urges Cheviot to refrain from theatrical posturing and behave more naturally. Under her influence, he abandons his impersonation of Savage and his chivalric fantasies, embraces affluence, and looks forward to becoming Echo's brother-in-law. As chameleons, Cheviot and Echo have been directionless, socially maladroit, and frustrated, and thus they welcome domestication and the prospect of a fixed marital identity.

In Cheviot's case, Lady Bloomfield's wealth liberates him from debtor's prison and a life of penury. Rather than achieving "virtuous independence" (V.iv.89), he and Echo submit to the moral guidance of their fiancées. Although the altruistic Cheviot appears to have little in common with the mercenary Diddler, he, like Diddler, plays a literary role that enables him to win the hand of a wealthy woman and "ravish rank and fortune" (V.i.70).[14] Cheviot forsakes his Della Cruscan correspondent Rosabella, who "has too much genius to be rich" (II.ii.24), and woos Lady Bloomfield with "the gallantries of a knight-errant." Kenney links Cheviot to Diddler by having them both quote from Richard's hypocritical declarations to Queen Elizabeth in Shakespeare's *Richard III*. When Cheviot imagines himself addressing Lady Bloomfield's father before embarking on "a modern crusade" that will prove his worthiness, he uses Richard's words: "*Crown'd with triumphant garlands will I come, / And lead your daughter to a conqueror's bed*" (V.i.70–71, italics in original; *Richard III* IV.iv.333–334). He increases the grandiloquence of Richard's boast by substituting "Crown'd" for the less regal "Bound." Cheviot's quotation from *Richard III* and his courtship of a rich widow suggest that there may be a little of the opportunistic king in even the most engaging male chameleon.

For both Kenney and Godwin, English society is a "system of imposture" (Godwin, *Political Justice Variants* 4.249), but whereas Godwin critiques political imposture, Kenney targets financial imposture. His opportunistic rogues, Diddler, Surfeit, Mrs. Dauntless, and Subtle, are economically rather than politically subversive: they misrepresent their financial circumstances to secure capital and credit. Like Holcroft's Monrose, they are duplicitous fortune hunters, but unlike him, they do not espouse egalitarianism. In *The World!*, the most exploitative character is the financial speculator Subtle, who gambles recklessly with money, conceals his insolvency, tries to get Cheviot arrested for debt, and plots to gain control of Echo's and Lady Bloomfield's fortunes. According to Index, Subtle was "[b]orn on board of a privateer" and "popp'd into the world just in time to share the prize-money." In the financial world, Subtle engages in "gambling speculations," and "in his haste to become a warm [i.e., rich] man, he has, now and then, burnt his fingers" (I.ii.13, 15). Kenney's negative portrayal of Subtle prefigures the Victorian antipathy toward improvisational financial speculators. As Esterhammer explains, "Nineteenth-century fiction represents financial speculation as an opportunistic activity interestingly akin to improvisation... Both speculators and improvisers are blamed for achieving profits too quickly, without corresponding labour; their products are at best an ephemeral, at worst a fraudulent, simulacrum of genuine production; and their continual reinvention of themselves for different audiences and under different conditions transgresses the ideal of a stable identity and a productive social role" ("Improvisation, Speculation, Risky Business" 3–4). Subtle's ephemeral "products" quickly evaporate—he has suffered "losses at Lloyd's" and has "differences to make up in [Exchange] alley"—and he blackens Cheviot's reputation to prevent Mr. Davenant from seeking "restitution of the sums he has advanced as the premium of [Cheviot's] initiation" into business (I.i.8).[15] Instead of performing a productive social role, Subtle bankrupts his firm, and his name appears on "the black-board of the Stock-Exchange." At the conclusion of the play, the rehabilitated Echo finds out that if he had signed his "articles of partnership" with his uncle, he would have been ruined. Although he is "sorry for [Subtle's] disgrace," he has "learnt to despise doctrines," which, in his uncle's "case, served chiefly as the shelter of a sordid heart." The most transgressive character in *The World!* is a financial imposter, "a lame duck" who masquerades as "the great commercial cormorant" (V.i.88).

Raising the Wind, *False Alarms*, and *The World!* feature five of the most acclaimed stage chameleons of the early nineteenth century: Diddler, Surfeit, Sedley, Echo, and Cheviot. Audiences and reviewers found Bannister's performance as Echo particularly endearing. On the page, Echo comes across as weak-willed and silly, but according to *The Edinburgh Annual Register*, Bannister's performance turned him into a sympathetic figure:

> Mr Bannister's Echo was admirable;—so humorous, and yet so chaste; so full of feeling, and so unpretendingly natural, that the whole play may be said to have received a tone from his excellent performance. Some scenes he raised to an importance, which they are not likely to retain after his secession from the stage... One situation, in particular, of alternate drollery and pathos, (where, amid the blunders of a ridiculous intoxication, Echo is suddenly melted by the recollection of his love for... Eleanor), would probably... have produced some disapprobation in the hands of any actor less judicious and moderate, by the dangerous intermixture of a grotesque imbecility with a pathetic remorse; but Mr Bannister made the scene ludicrous [i.e., humorous], not ridiculous;—poor Echo made us laugh in spite of his distress, yet interested us in spite of his weakness. (271)[16]

In the scene the reviewer singles out for praise, the drunken Echo fulminates against Loiter and Dauntless's mockery of Eleanor and declares his imperishable love for her: "They've talked of her... till they put me in a passion—and then I made myself look little. But it don't signify—here she is (*striking his heart*) here she is—yes, they laugh'd at her—laugh'd at her—and I can't think of that, but my eyes begin to swim, and my head turns round (*holding his hand to his head*) and nothing's there but Eleanor—there she's floating about—all Eleanor—all Eleanor! (*much affected*)" (IV.iii.69). The reviewer suggests that whereas a less gifted actor might have emphasized Echo's ridiculousness in this scene, Bannister's "unpretendingly natural" performance aroused the audience's interest in and sympathy for the farcical character. Bannister somehow naturalized a deracinated copyist. For Bannister's farewell performance in 1815, he chose to play Echo and another of his popular roles, Walter, in Thomas Morton's afterpiece *The Children in the Wood* (1793). William Hazlitt was in attendance and reported that "Mr. Bannister played the character of Echo, which is a whimsical mixture of simplicity, affectation, and good-nature, with his usual excellence." He and his fellow theatergoers parted with the beloved actor "as [they] should with one of [their] oldest and best friends" ("View of the English Stage" 229–230).

Epilogue: The Perkin Warbeck Debate

In the late autumn of 1491, 300 years before James Molesworth Hobart posed as the Duke of Ormond, a handsome, blond youth wearing a "doublet of brocade with sleeves" and a "long robe of silk" (Wroe 50) appeared on the streets of Cork, Ireland. As Ann Wroe explains, the silk robe would have made a strong impression on the people who gathered around the young man: "Silk was so precious that it was used, in England at that time, mostly for laces and ribbons. No one below the rank of knight could wear it" (53). After interrogating the youth, a group of Yorkists desperate to depose Henry VII proclaimed him Richard Plantagenet, Duke of York, the younger son of Edward IV and one of the princes imprisoned and allegedly murdered in the Tower of London at the behest of Richard III. Following his Irish debut, the purported Duke of York won recognition from Charles VIII, the King of France, and adventurers flocked to his cause. His claim to the English throne was also supported by Maximilian, the King of the Romans, and James IV, King of Scotland, who "introduced him to the [Scottish] nobility and gave him as wife Lady Catherine Gordon, daughter of the first earl of Huntly, who was [the king's] distant cousin" (Mackie 138). With the help of King Henry's enemies, the would-be Richard IV participated in three unsuccessful invasions of England. Following the failure of his third invasion in 1497, he surrendered to the king's men and confessed his imposture, possibly under duress. He twice attempted to escape from his captors and repeated his confession before he was hung at Tyburn in 1499. Like the bogus Duke of Ormond, he died in his mid-twenties.

Most historians of the fifteenth century believe that the man calling himself Richard, Duke of York, was actually Perkin Warbeck (*c.* 1474–1499), a Flemish boatman's son (Wroe viii). In *The History of the Reign of King Henry the Seventh* (1622), Francis Bacon claims that Perkin was the son of a converted Jew from Tournai. Bacon portrays "the counterfeit of Richard Duke of York" as a consummate chameleon: "he was a youth of fine favour and shape; but more than that, he had such a crafty and bewitching fashion both to move pity and to induce belief, as was like a kind of fascination and inchantment to those that saw him or heard him" (113). According to Bacon, King Henry's archenemy Lady Margaret, Duchess of Burgundy, discovered the "comely youth" and "thought she had now found a curious piece of marble to carve out an image of a Duke of York." Lady Margaret instructed her wily pupil "in princely behaviour and gesture; teaching him how he should keep state, and yet with a modest sense of his misfortunes: Then she informed him of all the circumstances and particulars that concerned the person of Richard Duke of York, which he was to act." Regarding "the manner of his brother's death" and Richard's escape from the Tower of London, "she taught him only to tell a smooth and likely tale of those matters; warning him not to vary from it...She taught him likewise how to avoid sundry captious and tempting questions, which were like to be asked of him. But in this she found him of himself so nimble and shifting, as she trusted much to his own wit and readiness" (114–115). In Bacon's view, Perkin was an artful "mercurial" (112) who played his role with panache, "not descending at all from his stage-like greatness" (158) even when James IV dismissed him. Bacon suspects that "with [Perkin's] long and continual counterfeiting and with often telling a lie, [he] was turned (by habit) almost into the thing he seemed to be, and from a liar to a believer" (118). The Flemish commoner's fluid identity and theatrical talent enabled him to transform into a convincing facsimile of a dispossessed English prince.

During the eighteenth and early nineteenth centuries, the debate over Perkin Warbeck's identity continued and mirrored the broader cultural debate over chameleonism. Whereas David Hume and the Scottish poet and novelist Alexander Campbell depicted Perkin as an imposter, Horace Walpole, the antiquarian John Bayley, and Mary Shelley contended that he was the actual Duke of York. Their assessments of Perkin's legitimacy were informed by their beliefs regarding the malleability of personal identity. Hume doubted the existence of fixed identities and thus readily believed that Perkin was the son of "a renegado Jew of Tournay" (*History of England* 3.374) who metamorphosed into a convincing royal impersonator. In contrast, Bayley and Shelley, who subscribed to the modern notion of the self as personal, innate, and unique, insisted that a foreign commoner would not have been able to impersonate English royalty.[1] According to them, the chameleon described by Bacon could not possibly have existed.

In *A Treatise of Human Nature* (1739–1740), Hume famously argues that humans "are nothing but a bundle or collection of different perceptions, which succeed each other with an inconceivable rapidity, and are in a perpetual flux and movement... The mind is a kind of theatre, where several perceptions successively make their apperance [*sic*]; pass, re-pass, glide away, and mingle in an infinite variety of postures and situations. There is properly no *simplicity* in it at one time, nor *identity* in different; whatever natural propension we may have to imagine that simplicity and identity" (300–301). Hume's portrayal of Perkin as a Flemish commoner who was quickly refashioned into a credible Duke of York is consistent with his theory that subjectivities "are in a perpetual flux and movement." In *The History of England, from the Invasion of Julius Cæsar to the Revolution in 1688* (1754–1761), Hume states that Perkin possessed "natural versatility and sagacity" and thus was "perfectly fitted to act any part, or assume any character." He regards Perkin as a clever, malleable youth who was transformed into a royal imposter by the Duchess of Burgundy: "She found him to exceed her most sanguine expectations; so beautiful did he appear in his person, so graceful in his air, so courtly in his address, so full of docility and good sense in his behaviour and conversation. The lessons, which were necessary to be taught him, in order to his personating the duke of York, were soon learned by a youth of such quick apprehension" (*The History of England* 3.375). The pretender's acting ability enabled him to gain "partizans among [the] ignorant and credulous" (3.376) Irish people, captivate the court of Charles VIII, recruit English followers, and hoodwink the naive King of Scotland. However, following his abortive invasion of Cornwall and surrender to King Henry, "Perkin...confessed his imposture more than once, and read his confession before the whole people...He renewed his confession at the foot of the gibbet on which he was executed." In Hume's opinion, the confessions are conclusive, and writers who "doubt" Perkin's imposture are "whimsical" (3.402–403n).[2]

Walpole disagreed with Hume's appraisal of Perkin and argues in his revisionist *Historic Doubts on the Life and Reign of King Richard the Third* (1768) that the young man was the true Duke of York. Whereas Bacon and Hume represent Lady Margaret as a female Pygmalion who carved a Flemish commoner into "an image of a Duke of York," Walpole points out that since Margaret left England seven years before the Duke was born, she could not have described the court of Edward IV, the royal family, and "what passed in the Tower" to an imposter: "It would not have been sufficient that Margaret had enjoined him *to tell a smooth and likely tale of those matters.* A man does not tell a *likely* tale, nor was a likely tale enough, of matters of which he is totally ignorant" (84–85, italics in original). According to

Walpole, not even the most astute imposter would have possessed the ability to improvise "a likely tale" unless he had a thorough knowledge of the Yorkist court. Moreover, Walpole cannot believe that a Fleming who had never lived in England would have been able to fake an English accent: he writes that "Perkin, in his supposed confession, [never] pretends to have ever set foot in England, till he landed there in pursuit of the crown; and yet an English birth and some stay, though in his very childhood, was a better way of accounting for the purity of his accent, than either of the preposterous tales produced by lord Bacon or by Henry [VII]" (90). Walpole is skeptical regarding the human capacity for improvisational and linguistic chameleonism. In his estimation, a Flemish imposter who knew virtually nothing about the court of Edward IV and learned English on the continent would not have been able to trick so many people into believing that he was Richard, Duke of York. Walpole indicates that Henry VII, not the young pretender, was the counterfeit king and declares that "commiseration will shed a tear over a hapless youth, sacrificed to the fury and jealousy of an usurper, and in all probability the victim of a tyrant, who has made the world believe that the duke of York, executed by his own orders, had been previously murdered by his predecessor" (93).

Like Walpole's *Historic Doubts*, John Bayley's two-volume *The History and Antiquities of the Tower of London, with Memoirs of Royal and Distinguished Persons* (1825) attempts to prove that Perkin was the genuine Duke of York. According to Bayley, it is impossible that "a mere wandering Flemish Jew" could have been transformed into "that perfect type of the royal progeny of the house of York" (350^{a}–350^{b}).[3] He asks "if this youth were of such obscure birth, such a wanderer, and brought up in such society, how are we to account for the many accomplishments that he possessed? whence that elegant person? whence that courteous and princely carriage? whence that easy, winning, and gracious behaviour? in fact that perfect type of the royal progeny of the house of York, with which he is acknowledged on all hands to have been adorned?" Bayley concludes that "[t]hese could not have been acquirements of a day or year: they must have been 'of nature in the root planted'" (350^{a}). While Hume has no difficulty in believing that a Flemish commoner could have convincingly performed the role of an English king's son, Bayley cannot believe that an imposter could have been such a flawless actor. For him, the fact that Perkin "never failed in his part,—and . . . neither his words nor actions were ever said to bear the semblance of imposition" (352^{b}) shows that he must have been the actual Duke of York. If Perkin had not been Richard of York, Bayley reasons, he would never have been able to convince so many rulers and aristocrats that he was a prince: his plebeian appearance, lack of courtly accomplishments, unfamiliarity with King Edward's family and court, and uncouth behavior would have betrayed his lowly origins.

Mary Shelley's conception of Perkin reflects the influence of both Walpole's *Historic Doubts* and Bayley's *The History and Antiquities of the Tower of London*.[4] In her novel *The Fortunes of Perkin Warbeck, A Romance* (1830), Shelley represents Perkin as Richard of York and as a tragic hero. Her idealistic and honorable Richard contrasts with his antagonist, Henry VII, who is portrayed as "a narrow-hearted, suspicious, exacting tyrant" (146). In her preface to *The Fortunes of Perkin Warbeck*, Shelley disputes Hume's skeptical account of the pretender. She states that "[i]t is not singular that [she] should entertain a belief that Perkin was, in reality, the lost Duke of York. For, in spite of Hume, and the later historians who have followed in his path, no person who has at all studied the subject but arrives at the same conclusion." But although she refers to "Records...in the Tower [of London]...which put the question almost beyond a doubt" and points out that Perkin "was believed to be the true man by his contemporaries" (5), she does not discuss Hume's representation of Perkin in any detail. While Hume contends that the pretender's "insinuating address and plausible behaviour...seduced [James IV] to believe the story of Perkin's birth and adventures" and "give him in marriage the lady Catherine Gordon" (3.390), Shelley insists that the Scottish king would never "have bestowed his near kinswoman...to one who did not bear evident signs of being of royal blood" (6).

In *The Fortunes of Perkin Warbeck*, the protagonist's identity is not only stable, it is also inscribed on his face. Like many of her contemporaries, Shelley was influenced by the pseudoscience of physiognomy, popularized by Johann Caspar Lavater's *Essays on Physiognomy* (1775–1778), which was translated into English in 1789.[5] Shelley's mother, Mary Wollstonecraft, had worked on an English translation of *Essays*, and although her father, William Godwin, was skeptical about the ability of physiognomists to read characters in faces, he concluded that "nothing can be more certain than that there is a science of physiognomy" (*Thoughts on Man* 233). According to Lavater, "The moral life of man...reveals itself in the lines, marks, and transitions of the countenance" (1.15). In Shelley's novel, the characters' exteriors display their inner selves: the scheming priest Richard Simon "looked the man he was—a prier into secrets" (35); Monina de Faro's "countenance was the mirror of her mind" (90);

anyone who "looked down upon" two conspirators "would have read villany [sic] and murder in their appearance" (245), and "there was something of ill omen in [the] physiognomy" (376) of a treacherous prison guard. Perkin Warbeck's inherent nobility manifests itself to everyone he encounters. When the spy Stephen Frion stumbles upon the young Perkin in rural Flanders, he immediately notices that "the plodding offspring of a rude Fleming" resembles "a king's son": "The boy speaks not like a cotter: his eye beams with nobleness" (66). In Ireland, Warbeck's "grace and gallantry . . . sh[ines] as a vision of light in [the] wild region" (126). His identity is both fixed and transparent, and "his honour call[s] on him to maintain his claims" (196) to the English throne. Richard of York's identity is so clearly delineated on his face that Henry VII does not dare to parade him through the streets of London after his capture. The novel's narrator asks, "What mark of reality did [Richard's] very forehead wear, that Henry, so prodigal of contumely on his foes, dared not bring him forward for the public gaze?" (343).[6] Richard's transparency contrasts with Frion's chameleonism: "the serpent-spirited . . . [Frion] had stores of science and knowledge within, which he seldom displayed . . . No words could describe his wiliness, his power of being all things to all men, . . . his unparalleled artifice" (65–66). However, perceptive characters are able to detect the spy's ignobility and craftiness, and "villainy is blazoned in [his] face" (273).

For Shelley, identity is inherent, unique, and denoted by "evident signs." In her apocalyptic novel *The Last Man* (1826), she has a character describe the self as the product of education and one's "innate disposition": "We are born; we choose neither our parents, nor our station; we are educated by others, or by the world's circumstance, and this cultivation, mingling with our innate disposition, is the soil in which our desires, passions, and motives grow" (47).[7] Although Shelley insists in her preface that *The Fortunes of Perkin Warbeck* mirrors historical fact, she departs from her sources to make Richard of York more heroic than he actually was. For example, whereas the historical Warbeck remained safely offshore during the Kent invasion, Shelley has him fighting valiantly against King Henry's forces on English soil (202–204).[8] She also invents adventures for Richard in Spain and elsewhere that demonstrate his valor. Rather than following Hume's lead and representing Perkin as a clever imposter and political pawn, she chose to create "a hero to ennoble the pages of a humble tale" (Shelley 6).

Like *The Fortunes of Perkin Warbeck*, Alexander Campbell's *Perkin Warbeck; or, The Court of James the Fourth of Scotland. An Historical*

Romance was published in 1830. In his novel, Campbell assumes that his readers are familiar with the tale of Perkin Warbeck and that they accept Hume's account of "the prince of imposters" (3.202):

> With regard to Perkin Warbeck, presuming that the reader is already acquainted with his story, as related by Hume and other historians, we shall be but brief. That personage, who was the son of a Jew of Tournay, possessing a remarkably striking resemblance to the family of Plantagenet, availed himself of that circumstance, to personate Richard duke of York, youngest son of Edward the Fourth, who...was, with his brother Edward, murdered in the Tower of London, by the command of their uncle, Richard duke of Gloucester. About thirteen years after this tragical event, and during the reign of Henry the Seventh, Warbeck appeared, and announced himself as Richard duke of York, supporting his pretensions to that character by representing, that sir Walter Tyrrel, to whom Gloucester had committed the charge of murdering himself and his brother, had relented,...and contenting himself with the death of the latter, not only saved the life of the former, but followed out that act of humanity, by having him conveyed safely out of the kingdom. It was in this character, then, in which he had succeeded in imposing himself upon the world, that Perkin Warbeck sought the Scottish court. The splendid and numerous retinue with which he was attended was furnished him by the duchess of Burgundy,...who, either deceived...by the plausibility of his tale, and his striking resemblance to her family, or, what is much more probable, glad of this opportunity of raising up a rival to Henry the Seventh,...had supplied him with the means of appearing...with all the state and consequence of a prince. (2.18–20)

Campbell presents Perkin as a charming but ruthless opportunist who conducts himself "with a self-possession and collectedness of manner which could be expected to be attained only by a long and familiar acquaintance with high ceremony and courtly etiquette" (2.60). When a monk recognizes Perkin as "an old though slight acquaintance of Tournay" (2.40), Perkin distracts him while a fellow conspirator stabs the monk in the back. The imposter's regal performances hoodwink the chivalric James IV, and his "noble bearing" and "graceful manner" (3. 258) win the heart of Lady Catherine Gordon. He is duplicitous and manipulative but not entirely unsympathetic. After he is captured by the English army, he confesses his imposture to Lady Catherine and prostrates himself before her: "'I am not, Catherine,' he [says], solemnly, 'the person whom thou believest me to be—I am not Richard duke of York, but an imposter. Now, lady Catherine,...trample on me, trample on the wretch who has betrayed and deceived the most virtuous and beautiful of women'" (3.257).[9] She forgives him and says that she fell in love with him—presumably his essential self—rather than his fictitious title. In response, he tells her that although he is not Richard Plantagenet, he is "a son, though an illegitimate one, of Edward's of England" (3.258).[10] Earlier in the novel, Campbell represents Perkin as "the son of a Jew of Tournay," so it is unclear whether Perkin's assertion that he is King Edward's illegitimate son is truthful or yet another imposture.

If Perkin Warbeck was an imposter, he was one of the most politically subversive imposters in English history. Whereas Hobart's impersonation of the Duke of Ormond enabled him to cheat a banker out of £200, Perkin's claim that he was the Duke of York was far more consequential: it undermined the legitimacy of the King of England and the Tudor dynasty he founded.[11] The Perkin described by Hume was a political chameleon who was justly "arraigned, condemned, and…hanged at Tyburn" (3.402). Like the Jacobin chameleons who haunted the imaginations of anti-Jacobin writers in the 1790s, Hume's imposter posed a threat to social and political stability and thus had to be eliminated. In contrast, Bayley and Shelley maintain that Henry VII, not Perkin Warbeck, was the imposter, a usurper pretending to be the legitimate ruler of England. Shelley, like Hume, abhors political chameleons: in *The Fortunes of Perkin Warbeck*, she represents the Machiavellian spy Frion as a "serpent-spirited" villain. She suggests, however, that the chameleonic capabilities of imposters are strictly limited. They cannot refashion their innate identities, and their characters are imprinted on their faces.

Notes

Introduction

1. In *Romantic Liars: Obscure Women Who Became Imposters and Challenged an Empire* (2006), Debbie Lee chronicles the exploits of six Romantic-era women whose impostures subverted class and gender boundaries. Among the women she examines is Mary Bateman (1768–1809), the so-called Witch of Leeds, who pretended to possess supernatural powers and necromantic assistants. Bateman cheated her superstitious victims out of money and, in some cases, poisoned them.
2. See, for example, the passage from Samuel Richardson's *Clarissa* (1747–48) excerpted later in this introduction.
3. Objectionable figures were also compared to air-feeding chameleons. For example, a character in Hannah Cowley's play *The Runaway, a Comedy* (1776) describes "a Court Dangler" as "one whose ambition is to be fostered with the cameleon food of smiles and nods" (IV.52).
4. Although a postmortem autopsy in 1810 revealed that the Chevalier D'Eon was biologically a man, he succeeded in convincing his contemporaries that he was female and lived as a woman for decades.
5. Wahrman's conception of the modern self is heavily influenced by the philosopher Charles Taylor, who argues that during the early Romantic period a stable, unitary, and interiorized notion of selfhood emerged and became normative. For Taylor, "the modern identity" is characterized by inwardness, uniqueness, and moral agency: "Something fundamental changes in the late eighteenth century. The modern subject is no longer defined just by the power of disengaged rational control but by [the] new power of expressive self-articulation as well—the power which has been ascribed since the Romantic period to the creative imagination. This [power] intensifies the sense of inwardness and leads to [a] radical subjectivism and an internalization of moral sources" (390).
6. Terry Castle offers several possible explanations for the sudden demise of masquerades (98–103).
7. Jeffrey N. Cox and Michael Gamer stress the pervasive influence of theater in Romantic-era British culture: "With the four patent theaters in London (the two winter dramatic theaters of Covent Garden

and Drury Lane, the summer theater at Haymarket, and the King's Theatre given over to Italian opera) standing as central national institutions, with theaters found in every major city from Bath to Edinburgh, and with forms of staged entertainment present in every kind of venue from taverns to carnivals, the theater held the same place in the late eighteenth and early nineteenth centuries that television, film, and video hold in the twenty-first" (xi).

8. Robert-François Damiens (1715–1757), who attempted to assassinate Louis XIV on January 5, 1757, was not related to Robespierre. He was condemned as a regicide and drawn and quartered.
9. Ormond rapes and murders "a Tartar girl" (202) and attempts to rape the novel's heroine, Constantia Dudley. Robert S. Levine has examined Ormond's association with the Illuminati and postrevolutionary conspiracy anxieties.
10. Will's and Tom's were popular London coffeehouses.
11. Smith quotes from an anonymous poem, possibly written by Daniel Defoe, titled *The English Gentleman Justified* (Part II, 47, 54).
12. In *An Enquiry Concerning Political Justice* (1793), Godwin writes: "It is evident...that a strict adherence to truth will have the best effect upon our minds in the ordinary commerce of life. This is the virtue which has commonly been known by the denomination of sincerity" (3.135). He also argues that "[t]he powerful recommendations attendant upon sincerity are obvious. It is intimately connected with the general dissemination of innocence, energy, intellectual improvement, and philanthropy" (*Political Justice Variants* 4.161).
13. *A Bold Stroke for a Wife* remained in the theatrical repertoire throughout the Romantic period.
14. Kenney's protagonist echoes a speech given by Letitia Hardy, the heroine of Cowley's *The Belle's Stratagem* (1780 premiere), at a masquerade (IV.i.59). I discuss this speech in chapter 4.
15. From 1792 to 1800, *The Irish Widow* was performed 18 times and *A Bold Stroke for a Husband* was performed only once in London (Hogan 1477, 1571, 1681–2, 1782, 1994, 2100, and 2204). Of course, as a two-act afterpiece, *The Irish Widow* was easier to fit into an evening's entertainment than was *A Bold Stroke for a Husband*, which is a five-act mainpiece.
16. A number of scholars have noted that Mayne's *Two Dissertations Concerning Sense and the Imagination* is a possible influence on Keats's conception of the chameleon poet (Roe 247).
17. Merry adopted the pseudonym Della Crusca in homage to the Accademia della Crusca, established in Florence, Italy in 1582–1583.
18. For a detailed discussion of Robinson's Tabitha Bramble avatar and her different voices, see Daniel Robinson (168–183).
19. Sharon Setzer observes that "it is possible...to understand [the Sylphid] as a feminist anticipation of Keats's chameleon poet" ("Mary Robinson's Sylphid Self" 505).

20. Cooke acknowledges that Keats would have disputed his characterization of Byron as the "consummate chameleon poet."
21. James Soderholm contends that Lady Blessington, who may have been the model for Lady Adeline Amundeville in *Don Juan*, was also chameleonic: "the *Conversations* presents the spectacle of dueling, conversing chameleons—a contest of verbal showiness and shiftiness that makes a hoax of the very possibility of candor, stable meanings, and sincerity as traditionally conceived" (150).
22. Richard Woodhouse, the recipient of Keats's chameleon poet letter, wrote that Byron, unlike Shakespeare and Keats, "does not come up to [the poetical] Character": "He can certainly conceive & describe a dark accomplished vilain [*sic*] in love—& a female tender & kind who loves him. Or a sated & palled Sensualist Misanthrope & Deist—But here his power ends.—The true poet can not only conceive this—but can assume any Character Essence idea or Substance at pleasure. & He has this imaginative faculty not in a limited manner, but in full universality" (*Letters* 1.390). It should be noted that Woodhouse penned his assessment of Byron's chameleonism in October 1818, before the publication of *Don Juan* (1819–1824) and Byron's dramas.
23. Simon Kövesi contends that Clare's poetic chameleonism "relates to, though [it] is noticeably different from, Keats' assertion that the poet 'has no Identity—he is continually in for—and filling some other body'; Clare instead wants lots of identities. Rather than an absence or denial of self he wants a free plurality of 'exist[e]nces'" (82).
24. Marshall Berman explains that "[t]he process of confessing, for Rousseau, was a process of unmasking, of differentiating, of integrating, of *bringing his authentic self into being*" (86, italics in original).
25. Elle m'avait donné cette confiance dont le défaut m'a presque toujours empêché d'être moi. Je le fus alors. Jamais mes yeux, mes sens, mon cœur et ma bouche n'ont si bien parlé" (*Les Confessions* 291).
26. As Jerome McGann observes, in Byron's work, "hypocrisy and the true voice of feeling cannot be separated (even if they can be distinguished)" (*Towards a Literature of Knowledge* 40). In a nuanced discussion of Lady Adeline's mobility, Angela Esterhammer argues that "[f]or Byron, sincerity is both spontaneous and performed; it manifests as an immediate, embodied response to stimuli, a response that is read by others through a semiotics of looks, gestures, and tone of voice, as well as words" ("The Scandal of Sincerity" 113).
27. In editions, reviews, and scholarly articles, the title of *Knave, or Not?* is punctuated in a variety of ways: *Knave, or Not?*, *Knave or Not?*, *Knave; or Not?*, or *Knave or Not.* The play was originally titled *Knave or No Knave?*
28. *A Biographical Dictionary of Actors, Actresses, Musicians, Dancers, Managers & Other Stage Personnel in London, 1660–1800* explains that Palmer "derived his nickname from Lord Plausible, the classic

coxcomb in Wycherley's Molièresque comedy *The Plain Dealer*, [and] was so called not only for his excellent delineation of the character but also because of his reputation for intrigue and hypocrisy" ("Palmer, John" 11.172).

1 The Case of the Pretended Duke of Ormond

1. Some of the pages in the 1663 edition of *The Case of Madam Mary Carleton* are misnumbered.
2. A "catch-dolt" is a cheat.
3. Ernest Bernbaum argues that *A Witty Combat* and *The German Princess*, which premiered in 1664 with Carleton in the title role, are the same play (25–26). Mary Jo Kietzman speculates that Carleton may have collaborated with Thomas Porter in the composition of *A Witty Combat* (142–143).
4. Kietzman explains that she "began...work on Carleton's life with the fact of her immense popularity" (2).
5. Hannah Cowley has bewildered patriarchal characters criticize English society as "one universal masquerade" in her comedies *The Belle's Stratagem* and *The Town before You* (1794 premiere) (*Stratagem* II.i.27; *The Town* V.vi.95).
6. In *Fictions and Fakes: Forging Romantic Authenticity, 1760–1845*, Russett "focus[es] on how spectacular fakes" like John Hatfield and Princess Caraboo "participated in defining the 'fictional identity' bequeathed to the modern subject by Romantic culture." She contends "that modern subjectivity should be understood as a subset and, to some extent, as a precipitate of the representational practices the Romantics called 'romance' but which, in their derogated forms, also go by such names as 'imposture,' 'forgery,' 'plagiarism,' and 'delusion'" (5).
7. In his 1817 account of the imposture, John Mathew Gutch concludes "That the talents of such a girl should have been hitherto directed to no better purpose [than deception], every one must lament" (55). Debbie Lee observes that Princess Caraboo's "popularity actually increased, rather than decreased" after she revealed that she was an imposter (193).
8. Some newspaper accounts of the imposter's activities and a transcription of his November 2, 1791 trial for shooting a constable's son in Vauxhall (near Birmingham) spell his name as Hubbard, but in *The Life and Extraordinary Adventures of James Molesworth Hobart, Alias Henry Griffin, Alias Lord Massey, the Newmarket Duke of Ormond, &c.* (1794), John Collard refers to him as Hobart. A note following *The Trial of Henry Griffin, Alias George Hubbard, (The Pretended Duke of Ormond)* and American references to Hobart and his father

spell the name as Hubard (*The Trial* 19; Reese 304 n8; "Duke of Ormond" 2).

9. Roxana fears that she will be compared to Carleton if her disreputable past is exposed: "I might as well have been the *German Princess*" (Defoe 271). Kietzman contends that "Defoe, through his heroines Moll Flanders and Roxana, provides a fictional representation of Carleton's behavioral style" (3). Hobart may also have inspired characters in Charles Brocken Brown's *Ormond; or The Secret Witness.* As Philip Barnard and Stephen Shapiro note in their recent edition of the novel, "Brown was likely familiar with the widely publicized case of American-born imposter James Molesworth Hubbard" (Brown 83n.), and his renderings of the novel's title-character and Thomas Craig, an imposter and forger, might have been influenced by the spurious Duke of Ormond. Brown's Ormond is a chameleonic figure who has "a remarkable facility in imitating the voice and gestures of others" (86) and "exchange[s] his complexion and habiliments for those of a negro and a chimney-sweep" (100) in order to spy on the novel's heroine. Unlike Hobart, however, Ormond is a wealthy and powerful member of a mysterious society modeled on the Illuminati.
10. *Memoirs of a Social Monster* states that "we have traced little less than an 100,000l. [*sic*] in [Price's] possession, near 10,000l of which he made in the last five years of his life, yet he professed to die *poor*" (335–336).
11. Hobart's entry in *The New and Complete Newgate Calendar*, published in 1795, identifies him as "HENRY GRIFFIN, *alias* GEORGE HOBART" (Jackson 124).
12. Collard states that advertisements asking for information about Henry Griffin mentioned "a small cicatrice, which had been remarked in the upper part of his fore-head" (Dralloc 193), but no reference to this identifying feature appears in the trial transcript.
13. As Collard points out, "since the fate of Dr. Dodd [executed in 1777], none, convicted of forgery, had been pardoned" (Dralloc 144).
14. *The Trial of Henry Griffin* states that "Hubard" was "not more than five or six and twenty" (20); according to *The New and Complete Newgate Calendar*, "He was 25 years old" (Jackson 125).
15. *The New and Complete Newgate Calendar* also attributes the soliloquy to Henry Griffin. A footnote in *Voices from Prison* states that "This criminal was executed at Newgate, February 13, 1793. The lines were found in his cell after his decease. A friend in England forwarded it for publication" (Spear 205).
16. *A Century of Birmingham Life: Or, A Chronicle of Local Events, from 1741 to 1841* provides some basic information about Collard: "On July 8 [1799], Mr. John Collard published his well known 'Praxis of Logic, for the use of Schools.' This gentleman was one of the Twelve Apostles who used to meet at 'Poet Freeth's;' and he consequently

figures in Eckstein's Tontine Painting. He was a hatter and tailor in High Street, and is described as 'being very fond of discussion.' He retired from business and lived in a 'pretty sylvan cottage, near the Bell and Cuckoo, on the Sutton-road.' Here he wrote his works, the 'Essentials of Logic,' the 'Praxis of Logic,' and 'other elaborate treatises'... His works obtained considerable reputation at the time, and are not quite unknown at the present day" (Langford 118–119).

17. According to Collard, *Authentic Memoirs of the Life and Adventures of James Molesworth Hobart* is an unauthorized reprinting of his newspaper sketch by a "needy printer" (*Life and Extraordinary Adventures* iv). *Authentic Memoirs* contains, however, materials that do not appear in *Life and Extraordinary Adventures* (e.g., a poem purportedly written by Hobart).
18. Robert K. Dent gives Collard and his fellow Birmingham liberals credit for disseminating the "principles" that inspired political reform in England: "'the nightly debates and clever productions of these worthies gave birth to and assisted in diffusing those great and glorious principles which in after years resulted in the passing of the Reform Bill, the Catholic Emancipation Bill, together with other progressive measures, and mainly contributed towards diffusing into the hearts of "the people" those sentiments of liberalism and loyalty which experience has proved to have been productive of highly beneficial effects.' By their political opponents they were nicknamed 'the Twelve Apostles,' and 'the Jacobin Club'" (212).
19. The newspaper story previously quoted from the New York *Daily Advertiser* claims that Hobart (or Hubard) ran the faro bank in France after his escape from the Dublin prison, but dissolved his partnership with "a famous English gambler" after "quarrelling about the profits."
20. Friedrich, Freiherr von der Trenck's account of his many escapes from Frederick the Great's prisons was well known in England. In 1788 Thomas Holcroft translated a French version of *The Life of Baron Frederic Trenck* into English.
21. The influence of criminal lives on *Caleb Williams* has been explored by numerous scholars. For example, Hal Gladfelder points out that "[John] Reynolds's collection *The Triumph of God's Revenge, against the Crying, and Execrable Sinne of Murther* was...singled out by Godwin as one of his...work's predecessors, along with the *Newgate Calendar*, the *Lives of the Pirates*, and other similar semihistorical pamphlets of breathless adventure" (1–2). I have not discovered any evidence that Godwin consulted Collard's biography of Hobart, but Godwin records in his diary that he read about the swindler Charles Price (entry for October 25, 1793).
22. Collard relates how Hobart was "nearly caught...in a very suspicious position" (Dralloc 135) by his mistress's husband and found refuge in a coal vault. Feeling a sudden urge to relieve himself, the

cuckolded husband opened the coal vault door and unwittingly urinated in Hobart's face.

23. Mary Robinson, the Beauty of Buttermere is not, of course, to be confused with the actress, royal courtesan, novelist, and poet of the same name, whose representations of chameleonism I discuss in chapter 5.
24. Zeluco is the eponymous archvillain of John Moore's Gothic novel *Zeluco. Various Views of Human Nature, Taken from Life and Manners, Foreign and Domestic* (1789). He is passionate, amoral, and sadistic, and preys on a succession of wealthy women.
25. Wordsworth's reflections on Hatfield were prompted by his viewing of Charles Dibdin the Younger's *Edward and Susan; or, The Beauty of Buttermere.*
26. The short biography of Hobart/Hubard in New York's *Daily Advertiser* quoted above states that Hobart "has a mother, two sisters, and a brother, now living at Williamsburgh [*sic*], in Virginia, with whom he has never corresponded since he lost the favour of Lords Cornwallis and Dunmore. His mother is a native of America; her maiden name was Morton; she retains very large possessions in the province of Virginia." See also *The Trial* (20).

2 Richard Cumberland's Imposters

1. *The Brothers* premiered on December 2, 1769 and was first published in 1770; the other plays listed were published in the same year they premiered.
2. In his "Advertisement" prefacing *The Fashionable Lover*, Cumberland rails against "those personal and unworthy aspersions, which writers who hide their own names, fling on them who publish their's" and the anonymous reviewers' "unhandsome practice of abuse" (vii).
3. Dircks notes that Cumberland was "unrestrained in his praise of [Edmund] Burke's tract about the French Revolution, and he quote[d] a letter from Burke replying to his congratulatory letter on the occasion of its publication" (19). "Burke's tract" was his conservative critique of the French Revolution, *Reflections on the Revolution in France* (1790).
4. All parenthetical references to Cumberland's plays cite act and page numbers; scene numbers are provided when the scenes are numbered in the text.
5. Elizabeth M. Yearling is skeptical about the effectiveness of Cumberland's campaign against ethnic prejudice and argues that he actually reinforces stereotypes: "his victim figures tend to conform to national stereotypes and to establish the mental inferiority and oddity of anyone who is not English" (30).

6. In *Romantic Drama: Acting and Reacting*, Frederick Burwick discusses the ways in which *The Imposters* employs "the dramatic strategies of dissembling and performative self-reflection" (102).
7. A seventh performance was scheduled for January 28, but had to be canceled because Dorothy Jordan, who played Eleanor Sapient, was ill (Hogan 1126).
8. The *Public Advertiser* was also impressed by the audience's enthusiastic response: "The comedy was received by the audience with very great applause throughout, and will, we may venture to predict, become a favourite with the town, as well as prove a valuable addition to the stock-list of the Theatre" (January 27, 1789). Both *The Imposters* and *The Box-Lobby Challenge* were selected by Elizabeth Inchbald for inclusion in *The Modern Theatre; a Collection of Successful Modern Plays, as Acted at the Theatres Royal, London* (1811).
9. In his essay "On the Artificial Comedy of the Last Century" (1822), Lamb praises Palmer for transforming Joseph Surface, the villain of Sheridan's *The School for Scandal* (1777), into an endearing character.
10. C. R. Snyder and Howard L. Fromkin have argued that clothing and names are both important "uniqueness attributes" (118–142) and "that the name serves as a source of identity by which one is differentiated from others" (141).
11. When they are alone, Singleton addresses Polycarp as "Jack." Polycarp is also the name of a Christian martyr and saint.
12. Citing the *Dictionary of the Vulgar Tongue*, Roberta F. S. Borkat explains that "[t]o 'die dunghill' means 'to repent or show any signs of contrition at the gallows'" ("Notes to *The Imposters*" 5).
13. The *Morning Post* reviewer did not know that Cumberland had written *The Box-Lobby Challenge.*
14. The review in the *World (1787)* was also positive and remarked that *The Box-Lobby Challenge* "was altogether very well received, and given out for this evening with much applause" (February 24, 1794).
15. The *World (1787)* praised Bannister's performance in *The Box-Lobby Challenge*: "The Performers, particularly Young BANNISTER, BARRYMORE, Mrs. HARLOWE, and Mrs. GIBBS, deserve much commendation" (February 24, 1794).
16. Both Sir Charles Freemantle in *The Imposters* and Captain Waterland in *The Box-Lobby Challenge* were played by William Barrymore (1759–1830).
17. Jack utters only one Latin phrase in the play, the well-known "*ecce signum*" (V.i.51), which means behold the sign, or look at the proof.
18. This aside is not identified as such in the text, so I have inserted *aside* in brackets.
19. A huncks or hunks is "a close-fisted, stingy man; a miser" (*OED*).

20. The theater historian John Genest notes that this passage "deserves to be quoted" and reproduces an edited version of it in *Some Account of the English Stage* (7.149).
21. The term counsel refers to "A body of legal advisers, engaged in the direction or conduct of a cause" (*OED*).
22. This passage does not appear in the Larpent Licensing manuscript (Borkat, "Notes to *The Box-Lobby Challenge*" 12).

3 Thomas Holcroft's Politicized Imposter and Sycophantic Chameleon

1. The only influences on *Knave, or Not?* that Holcroft acknowledged are three comedies by Carlo Goldoni (1707–1793): *Il Raggiratore* (1758), *La Serva Amorosa* (1753), and *Il Padre di Famiglia* (1751). It is clear, however, that he also borrowed heavily from Cumberland's comedies. The main source for one of his most successful plays, *The Deserted Daughter* (1795), was Cumberland's *The Fashionable Lover* (1772), and, as I demonstrate in this chapter, *Knave, or Not?* owes a debt to both *The Imposters* and *The Box-Lobby Challenge.*
2. Moody maintains that the cuts were made by the acting manager rather than by Holcroft ("Censorship of Jacobin Theatre" 208).
3. Thomas Pfau has argued that "paranoia constitutes... the paradigmatic mood of the 1790s in England" and analyzes the conspiracy theory advanced by the British government, which claimed that "various kinds of radicals, millenarian visionaries and misguided reformers, all operating in collusion with the French Jacobins" threatened the English "crown and constitution" (77, 159–160).
4. Newspaper articles published in 1794 characterized Robespierre's confederate Bertrand Barère as "a true revolutionary cameleon" who "affected to pass for a Noble [under the old regime], but unconstant as the camelion,... changes his opinions as often as his dress, and has been successively a Feuillant, a Jacobin, and an Aristocrat" (*Whitehall Evening Post [1770]*, December 16–18, 1794 and "CHARACTER OF BARRERE [From a Parisian Paper]," *London Packet or New Lloyd's Evening Post*, December 17–19, 1794).
5. In his advertisement, Holcroft asks the readers of his comedy to "decide whether the author could have been so insane as actually to intend to enflame the spectators, and increase a spirit of enmity between men of different factions" (iv).
6. Garnai identifies the censored passage from the Larpent manuscript in the Huntington Library:

   "Monrose. If I am not a lord, it seems I ought to have been. I find no difficulty in being as extravagant as a lord, as proud as a lord and as idle as a Lord. Let Lords look to it then[.] Let them be as superior to the poor in virtue as they are in power, and I will blush for being an imposter" (II.xx) (Garnai 476, LA 1192). Also see Morgan 55–56.

7. John Bannister played Jonas Ferment in *Knave, or Not?*
8. On the day after the premiere, Holcroft was identified as the author of *Knave, or Not?* by the *Oracle and Public Advertiser*: "It is said to be from the pen of Mr. HOLCROFT, the author of several successful pieces, and whose industry and talents have on some occasions deserved and obtained the most flattering encouragement" (January 26, 1798). The *Star* confirmed this report: "This comedy is generally understood to be the production of Mr. HOLCROFT" (January 27, 1798). Garnai states that Holcroft's "authorship was apparently an open secret" (476) during the play's opening night.
9. The epilogue to *Knave, or Not?*, composed by Matthew Lewis, advises the "Author" to emulate Colman and "stick on [his] Villains a beard of pale blue" (vii). According to the *Morning Herald*, during the premiere of *Knave or Not?* "The House was very full" (January 26, 1798).
10. The *Morning Herald* attacked the moral and political sentiments expressed in *Knave or Not?* but praised the actors' performances: "PALMER was an able representative of a Knave, who was suffered to hold up to contempt and ridicule some of the most amiable traits of civilized man" (January 26, 1798).
11. Sir Thomas Burnet's satire *A Second Tale of a Tub: Or, The History of Robert Powel the Puppet-Show Man* (1715) notes that "*Fur-Gowns* and *Gold Chains*" are the "Emblems of *Aldermanship*" (198). White wands were carried by a variety of governmental officials.
12. Susan Monrose was played by the comedienne Dorothy Jordan, who was renowned for her portrayals of naive countrywomen.
13. One of the definitions of "knave" that persisted throughout the seventeenth century is "a boy or lad employed as a servant; hence, a male servant or menial in general; one of low condition" (*OED*).
14. The quotation marks (or inverted commas) in the quoted passage indicate that it was censored after the play's first performance.
15. Alison Hickey has examined the political connotations of "system" in Britain during and after the French Revolution: "In the 1790s, 'system' was associated with a dangerous abstraction or generalizing tendency harboring the potential to erase ancient hierarchies... 'System' conjured up anxieties about the supposedly denaturing energies of the French political metaphysicians (the Baron d'Holbach's *Système de la Nature*) and was used to express and create suspicion of Jacobinism at home" (20). In the "Advertisement" prefacing *Knave, or Not?* Holcroft writes that "[h]is design was to draw a man of genius,...reasoning on his actions, [and] *systematizing* them" (iii, italics added).

16. Philip Cox argues that "far from being the 'harmless and secure' production that [*The Monthly Mirror*] thought [*He's Much to Blame*] was, the play continued not only the sustained generic experimentation but also the social critique of [Holcroft's previous plays]" (101).
17. In his notes on *He's Much to Blame*, Joseph Rosenblum reports that "lords, and commons" was "crossed out in MS, probably by John Larpent" (cxxviii).
18. The masquerade scene in *The Belle's Stratagem* will be discussed in chapter 4.
19. "L'homme du monde est tout entier dans son masque. N'étant presque jamais en lui-même, il y est toujours étranger, et mal à son aise quand il est forcé d'y rentrer. Ce qu'il est n'est rien, ce qu'il paraît est tout pour lui" (*Émile ou de l'Éducation* 271).
20. The second quotation from *A Narrative of Facts* is taken from the separately numbered "Defence" section of the volume.
21. The phrase "benevolent lies" is from Holcroft's review of *Every One Has His Fault* (303).
22. Garnai wonders if Holcroft had come "to the conclusion that social harmony and justice could only be achieved through deception" (482) by the time he wrote *Knave, or Not?*.

4 Fluid Identities in Hannah Cowley's Universal Masquerade

1. Parenthetical references to the first editions of Cowley's plays provide act, scene, and page numbers. I have numbered scenes that are unnumbered in the texts. References to the 1813 edition of *The Town before You* provide only volume and page numbers.
2. Letitia's masquerade scene has been variously interpreted in recent analyses of *The Belle's Stratagem*. According to Elizabeth Kowaleski Wallace, Letitia exemplifies "Cowley's performance-based theory of human subjectivity," which "endorses masking as movement or as the free play of identity that refuses to fix character as only this or that" (430). Wallace argues that Cowley's theatrical "cosmopolitanism affords the opportunity for a social performance with liberating potential" (417). Although Wendy Arons maintains that Letitia's "romantic longings are wholly conventional, ceding power to the male gaze to define her as an object of eros," she agrees with Wallace that *The Belle's Stratagem* "celebrates the liberating effects of performance for women" (253). According to Arons, "Letitia's performance is a desperate response to Doricourt's indifferent gaze" that "depends upon her skill in reading and deciphering his desire and then shaping her performance to it" (253–254). Lisa A. Freeman contends that "Cowley posits conventional eighteenth-century English female character, even as she subverts the very frame of that representation

by self-consciously staging character as no more or less than a performative, or constitutional parody of, identity" (183). Citing Letitia's willingness to be "any thing—and all" for her beloved, Erin Isikoff argues that "Letitia . . . is not highlighting the invention and poetry of the female mind, but rather proposing her own insignificance: without a man she represents a blank, a cipher" (114). Anne K. Mellor disputes Isikoff's assessment and points out that by the play's end Letitia "has assumed the mastery of [her and Doricourt's] marriage" and "has amply gratified her own sexual desire" (56). Gillian Russell writes that "[t]he freedom of masquerade disguise enables [Letitia] to articulate a vision of marriage as a globe-trotting egalitarian adventure, culminating in the appropriation of that emblem of eroticized sexuality, the harem, to create a haven of 'liberty and love'" (220). Angela Escott emphasizes Letitia's cosmopolitanism (42).

3. As Jeffrey N. Cox points out, "the women in Cowley's *Bold Stroke* find that . . . they can discover new comic power in self-consciously manipulating the conventions that would constrain them" (372).
4. The roles of Letitia Hardy and Lady Horatia Horton were originated by the same actress, Elizabeth Younge (later Mrs. Pope) (*c.* 1740–1797).
5. The *Morning Chronicle* identified Lady Horatia as "the representative of Mrs. D——" (December 8, 1794). See also *The Monthly Review* (January–April 1795) (330–331), quoted later in this chapter.
6. As Wahrman has demonstrated, numerous eighteenth-century writers, including Henry Fielding, Tobias Smollett, and Oliver Goldsmith, described the world, human life, society, or London as a masquerade (167).
7. Melinda C. Finberg provides an insightful analysis of Kitty Willis in her dramaturgical assessment of *The Belle's Stratagem* ("Staging the 18th-Century Prostitute" n. pag.).
8. See *London Courant and Westminster Chronicle* (February 26, 1781) and "Postscript. Theatre," *St. James's Chronicle or the British Evening Post* (February 24–27, 1781). The following lines in the epilogue refer to D'Eon: "We all have heard / That D'Eon with the veil conceals her beard. / The Chevalier, had she been made a nun / In the same convent [that is featured in the play], might have shown some fun" ("Epilogue to the World as it Goes," *The Scots Magazine* 216).
9. See "Postscript. Theatre," *St. James's Chronicle or the British Evening Post* (March 24, 1781). The "Theatrical Intelligence" column of the *London Courant and Westminster Chronicle* complained that in revising rather than abandoning her condemned comedy, "Mrs. Cowley has shewn a masculine resolution and boldness, which operated against her" (March 26, 1781).
10. All quotations from *The World as It Goes* are taken from the Larpent licensing manuscript in the Huntington Library in San Marino,

California (LA 548). The parenthetical citations provide act, scene, and page number; since the manuscript pagination restarts with 1 beginning with Act III, I have renumbered the pages in the last three acts to make the pagination consistent throughout.

11. By "science," Mrs. Sparwell means knowledge rather than natural and physical science.
12. The *Morning Herald and Daily Advertiser* criticized the fake Hercules statue scene for its comedic ineffectiveness rather than for its indecency: "The living figure of an *Hercules*, set up in order to expose Mrs. *Sparwell*'s false pretensions to a critical knowledge of the antique, is an idea taken from the well known anecdote of the critic, who damned the production of an artist, for vilely painting a fly, which, however, contrived to fly from the canvas, while he was pointing out its defects.—But Mrs. Cowley's *Hercules* was a figure so evidently defective in every part of symmetry and proportion, that instead of making Mrs. *Sparwell*'s criticisms, ill founded, and exposing her to the ridicule of the company, it served to justify every stricture she had made, and consequently destroyed the effect that was intended from the scene" (February 26, 1781).
13. In Greek mythology, Actaeon was transformed into a stag. Colonel Sparwell is saying that his wife would make him a cuckold (give him horns).
14. According to a review of *The Town before You* that Angela Escott found in an unattributed newspaper cutting, Lady Horatia's character "affords . . . some tolerable good lessons of morality and propriety of female deportment" (quoted from Escott 185).
15. One of the definitions of bronze in the *OED* is "Impudence, unblushingness."
16. At the conclusion of James Townley's farce, *High Life below Stairs* (1759), a character moralizes that "[i]f Persons of Rank would act up to their Standard, it would be impossible that their Servants could ape them——But when they affect every thing that is ridiculous, it will be in the Power of any low Creature to follow their Example" (II.54).
17. See "To Della Crusca," *The World* (August 4, 1787):

    O Time! . . .
    bid the soft Carnation fly;
    My tresses sprinkle with thy snow,
    Which boasted once the *auburn glow*,
    Warp the slim form that was ador'd
    By him, so lov'd, my *bosom's* LORD— But leave me, when all these you steal,
    The mind to *taste*, the nerve to *feel!* (lines 31–40)

18. Daniel Robinson disputes Reynolds's account of the Merry-Cowley meeting, particularly the assertion that Merry "seriously harbored

a romantic interest" in Anna Matilda, and suggests that Reynolds wanted to make Merry seem foolish because he abhorred the poet's radical politics (64).

19. In his poem "The Interview" (1790), Merry has Anna Matilda banish the forlorn Della Crusca, thus ending their poetic correspondence:

   "Farewel! ANOTHER claims my heart,
   Then wing thy sinking steps, for here we part,
   WE PART! and listen, for the word is MINE,
   ANNA MATILDA NEVER CAN BE THINE!" (*The British Album* 2.166, lines 88–91)

20. Antje Blank suggests that Cowley ended her dramatic career because of her disappointment with the "moderate" success of *The Town before You* (nine performances) (198). By contrast, *The Belle's Stratagem* had an initial run of 28 nights. A notice in the *Oracle and Public Advertiser* suggests, however, that the revised version of the play was well-received: "*The Town before You* had a magnificent house on Friday [December 19]—such boxes have hardly been seen during the season. Considering the time of year, this is a circumstance highly honourable for the Comedy—and the applause with which it went off was still more so" (Monday, December 22, 1794).
21. As Frederick Burwick points out, in *The Town before You* Cowley "entertained her audience with more elaborate antics of the transvestite male con artist than were customary on the stage of her period" (*Romantic Drama* 127). For the 1813 edition of the play, Cowley abbreviated Brisk's (Tippy's) celebration of cross-dressing: "A plan that forced me, the other morning, into a strange Disguise! like Hercules, to exchange my Cane for a Distaff, and—but mum!" (*Works* II.349).
22. Tippy is not the only female impersonator in Cowley's comedies. For example, in *Who's the Dupe?*, a male character named Granger delivers a convincing performance as a female French mantua-maker. In *A Bold Stroke for a Husband*, an old servant called Gaspar improbably claims that he is "always Queen Cleopatra . . . [i]n . . . plays at home" and "hits her off to a nicety" (V.i.72).
23. The preface to *The Works of Mrs. Cowley* stipulates that the edition includes "[a]ll the retouchings to be found amongst [Cowley's] Papers" (I.xx). Frederick M. Link explains that Cowley's "revisions tend to make the [1813] *Works* texts bland, somewhat overwritten, and conventional—altogether less interesting than the early ones." Although Link does not "doubt the authority of the 1813 texts," he "prefer[s] the Hannah Cowley actively engaged in the London theatre to the older one blue-pencilling herself in retirement at Tiverton" (xlviii).
24. Although Fancourt's speech appears to endorse Jean-Jacques Rousseau's valorization in the *Discourse on the Origin and Foundations*

of Inequality Among Men (1755) of "man in the state of nature" (14), his commendation of "natural" transparency is clearly a ploy intended to convince his prospective victim that he champions honesty. Obviously, Sir Robert's servants are not exemplars of primitive naturalness; in fact, one of them, Jenny, is Tippy's scheming sister and accomplice.

25. Alison Yarrington argues that in Darwin's lines, "It is the image of feminine charm overcoming the cold, intractable marble and bringing it to life, the soft touch that is more easily associated with modeling rather than carving that dominates—the female Pygmalion" (37).
26. Damer's maiden surname was Conway. In the 1813 edition of *The Town before You*, Horton extols "the vigour of Michael Angelo" (*Works* II.401).
27. Elfenbein (*Romantic Genius: The Prehistory of a Homosexual Role* 97–103, 110–111, 120) and Jonathan Gross (*The Life of Anne Damer: Portrait of a Regency Artist* 69) provide illuminating discussions of Damer's controversial public image.
28. Elfenbein admits that "Cowley seems to poke a bit of fun at Horton in the rhapsodic tone of [her] speeches" to Sir Simon but argues that since "a variety of characters praise [her as] a touchstone of judgment" she "is basically meant to be taken seriously" ("Lesbian Aestheticism" 5–6). Cowley borrowed the phrase "more than gothic ignorance" from Henry Fielding's *The History of Tom Jones* (1749), in which Mrs. Western decries the "more than Gothic Ignorance" of her boorish brother, Squire Western (336).
29. Mellor characterizes Cowley as a conservative feminist who "endorses heterosexual marriage, the British constitution, inherited wealth, and the class system, but... nonetheless envisions women as the agents who can best govern those institutions" (*Mothers of the Nation* 52).
30. In Cowley's advertisement to *A Day in Turkey*, she rejects the notion that her comic opera is "tainted with POLITICS": "I protest I know nothing about politics;—will Miss Wolstonecraft [*sic*] forgive me-whose book contains such a body of mind as I hardly ever met with—if I say that politics are *unfeminine*? I never in my life could attend to their discussion" (n. pag.).
31. Siddons also played Chelonice in Cowley's tragedy *The Fate of Sparta; or, The Rival Kings* (1788 premiere). Other actresses who won acclaim for their performances in Cowley's plays include Elizabeth Farren, who played Seraphina in *A School for Greybeards*, Elizabeth Kemble (John Philip Kemble's sister-in-law), who created the role of Arabella in *More Ways than One* (1783 premiere), and Elizabeth Younge, who originated roles in *The Runaway* (as Bella), *The Belle's Stratagem* (as Letitia Hardy), *The World as It Goes* (as Mrs. Danvers), *Which is the Man?* (1782 premiere, as Lady Bell Bloomer), *More Ways than One* (as Miss Archer), and, under her married name, Mrs. Pope,

performed in *A Day in Turkey* (as Alexina) and *The Town before You* (as Lady Horatia Horton).

32. In *The Town before You*, Cowley has Fancourt compare himself to Marplot, a comic character in Centlivre's *The Busybody* (1709) who inadvertently spoils his friends' plots (V.iii.87).
33. Horton is prefigured in some ways by the wealthy widow Lady Bell Bloomer, the heroine of *Which is the Man?*. Bloomer, like Horton, is economically self-sufficient, in control of her destiny, and in love with a virtuous military man. She boasts that she is "mistress of [her] own situation, and cannot be surpris'd" (II.i.13). Unlike Horton, however, Bloomer enjoys fashionable society and witty badinage and has no interest in creating art.

5 Mary Robinson's Polygraphs

1. In her biography of Robinson, Sarah Gristwood points out that Hawkins was "very far from a partial witness for [Robinson], of whom she heartily disapproved" (74).
2. Paula Byrne argues that Robinson suffered from acute rheumatic fever (228–229); Gristwood writes that the progress of Robinson's disease "does seem to fit the pattern of the 'fever' and 'rheumatism' her daughter [Maria Elizabeth Robinson] mentioned—what we call rheumatic fever today" (206).
3. Daniel Robinson thoroughly examines Robinson's poetic avatars in his monograph *The Poetry of Mary Robinson: Form and Fame.*
4. In *Present State of the Manners, Society, & c. &c. of the Metropolis of England*, Robinson alludes to Jordan's "magical fascinations" (195).
5. Sharon Setzer writes that "it is never quite clear how the mercurial nature of Fashion is different from that of the shape-changing Sylphid" ("Mary Robinson's Sylphid Self" 510–511). I contend that while they are both chameleons, the Sylphid's moralistic observations and reformative inclinations distinguish her from amoral Fashion.
6. I borrow the phrase "moral orientation" from Charles Taylor, who argues that a "fundamental moral orientation [is] essential to being a human interlocutor, capable of answering for oneself" (29). For Taylor, one's identity is largely defined by one's moral commitments.
7. Wahrman's argument regarding the historical shift from the *ancien régime* of identity to the modern regime of selfhood is discussed in the introduction to this book.
8. Jasper Woodville's "innate" superiority remains intact despite poverty and "immitigable sorrows": "his address, his voice, his words were such as marked the disparity between his fortune and his intellects; for the meanest garb of poverty cannot conceal the innate lustre of superior organization . . . The stamp which Nature sets upon her best works is not subject to the power of Fortune" ("Jasper" 264).

9. Robinson's birthdate has not been definitively established. Byrne argues that she was born on November 27, 1757, and Alix Nathan and Hester Davenport believe that she was born in 1756 (Byrne 430; Davenport 7; Nathan 139–141). Thus on April 30, 1778 she may have been either 20 or 21.
10. Strolling actors were not attached to a specific theater and performed in various venues throughout Britain.
11. Mellor and Setzer briefly discuss polygraphing in *Walsingham* (Mellor, "Mary Robinson and the Scripts of Female Sexuality" 254; Setzer, "The Dying Game" 319).
12. Samuel Taylor Coleridge uses the term polygraph in his December 17, 1794 letter to Robert Southey. Referring to his sonnet, "To R. B. Sheridan Esq.—," Coleridge writes that "[t]he mode of bepraising a man by enumerating the beauties of his *Polygraph* is at least an original one" (1.141).
13. "Je ne suis fait comme aucun de ceux que j'ai vus; j'ose croire n'être fait comme aucun de ceux qui existent. Si je ne vaux pas mieux, au moins je suis autre" (*Les Confessions* 3). Walsingham admires Rousseau's political philosophy (*Walsingham* 347).
14. For an example of Rousseau's impulsive and irrational behavior, see *Les Confessions*, 91–95, the famous ribbon-stealing episode.
15. As Sharon Setzer informed me in an email message (May 29, 2007), Walsingham's rape of the masked Amelia recalls *The Masqueraders: Or, Fatal Curiosity* (1724–1725), a two-part story by Eliza Haywood in which Philecta successfully impersonates Dorimenus's beloved at a masquerade. Her subsequent affair with the inconstant Dorimenus leads to the loss of her reputation, her pregnancy, and possibly her death. In the second part of *The Masqueraders*, Dorimenus attends another masquerade in the costume of a friar and ravishes his wife Lysimena, whose disguise as a nun prevents him from recognizing her. His libertinism and her "fatal curiosity" destroy their marriage.
16. Citing the work of Judith Butler, Eleanor Ty, Chris Cullens, and Sharon Setzer have argued that in *Walsingham* gender is performative. But as Ty acknowledges, "Robinson does not articulate the theories of sexual identities in the sophisticated way that Butler does" (46).
17. Shaffer points out that "Robinson may suggest that even Sidney's prowess at 'manly exercises' should be shared by women; we might reach this conclusion from Robinson's *Letter to the Women of England*,...in which she supports women's right to engage in physical activity normally limited to males" (77).
18. John Hope Mason notes that "[t]he importance of Edward Young's *Conjectures on Original Composition* (1759), in France and Germany as well as in Britain, is generally recognized" (37). Mary Robinson admired Young and used five passages from his poetry as chapter epigraphs in *Hubert de Sevrac* (3, 134, 147, 156, 235). Young is also mentioned in *Walsingham* (230).

19. The original/copy binary is also an important issue in Robinson's poetry. Ashley J. Cross persuasively argues that Robinson's *Lyrical Tales* (1800) is "a revisionary response to *Lyrical Ballads* (1798)" that "radically destabilizes the relationship between original and copy, self and other" ("From *Lyrical Ballads* to *Lyrical Tales*" 574, 593).
20. Contemporary readers identified Treville as a surrogate for Robinson's former lover Banastre Tarleton, who announced his engagement to the illegitimate heiress Susan Priscilla Bertie a couple of months before the novel's publication. Hester Davenport writes, however, that "Treville represents more than Tarleton. In 1798 Mary was writing not just *The False Friend* but her *Memoirs* and, consciously or unconsciously, Treville is surely a composite of all those libertines who aimed at or succeeded in charming her into their beds, from Lord Lyttelton onwards" (202). Paula Byrne contends that "the character of Treville is actually more a literary type than a portrait of Tarleton. He is a rake in the mold of Lovelace in Samuel Richardson's *Clarissa*" (342). In fact, Gertrude makes an explicit comparison between Lovelace and Treville (149).
21. The phrase "pupil of nature" is also used to describe the title-character of *Walsingham*; in *The False Friend*, Gertrude regards the impulsive Edward Ashgrove as a "child of nature" (227). Gertrude has seen Elizabeth Inchbald's play *The Child of Nature* (1788), a translation of *Zélie* by Madame de Genlis, at Drury Lane (171, 421n58).
22. As Daniel Robinson observes, a September 1, 1797 article in the *Morning Post* referred to Anna Seward as "the SAPHO of the Age" (115). Regarding Hemans's response to Sappho, see Ross 298–299; for a discussion of Landon and Sappho, see Prins 191–200. According to Linda H. Peterson, "Sappho represents, for Robinson and other woman poets, an ancient, original, and originating figure who fulfills the criteria for Romantic artistry yet adds specifically female features to the myths of becoming a poet" (41).
23. Robinson is referred to as "our British Sappho" in a December 1796 review of her *Sappho and Phaon* in the *English Review* (*Selected Poems* 385). Gill Perry claims that a painting titled *The British Sappho* by Robinson's friend Angelica Kauffman, a famous Swiss artist, is a portrait of the poet (44).
24. In Jerome McGann's discussion of *Sappho and Phaon*, he argues that Robinson considers herself as "the avatar of Sappho," seeking to redeem "man," as Sappho attempts to redeem her benighted lover Phaon, through "POESY" (114; *Sappho and Phaon* I.9–10).
25. In her memoirs, Robinson suggests that she learned Latin, French, and Italian from her teacher Meribah Lorrington but does not claim to have acquired even the rudiments of ancient Greek (see "Memoirs" 201).

26. Margaret Reynolds blames Pope for turning the name "Sappho" into a code word for a "lewd and infamous Creature" (124–125).
27. There is at least one disrespectful reference to Sappho in Robinson's writings: the narrator of *The Natural Daughter* condemns the licentious and villainous Julia Bradford for her ability to "make love like Sappho" (35).
28. See Ovid's *Epistvla Sapphvs ad Phaonem*, 15–20: "nec me Pyrrhiades Methymniadesue puellae, / nec me Lesbiadum cetera turba iuuant. / uilis Anactorie, uilis, mihi crede, Gyrinno, / non oculis grata est Atthis, ut ante, meis, / atque aliae centum, quas non sine crimine amaui. / improbe, multarum quod fuit, unus habes" (*Heroides: Selected Epistles* 78), translated by Harold Isbell as "[n]o Pyrrhan girls please me now, nor do those from / Methymna, nor any from Lesbos. / Anactoria is nothing to me now, / nor is that dazzling beauty, Cydro. / Atthis no longer brings joy to my eyes as / she did once. Nor do I find pleasure / in the hundred others I have loved in shame" (*Heroides* 134). Pope downplays this passage by reducing it to two lines: "No more the *Lesbian* Dames my Passion move, / Once the dear Objects of my guilty Love" (*Sapho to Phaon*, 17–18).
29. Robinson also cites Barthélemy's account of Sappho in her *A Letter to the Women of England*: "Some anecdotes of this celebrated WOMAN, who lived near 600 years before Christ, may be found in the Abbé Barthelimi's [*sic*] Travels of Anacharsis the Younger" (143).
30. *Epistvla Sapphvs ad Phaonem*, 117–122, *Sapho to Phaon*, 135–142. Pope has "Sapho" express her unhappiness as a parent: "An Infant Daughter late my Griefs increast [*sic*] / And all a Mother's Cares dis tract my Breast" (77–78). No daughter is mentioned in Robinson's *Sappho and Phaon*.
31. *Poems* 1.327; "Memoirs" 201–202.
32. Although Denmore states that Sappho "was not famed for personal attractions," the bust is modeled on a beautiful woman who resembles the lovely Gertrude. This inconsistency is not explained in the novel.
33. For the definitive edition of this poem in its original Greek, see Lobel and Page 32.
34. Addison's *Spectator* essays on Sappho, to which Robinson alludes in her "Account of Sappho" (*Selected Poems* 152), contain English translations by Addison's friend Ambrose Philips of Sappho's two most famous fragments (2.367–369, 2.392). Gertrude may have access to the *Spectator* essays in Lord Denmore's extensive library.
35. See Addison 2.366.
36. See Robinson's extract from Barthélemy in her "Account of Sappho": "The sensibility of SAPPHO was extreme! she loved PHAON, who forsook her; after various efforts to bring him back, she took the leap of Leucata, and perished in the waves!" (*Poems* 1.327).

37. Cross writes that Miss Stanley "is the substitute mother" who "comes too late to save [Gertrude]" ("He-She Philosophers and Other Literary Bugbears" 61).
38. Laura was one of Robinson's pennames.
39. Since *The False Friend* was published in February 1799, it is likely that Robinson read *Memoirs of the Author of "The Rights of Woman"* as she composed her novel.

6 JAMES KENNEY'S OPPORTUNISTIC, REFORMATIVE, AND IMITATIVE CHAMELEONS

1. "Man Was Made to Mourn: A Dirge" (1784) was written by Robert Burns.
2. Mr. Poe also performed the role of Dauntless in Kenney's *The World!* (1808) at least four times, and Mrs. Poe played Emily in Kenney's *False Alarms* (1807) (Quinn 718–719).
3. The quotations from *Raising the Wind*, *Cheap Living*, and *False Alarms* reproduce the square brackets that set off the stage directions in the original texts.
4. My summary of Diddler's cultural influence is indebted to Terry F. Robinson's "James Kenney's Comedic Genius" (1086–1088). In *The Life & Adventures of Nicholas Nickleby*, the stage manager Mr. Crummles orders Nicholas to study the dissimilar roles of Romeo, Rover, Cassio, and Jeremy Diddler because "one part helps the other so much" (298). In Bulwer-Lytton's *Money*, Alfred Evelyn's friends fear that he has diddled them:

   BLOUNT... he borrowed 700*l.* of me!
   GLOSSMORE. And 600*l.* of me!
   SIR JOHN. And 500*l.* of me!
   STOUT. Oh! a regular Jeremy Diddler! (IV.v.73)

5. In Adam Smith's *An Inquiry into the Nature and Causes of the Wealth of Nations* (1776), he maintains that tradesmen are motivated by "self-love" rather than "humanity": "It is not from the benevolence of the butcher, the brewer, or the baker, that we expect our dinner, but from their regard to their own interest. We address ourselves, not to their humanity but to their self-love, and never talk to them of our own necessities but of their advantages" (1.27).
6. As Jeffrey N. Cox has pointed out, "Kenney's *The World*" is "the precursor of... Woody Allen's *Zelig*," and "Echo, like Woody Allen's Zelig, is a man who fits himself to those who surround him" (366, 372).
7. According to William Jerdan, "Taylor was a being of the artificial stage, not of the actual living world... He was... knowing in one sense, yet absurdly plotting as in a play; and looking for surprises

and *dénouements*; as if the game of life were a comedy or a farce" (2.73).

8. *The Pleasures of Imagination*, II.545: "O wake thee, rouse thy spirit!"
9. Julia was one of Mary Robinson's pseudonyms.
10. The lines are not numbered in *British Theatre*, so I have provided the page number of the passage.
11. In *Reflections on the Revolution in France*, Burke writes: "the age of chivalry is gone.—That of sophisters, oeconomists, and calculators, has succeeded; and the glory of Europe is extinguished for ever" (76).
12. Later in the play, Emily tells Plod that she has never seen Surfeit before (II.ii.55).
13. In the first edition of *English Bards and Scotch Reviewers*, Byron's criticism of *The World!* is milder: "While Kenney's World just suffer'd to proceed, / Proclaims the audience very kind indeed?" (*The Complete Poetical Works* 1.247n).
14. Robinson points out that "[b]oth Jeremy Diddler and Cheviot employ romance to gain suitable financial ends" (1096).
15. Originally located in Lloyd's Coffee-House, Lloyd's was the center of marine insurance and shipbroking in Great Britain (Martin).
16. In the eighteenth century, one of the definitions of ludicrous was "in a favourable sense, witty, humorous" (*OED*).

EPILOGUE: THE PERKIN WARBECK DEBATE

1. For a definition of the modern self, see Wahrman (276). Like Bayley and Shelley, Thomas De Quincey believed that Perkin Warbeck was "the true Plantagenet" ("Historico-Critical Inquiry" 2 and n).
2. Hume dismisses the notion that Perkin's "confession was drawn from him by torture," noting that "no ancient [i.e., medieval] historian gives any ground for this surmise" (3.403n).
3. In *The History and Antiquities of the Tower of London*, some of the page numbers are repeated and marked with a superscript [a] or [b]. I have reproduced the superscript letters in the parenthetical citations of this text.
4. Doucet Devin Fischer notes that the allusion in the preface to *The Fortunes of Perkin Warbeck* to "those who have access to... Records... in the Tower" "[a]lmost certainly refer[s] to works by Horace Walpole... and the antiquarian John Bayley" (5 and n.c). Shelley follows Walpole and Bayley's lead in dismissing "the history of the pretender" issued by Henry VII. She writes that "History has in its caprice given more credence to this composition, than its contemporaries gave; it was ridiculed and despised at the time even by the partizans of Lancaster" (157 and n).

5. Graeme Tytler has explored Lavater's influence on English fiction during the Romantic period, and Scott J. Juengel discusses Lavater's influence on *Frankenstein* (354–355).
6. Walpole (85–86) and Bayley (352[a]–353[b]) both speculate that the reason Henry VII never confronted the pretender with his alleged mother (the Queen Dowager) and sisters (one of whom was Henry's wife) was that he feared they would identify him as Richard, Duke of York.
7. The character who articulates this conception of the self is the Byronic Lord Raymond.
8. Bacon writes that the "wily" Perkin "would not set one foot out of his ship, till he might see things were sure" (133).
9. Campbell invents Perkin's capture during the Scottish incursion into England. The historical Perkin sailed from Scotland to Ireland and was captured after invading Cornwall.
10. The rumor that Perkin was the illegitimate son of Edward IV is mentioned by Bacon (113) and Hume (3.375).
11. According to Wroe, Perkin "caused far more trouble, and more nearly upended Henry, than he is usually given credit for" (viii).

Works Cited

Addison, Joseph. *The Spectator*. Ed. Donald F. Bond. Vol. 2. Oxford: Clarendon, 1965.

Adolphus, John. *Memoirs of John Bannister, Comedian*. 2 vols. London: Richard Bentley, 1839.

Allen, Emily. "Loss Incommensurable: Economics of Imbalance in Mary Robinson's *Walsingham*." *The Eighteenth-Century Novel* 5 (2006): 67–92.

The Analytical Review 19.3 (July 1794): 275–276.

Angus, William. "An Appraisal of David Garrick: Based Mainly upon Contemporary Sources." *The Quarterly Journal of Speech* 25 (1939): 30–42.

Arons, Wendy. "Performance, Mobility, and the Domestication of Female Desire in *The Belle's Stratagem*." *1650–1850: Ideas, Aesthetics, and Inquiries in the Early Modern Era* 11 (2005): 251–264.

Article XIX. *The Town before You*. *The Monthly Review; or, Literary Journal, Enlarged: From January to April, Inclusive, 1795*. Vol. 16. London: R. Griffiths, 1795.

Authentic Memoirs of the Life and Adventures of James Molesworth Hobart, (Alias Lord Massey, Alias the Duke of Ormond,) From His Birth in the Year 1765, to His Execution on the 13th of February 1793. Birmingham: I. Hawkins, 1793.

Bacon, Francis. *The History of the Reign of King Henry the Seventh*. Ed. Jerry Weinberger. Ithaca, NY: Cornell UP, 1996.

Barker-Benfield, G. J. *The Culture of Sensibility: Sex and Society in Eighteenth-Century Britain*. Chicago, IL: U of Chicago P, 1992.

Bayley, John. *The History and Antiquities of the Tower of London, with Memoirs of Royal and Distinguished Persons*. Vol. 2. London: T. Cadell, 1825.

Beattie, J. M. *Crime and the Courts in England, 1660–1800*. Princeton, NJ: Princeton UP, 1986.

Beckford, William. *Vathek and Other Stories: A William Beckford Reader*. Ed. Malcolm Jack. London: Penguin, 1993.

Berman, Marshall. *The Politics of Authenticity: Radical Individualism and the Emergence of Modern Society*. New York: Atheneum, 1972.

Bernbaum, Ernest. *The Mary Carleton Narratives, 1663–1673: A Missing Chapter in the History of the English Novel*. Cambridge: Harvard UP, 1914.

Bisset, Robert. *The Historical, Biographical, Literary, and Scientific Magazine. The History of Literature & Science, for the Year 1799.* Vol. 2. London: G. Cawthorn, 1800.

Blank, Antje, ed. *Hannah Cowley. Eighteenth-Century Women Playwrights.* Gen. Ed. Derek Hughes. Vol. 5. London: Pickering & Chatto, 2001.

Blessington, Lady Marguerite. *Lady Blessington's Conversations of Lord Byron.* Ed. Ernest J. Lovell, Jr. Princeton, NJ: Princeton UP, 1969.

Boaden, James. *Memoirs of the Life of John Philip Kemble, Esq.* Philadelphia, PA: Robert H. Small, 1825.

Bolton, Betsy. *Women, Nationalism, and the Romantic Stage: Theatre and Politics in Britain, 1780–1800.* Cambridge: Cambridge UP, 2001.

Boreman, Thomas. *A Description of Three Hundred Animals, Viz. Beasts, Birds, Fishes, Serpents, and Insects.* 7th ed. London: R. Ware, 1753.

Borkat, Roberta F. S. "Notes to *The Box-Lobby Challenge.*" In *The Plays of Richard Cumberland.* Ed. Roberta F. S. Borkat. Vol. 4. New York and London: Garland, 1982. 1–12.

———. "Notes to *The Imposters.*" In *The Plays of Richard Cumberland.* Vol. 4. 1–6.

Boswell, James. *Boswell's Life of Johnson.* Ed. George Birbeck Hill. 6 vols. Oxford: Clarendon, 1934.

The British Album. Containing the Poems of Della Crusca, Anna Matilda, Arley, Benedict, the Bard, &c. &c. &c. 2nd ed. 2 vols. London: J. Bell, 1790.

British Theatre; or, A Collection of Plays, which Are Acted at the Theatres Royal, Drury Lane, Covent Garden, and Haymarket. Printed under the Authority of the Managers from the Prompt Books. With Biographical and Critical Remarks, by Mrs. Inchbald. Vol. I. *Comedy of Errors. Romeo and Juliet. Hamlet. King John. King Richard III.* London: Longman, Hurst, Rees, and Orme, 1808.

Brooks, Helen E. M. "'One Entire Nation of Actors and Actresses': Reconsidering the Relationship of Public and Private Theatricals." *Nineteenth Century Theatre & Film* 38.2 (Winter 2011): 1–13.

Brown, Charles Brockden. *Ormond; or The Secret Witness.* Ed. Philip Barnard and Stephen Shapiro. Indianapolis, IN: Hackett, 2009.

[Bullokar, John]. *The English Expositor Improv'd: Being a Complete Dictionary, Teaching the Interpretation of the Most Difficult Words, which Are Commonly Made Use of in Our English Tongue.* Revised by R. Browne. 10th ed. London: A. and J. Churchill, 1707.

Bulwer-Lytton, Edward. *Money: A Comedy.* New ed. London: Chapman & Hall, 1856.

Burke, Edmund. *A Letter to a Member of the National Assembly.* In *Reflections on the Revolution in France.* Ed. L. G. Mitchell. Oxford: Oxford UP, 1993. 251–292.

———. *Reflections on the Revolution in France.* Ed. L. G. Mitchell. Oxford: Oxford UP, 1993.

Burnet, Sir Thomas. *A Second Tale of a Tub: Or, The History of Robert Powel the Puppet-Show Man*. London: J. Roberts, 1715.
Burney, Frances. *Memoirs of Doctor Burney, Arranged from His Own Manuscripts, from Family Papers, and from Personal Recollections. By His Daughter, Madame D'Arblay*. 3 vols. London: Edward Moxon, 1832.
Burwick, Frederick. *Playing to the Crowd: London Popular Theater, 1780–1830*. New York: Palgrave Macmillan, 2011.
———. *Romantic Drama: Acting and Reacting*. Cambridge: Cambridge UP, 2009.
Byrne, Paula. *Perdita: The Literary, Theatrical, Scandalous Life of Mary Robinson*. New York: Random House, 2004.
Byron, George Gordon, Lord. *Byron's Letters and Journals*. Ed. Leslie A. Marchand. 12 vols. Cambridge: Harvard UP, 1973–1982.
———. *Don Juan. Lord Byron: The Complete Poetical Works*. Ed. Jerome J. McGann. Vol. 5. Oxford: Clarendon, 1986.
———. *Lord Byron: The Complete Poetical Works*. Ed. Jerome J. McGann. Vol. 1. Oxford: Clarendon, 1980.
Campbell, Alexander. *Perkin Warbeck; or, The Court of James the Fourth of Scotland. An Historical Romance*. 3 vols. London: A. K. Newman, 1830.
Carleton, Mary. *The Case of Madam Mary Carleton, Lately stiled The German Princess, Truely Stated: With an Historical Relation of Her Birth, Education, and Fortunes; in an Appeal to His Illustrious Highness Prince Rupert*. London: Printed for Sam Speed and Henry Marsh, 1663.
Castle, Terry. *Masquerade and Civilization: The Carnivalesque in Eighteenth-Century Culture and Fiction*. Stanford, CA: Stanford UP, 1986.
"Characteristics of Authors and Players, No. XI. *MR. PALMER*." *The Monthly Mirror: Reflecting Men and Manners. With Strictures on Their Epitome, The Stage. For July, 1798*. Vol. VI. London: J. Wright, 1798. 110–112.
Chesterfield, Philip Dormer Stanhope. *Letters Written by the Late Right Honourable Philip Dormer Stanhope, Earl of Chesterfield, to His Son, Philip Stanhope, Esq*. 4 vols. 5th ed. London: J. Dodsley, 1774.
Clare, John. *John Clare* (Oxford Authors). Ed. Eric Robinson and David Powell. Oxford: Oxford UP, 1984.
———. *John Clare by Himself*. Ed. Eric Robinson and David Powell. Manchester: Carcanet, 1996.
———. *The Letters of John Clare*. Ed. Mark Story. Oxford: Clarendon, 1985.
Coleridge, Samuel Taylor. *Collected Letters of Samuel Taylor Coleridge*. Ed. Earl Leslie Griggs. 2 vols. Oxford: Clarendon, 1956.
———. *Essays on His Times in* The Morning Post *and* The Courier. Ed. David V. Erdman. *The Collected Works of Samuel Taylor Coleridge*. Vol. 1. Princeton, NJ: Princeton UP, 1978.
Colman, George. *The Connoisseur. By Mr. Town, Critic and Censor-General*. Vol. 3. 6th ed. Oxford: J. Rivington, T. Caslon, T. Becket, F. Newbery, R. Baldwin, and W. Goldsmith, 1774.

Cooke, Michael G. *Acts of Inclusion: Studies Bearing on an Elementary Theory of Romanticism*. New Haven, CT: Yale UP, 1979.

Cowley, Hannah. *The Belle's Stratagem, a Comedy*. London: T. Cadell, 1782.

———. *A Bold Stroke for a Husband, a Comedy*. London: T. Evans, 1784.

———. *A Day in Turkey; or, The Russian Slaves. A Comedy*. London: G. G. J. and J. Robinson, 1792.

———. "To Della Crusca," *The World* (August 4, 1787).

———. "Epilogue to the World as it Goes." *The Scots Magazine*. Vol. 43. Edinburgh: A. Murray and J. Cochran, 1781. 216.

———. *The Runaway, a Comedy*. 2nd ed. London: Printed for the Author, 1776.

———. *A School for Greybeards; or, The Mourning Bride*. London: G. G. J. and J. Robinson, 1786.

———. *The Town before You, a Comedy*. London: T. N. Longman, 1795.

———. *Which Is the Man?* London: C. Dilly, 1783.

———. *Who's the Dupe? A Farce*. London: J. Dodsley, L. Davis, W. Owen, S. Crowder, T. Longman, T. Cadell, T. Becket, and Messrs. Carnan and Newbery, 1779.

———. *The Works of Mrs. Cowley. Dramas and Poems. In Three Volumes*. London: Wilkie and Robinson, 1813.

———. *The World as It Goes; or a Party at Montpelier*. Larpent Manuscript (LA 548). San Marino, CA: Huntington Library, 1781.

Cox, Jeffrey N. "Cowley's Bold Stroke for Comedy." *European Romantic Review* 17.3 (July 2006): 361–375.

Cox, Jeffrey N., and Michael Gamer. Introduction. In *The Broadview Anthology of Romantic Drama*. Ed. Jeffrey N. Cox and Michael Gamer. Peterborough, ON: Broadview, 2003. vii–xxiv.

Cox, Philip. "'Perfectly harmless and secure'? The Political Contexts of Thomas Holcroft's *He's Much to Blame*." In *Re-Viewing Thomas Holcroft, 1745–1809: Essays on His Works and Life*. Ed. Miriam L. Wallace and A. A. Markley. Farnham and Burlington: Ashgate, 2012. 87–101.

Critical Review 22 (February 1798): 232–234.

Crook, G. T., ed. *The Complete Newgate Calendar*. Vol. 4. London: Privately Printed for the Navarre Society, 1926.

Cross, Ashley J. "From *Lyrical Ballads* to *Lyrical Tales*: Mary Robinson's Reputation and the Problem of Literary Debt." *Studies in Romanticism* 40 (Winter 2001): 571–605.

———. "He-She Philosophers and Other Literary Bugbears: Mary Robinson's *A Letter to the Women of England*." *Women's Writing* 9.1 (2002): 53–68.

Cullens, Chris. "Mrs. Robinson and the Masquerade of Womanliness." *Body and Text in the Eighteenth Century*. Ed. Veronica Kelly and Dorothea von Mücke. Stanford, CA: Stanford UP, 1994. 266–289.

Cumberland, Richard. *The Battle of Hastings, a Tragedy*. London: Edward and Charles Dilly, 1778.

———. *The Box-Lobby Challenge, a Comedy*. London: J. Debrett, 1794.

———. *The Fashionable Lover; a Comedy*. London: W. Griffin, 1772.
———. *The Imposters: A Comedy*. London: C. Dilly, 1789.
———. *The Jew: A Comedy*. London: C. Dilly, 1794.
———. *Memoirs of Richard Cumberland*. Ed. Henry Flanders. New York: Benjamin Blom, 1969.
———. "Remarks upon the Present Taste for Acting Private Plays." *The European Magazine and London Review* 14 (August 1788). London: J. Sewell, 1788. 115–118.
Curran, Stuart. "Mary Robinson's *Lyrical Tales* in Context." In *Re-Visioning Romanticism: British Women Writers, 1776–1837*. Ed. Carol Shiner Wilson and Joel Haefner. Philadelphia: U of Pennsylvania P, 1994. 17–35.
———. "Women Readers, Women Writers." In *The Cambridge Companion to British Romanticism*. Ed. Stuart Curran. 2nd ed. Cambridge: Cambridge UP, 2010. 169–186.
Damrosch, Leo. *Jean-Jacques Rousseau: Restless Genius*. Boston: Houghton Mifflin, 2005.
Darwin, Erasmus. *The Economy of Vegetation*. In *The Botanic Garden; A Poem, in Two Parts*. Part I. London: J. Johnson, 1791. xi–214.
Davenport, Hester. *The Prince's Mistress: A Life of Mary Robinson*. Thrupp, Stroud: Sutton, 2004.
De Quincey, Thomas. "Historico-Critical Inquiry into the Origins of the Rosicrucians and the Free-Masons." In *The Works of Thomas De Quincey*. Vol. 4. Ed. Frederick Burwick. London: Pickering & Chatto, 2000. 1–49.
———. *Recollections of the Lakes and the Lake Poets*. Ed. David Wright. Harmondsworth: Penguin, 1970.
Defoe, Daniel. *Roxana: The Fortunate Mistress*. Ed. John Mullan. Oxford: Oxford UP, 1996.
Dent, Robert K. *Old and New Birmingham: A History of the Town and Its People*. Birmingham: Houghton and Hammond, 1880.
Dickens, Charles. *The Life & Adventures of Nicholas Nickleby*. Oxford: Oxford UP, 1950.
Dircks, Richard J. *Richard Cumberland*. Boston: Twayne, 1976.
Dralloc, N. [John Collard]. *An Epitome of Logic. In Four Parts*. London: J. Johnson, 1795.
———. *The Life and Extraordinary Adventures of James Molesworth Hobart, Alias Henry Griffin, Alias Lord Massey, the Newmarket Duke of Ormond, &c*. London: G. Sael, 1794.
"Duke of Ormond." *The Daily Advertiser* (New York) (February 21, 1792): 2.
Dunlap, William. *Memoirs of the Life of George Frederick Cooke*. 2 vols. New York: P. Longworth, 1813.
The Edinburgh Annual Register, for 1808. Vol. 1, Part 2. Edinburgh: John Ballantyne, 1810.
Elfenbein, Andrew. "Lesbian Aestheticism on the Eighteenth-Century Stage." *Eighteenth-Century Life* 25 (Winter 2001): 1–16.

Elfenbein, Andrew. *Romantic Genius: The Prehistory of a Homosexual Role.* New York: Columbia UP, 1999.

The English Gentleman Justified. London: J. Nutt, 1701.

Escott, Angela. *"The Celebrated Hannah Cowley": Experiments in Dramatic Genre, 1776–1794.* London: Pickering & Chatto, 2012.

Esterhammer, Angela. "Improvisation, Speculation, Risky Business: Fiction and Performance, 1824–1826." *Essays in Romanticism* 21.1 (2014): 1–16.

———. *Romanticism and Improvisation, 1750–1850.* Cambridge: Cambridge UP, 2008.

———. "The Scandal of Sincerity: Wordsworth, Byron, Landon." In *Romanticism, Sincerity, and Authenticity.* Ed. Tim Milnes and Kerry Sinanan. Houndmills and New York: Palgrave Macmillan, 2010. 101–119.

Farquhar, George. *The Beaux Stratagem.* Ed. Simon Trussler. London: Nick Hern Books, 1995.

Fielding, Henry. *The History of Tom Jones, a Foundling.* Ed. Fredson Bowers. Middletown, CT: Wesleyan UP, 1975.

Fielding, Sarah. *Familiar Letters between the Principal Characters in David Simple, and Some Others.* Vol. 4. 2nd ed. London: A. Millar, 1752.

Finberg, Melinda C. Introduction. *Eighteenth-Century Women Dramatists.* Ed. Melinda C. Finberg. Oxford: Oxford UP, 2001. ix–xlvii.

———. "Staging the 18th-Century Prostitute for the 21st Century: A Dramaturgical Approach to Teaching Cowley's *The Belle's Stratagem.*" *Teaching Romantic Drama*, *Special Issue of the Romantic Pedagogy Commons*, ed. Thomas C. Crochunis, *Romantic Circles* (May 2011), n. pag. Web. May 11, 2011.

Ford, Susan Allen. "'A name more dear': Daughters, Fathers, and Desire in *A Simple Story*, *The False Friend*, and *Mathilda.*" In *Re-Visioning Romanticism: British Women Writers, 1776–1837.* Ed. Carol Shiner Wilson and Joel Haefner. 51–71.

Freeman, Lisa A. *Character's Theater: Genre and Ideology on the Eighteenth-Century Stage.* Philadelphia: U of Pennsylvania P, 2002.

Gamer, Michael. "'Bell's Poetics': *The Baviad*, the Della Cruscans, and the Book of *The World.*" *The Satiric Eye: Forms of Satire in the Romantic Period.* Ed. Steven E. Jones. New York: Palgrave Macmillan, 2003. 31–53.

Garnai, Amy. "'A Lock Upon My Lips': The Melodrama of Silencing and Censorship in Thomas Holcroft's *Knave, or Not?*" *Eighteenth-Century Studies* 43.4 (2010): 473–484.

Garrick, David. *The Irish Widow.* London: T. Becket, 1772.

Genest, John, ed. *Some Account of the English Stage from the Restoration in 1660 to 1830.* 10 vols. New York: Burt Franklin, 1832.

Gifford, William. *The Baviad, a Paraphrastic Imitation of the First Satire of Persius.* London: Printed for R. Faulder, 1791.

Gilbert, Sandra M., and Susan Gubar. *The Madwoman in the Attic: The Woman Writer and the Nineteenth-Century Literary Imagination.* New Haven, CT: Yale UP, 1979.

Gladfelder, Hal. *Criminality and Narrative in Eighteenth-Century England: Beyond the Law.* Baltimore, MD: Johns Hopkins UP, 2001.

Godwin, William. *Caleb Williams.* Ed. Gary Handwerk and A. A. Markley. Peterborough, ON: Broadview, 2000.

———. *The Diary of William Godwin.* Ed. Victoria Myers, David O'Shaughnessy, and Mark Philp. Oxford: Oxford Digital Library, 2010. Web. January 19, 2012.

———. *An Enquiry Concerning Political Justice.* Ed. Mark Philp. *Political and Philosophical Writings of William Godwin.* Vol. 3. London: William Pickering, 1993.

———. *An Enquiry Concerning Political Justice Variants.* Ed. Mark Philp. *Political and Philosophical Writings of William Godwin.* Vol. 4. London: William Pickering, 1993.

———. *The Enquirer. Reflections on Education, Manners, and Literature. In a Series of Essays. Educational and Literary Writings.* Ed. Pamela Clemit. *Political and Philosophical Writings of William Godwin.* Vol. 5. London: William Pickering, 1993. 73–289.

———. *Memoirs of the Author of "The Rights of Woman." A Short Residence in Sweden* and *Memoirs of the Author of "The Rights of Woman."* By Mary Wollstonecraft and William Godwin. Ed. Richard Holmes. London: Penguin, 1987. 201–277.

———. *Thoughts on Man, His Nature, Productions, and Discoveries.* Ed. Mark Philp. *Political and Philosophical Writings of William Godwin.* Vol. 6. London: William Pickering, 1993. 33–292.

Goldsmith, Oliver. *An Enquiry into the Present State of Polite Learning in Europe.* 2nd ed., rev. London: J. Dodsley, 1774.

———. *An History of the Earth, and Animated Nature.* 8 vols. London: J. Nourse, 1774.

Gristwood, Sarah. *Perdita: Royal Mistress, Writer, Romantic.* London: Bantam, 2005.

Gross, Jonathan David. *The Life of Anne Damer: Portrait of a Regency Artist.* Lanham, MD: Lexington Books, 2014.

Gutch, John Mathew. *Caraboo. A Narrative of a Singular Imposition, Practised Upon the Benevolence of a Lady Residing in the Vicinity of the City of Bristol, By a Young Woman of the Name of Mary Willcocks, alias Baker, alias Bakerstendht, alias Caraboo, Princess of Javasu.* London: Baldwin, Cradock and Joy, 1817.

Harris, Jocelyn. "Protean Lovelace." *Eighteenth-Century Fiction* 2.4 (1990): 327–346.

Hawkins, Laetitia-Matilda. *Memoirs, Anecdotes, Facts, and Opinions.* 2 vols. London: Longman, Hurst, Rees, Orme, Brown, and Green, 1824.

Haywood, Eliza. *Fantomina: Or, Love in a Maze. Being a Secret History of an Amour between Two Persons of Condition. Secret Histories, Novels, and*

Poems, Written by Mrs. Eliza Haywood. Vol. 3. 2nd ed. 3 vols. London: Dan. Browne, jun. and S. Chapman, 1725. 256–291.

———. *The Masqueraders: Or, Fatal Curiosity. Being the Secret History of a Late Amour.* London: J. Roberts, 1724–1725.

Hazlitt, William. "On Personal Identity." In *The Complete Works of William Hazlitt.* Ed. P. P. Howe. Vol. 17. New York: AMS, 1967. 264–275.

———. "A View of the English Stage." In *The Complete Works of William Hazlitt.* Ed. P. P. Howe. Vol. 5. New York: AMS, 1967. 167–379.

Henderson, Andrea K. *Romantic Identities: Varieties of Subjectivity, 1774–1830.* Cambridge: Cambridge UP, 1996.

Hickey, Alison. *Impure Conceits: Rhetoric and Ideology in Wordsworth's "Excursion."* Stanford, CA: Stanford UP, 1997.

Highfill, Philip H., Jr., Kalman A. Burnim, and Edward Langhans. "Bannister, John." *A Biographical Dictionary of Actors, Actresses, Musicians, Dancers, Managers & Other Stage Personnel in London, 1660–1800.* Vol. 1. Carbondale and Edwardsville: Southern Illinois UP, 1973. 267–273.

———. "Palmer, John." *A Biographical Dictionary of Actors, Actresses, Musicians, Dancers, Managers & Other Stage Personnel in London, 1660–1800.* Vol. 11. 161–177.

The History of the Swindling and Amorous Adventures of James George Semple, &c. &c. since His Liberation from the Hulks; Compressing His Various Deceptions Practised upon the Convention at Paris, Dumourier, and the Generals of the Allied Armies. London: Mason [1795?].

Hogan, Charles Beecher, ed. *The London Stage 1660–1800.* Part 5: 1776–1800. Vols. 2 and 3. Carbondale: Southern Illinois UP, 1968.

Hogg, James. *The Private Memoirs and Confessions of a Justified Sinner.* Ed. Adrian Hunter. Peterborough, ON: Broadview, 2001.

Holcroft, Thomas. *He's Much to Blame, A Comedy.* London: G. G. and J. Robinson, 1798.

———. *Knave, or Not? A Comedy.* London: G. G. and J. Robinson, 1798.

———. *A Narrative of Facts, Relating to a Prosecution for High Treason.* London: H. D. Symonds, 1795.

———. Review of *Every One Has His Fault. The Monthly Review.* Vol. 10. London: R. Griffiths, 1793. 302–308.

Holcroft, Thomas, and William Hazlitt. *The Life of Thomas Holcroft.* Ed. Elbridge Colby. 2 vols. New York: Benjamin Blom, 1968.

Hume, David. *The History of England, from the Invasion of Julius Cæsar to the Revolution in 1688.* Vol. 3. New ed. London: A. Millar, 1767.

———. *A Treatise of Human Nature.* Ed. Ernest C. Mossner. New York: Penguin, 1984.

Inchbald, Elizabeth. *Nature and Art.* Ed. Shawn L. Maurer. London: Pickering & Chatto, 1997.

Isikoff, Erin. "Masquerade, Modesty, and Comedy in Hannah Cowley's *The Belle's Stratagem.*" *Look Who's Laughing: Gender and Comedy.* Ed. Gail Finney. Langhorne, PA: Gordon and Breach, 1994. 99–117.

Jackson, William. *The New and Complete Newgate Calendar; or, Villany Displayed in All Its Branches.* 6 vols. London: Alex. Hogg, 1795.
Jerdan, William. *The Autobiography of William Jerdan.* Vol. 2. London: Arthur Hall, Virtue, 1852.
Johnson, Samuel. *An Account of the Life of Mr Richard Savage, Son of the Earl Rivers.* London: J. Roberts, 1744.
Juengel, Scott J. "Face, Figure, Physiognomics: Mary Shelley's *Frankenstein* and the Moving Image." *Novel: A Forum on Fiction* 33.3 (Summer 2000): 353–376.
Keats, John. *The Letters of John Keats: 1814–1821.* Ed. Hyder Edward Rollins. 2 vols. Cambridge: Harvard UP, 1958.
Kenney, James. *Debtor and Creditor; A Comedy.* New York: D. Longworth, 1816.
———. *False Alarms. A Comic Opera.* New York: D. Longworth, 1807.
———. *Raising the Wind, A Farce.* New York: D. Longworth, 1804.
———. *The World! A Comedy.* New York: David Longworth, 1808.
Kietzman, Mary Jo. *The Self-Fashioning of an Early Modern Englishwoman: Mary Carleton's Lives.* Aldershot: Ashgate, 2004.
Knox, Vicesimus. "On the Prevailing Practice of Acting Plays by Private Gentlemen and Ladies, Writing and Speaking Prologues and Epilogues, and Building Private Theatres." *Winter Evenings: Or, Lucubrations on Life and Letters.* Vol. 3. London: Printed for Charles Dilly, 1788. 31–39.
Kövesi, Simon. "John Clare's 'I' and 'Eye': Egotism and Ecologism." In *Green and Pleasant Land: English Culture and the Romantic Countryside.* Ed. Amanda Gilroy. Leuven: Peeters, 2004. 73–88.
Lamb, Charles. "On Some of the Old Actors." *The Works of Charles Lamb.* Vol. 2. New York: Harper & Brothers, 1838. 151–160.
Langford, John Alfred, comp. and ed. *A Century of Birmingham Life: Or, A Chronicle of Local Events, from 1741 to 1841.* Vol. 2. Birmingham: E. C. Osborne, 1868.
Lavater, Johann Caspar. *Essays on Physiognomy; for the Promotion of the Knowledge and the Love of Mankind.* Trans. Thomas Holcroft. 3 vols. London: G. G. J. and J. Robinson, 1789.
Lee, Debbie. *Romantic Liars: Obscure Women Who Became Imposters and Challenged an Empire.* New York: Palgrave Macmillan, 2006.
Lee, Elizabeth. "Miller, Anna, Lady." In *Dictionary of National Biography.* Ed. Sidney Lee. Vol. 13. New York: Macmillan, 1909. 405–406.
Lemire, Beverly. "Consumerism in Preindustrial and Early Industrial England: The Trade in Secondhand Clothes." *Journal of British Studies* 27 (January 1988): 1–24.
Levine, Robert S. "Villainy and the Fear of Conspiracy in Charles Brockden Brown's 'Ormond.'" *Early American Literature* 15.2 (Fall 1980): 124–140.
Lewis, Matthew. *The Monk.* Ed. Howard Anderson. Oxford: Oxford UP, 1973.
Link, Frederick M. "Textual Note." In *The Plays of Hannah Cowley.* Ed. Frederick M. Link. 2 vols. New York: Garland, 1979. Vol. 1, xlvi–xlviii.

Lobel, Edgar and Denys Page, eds. *Poetarum Lesbiorum Fragmenta*. Oxford: Oxford UP, 1955.

Locke, John. *An Essay Concerning Human Understanding*. Ed. Alexander Campbell Fraser. 2 vols. New York: Dover, 1959.

Lytton, Edward George Earle Lytton Bulwer. *Money: A Comedy*. London: Chapman & Hall, 1853.

Mackenzie, Henry. *The Man of Feeling*. New York: Norton, 1958.

Mackie, J. D. *The Earlier Tudors: 1485–1558*. Oxford: Clarendon, 1952.

Martin, Frederick. *The History of Lloyd's and of Marine Insurance in Great Britain*. New York: Burt Franklin, 1971.

Mason, John Hope. "Originality: Moral Good, Private Vice, or Self-enchantment." In *Jean-Jacques Rousseau and the Sources of the Self*. Ed. Timothy O'Hagan. Brookfield, VT: Ashgate, 1997. 37–55.

Mayne, Zachary. *Two Dissertations Concerning Sense and the Imagination. With an Essay on Consciousness*. London: J. Tonson, 1728.

McGann, Jerome J. *The Poetics of Sensibility: A Revolution in Literary Style*. Oxford: Clarendon, 1996.

———. *Towards a Literature of Knowledge*. Chicago, IL: U of Chicago P, 1989.

Mellor, Anne K. "Mary Robinson and the Scripts of Female Sexuality." In *Representations of the Self from Renaissance to Romanticism*. Ed. Patrick Coleman, Jayne Lewis, and Jill Kowalik. Cambridge: Cambridge UP, 2000. 230–259.

———. *Mothers of the Nation: Women's Political Writing in England, 1780–1830*. Bloomington: Indiana UP, 2000.

Melville, Herman. *The Confidence-Man*. Ed. Stephen Matterson. New York: Penguin, 1990.

Memoirs of a Social Monster; or, The History of Charles Price, Otherwise Bolingbroke, Otherwise Johnson, Otherwise Parks, Otherwise Wigmore, Otherwise Brank, Otherwise Wilmott, Otherwise Williams, Otherwise Schutz, Otherwise Trevors, Otherwise Polton, Otherwise Taylor, Otherwise Powel, &c. &c. &c. and Commonly Called Old Patch. Containing an Accurate Account of the Astonishing Fraud and Ingenious Forgeries of that Truly Great Man, on the Governor and Company of the Bank of England for a Series of Six Years. Including a Faithful Detail of his Devices and Depredations on Society for a Period of Fifty-Five Years. London: Printed for G. Kearsley, 1786.

Memoirs of the New Insect: Interspersed with Sketches of Other Singular Characters. London: J. Ridgway, 1792.

"Memoranda Dramatica, &c." *The Monthly Mirror*. Vol. 1. London: J. Wright, 1807. 66–77.

Modder, Montagu. *The Jew in the Literature of England*. Philadelphia, PA: Jewish Publication Society of America, 1939.

Mole, Tom. "Mary Robinson's Conflicted Celebrity." *Romanticism and Celebrity Culture, 1750–1850*. Cambridge: Cambridge UP, 2009. 186–205.

The Monthly Review, vol. 16. London: R. Griffiths, 1795.

Moody, Jane. *Illegitimate Theatre in London, 1770–1840*. Cambridge: Cambridge UP, 2000.

———. "Inchbald, Holcroft and the Censorship of Jacobin Theatre." In *Women's Romantic Theatre and Drama: History, Agency, and Performativity*. Ed. Lilla Maria Crisafulli and Keir Elam. Farnham: Ashgate: 2010. 197–211.

Morgan, Stewart S. "The Damning of Holcroft's *Knave or Not?* and O'Keeffe's *She's Eloped*." *Huntington Library Quarterly* 22.1 (November 1958): 51–62.

Nathan, Alix. "Mistaken or Misled? Mary Robinson's Birth Date." *Women's Writing* 9.1 (2002): 139–142.

The Northern Imposter; Being a Faithful Narrative of the Adventures, and Deceptions, of James George Semple, Commonly Called Major Semple, Alias Major Harrold, Major Maxwell, Major Grant, Major Cunningham, Major Winter, &c. &c. &c. With an Account of His Devices at Lord Salisbury's, Sir Thomas Dundass's, Mr. Pitt's, the Marquis of Landsdown's, Baron Hompesch, Dr. Prettyman, &c. &c. London: Printed for G. Kearsley, 1786.

Novak, Maximillian E. "'Appearances of Truth': The Literature of Crime as a Narrative System (1660–1841)." *The Yearbook of English Studies* 11 (1981): 29–48.

Ovid (Publius Ovidius Naso). *Heroides*. Trans. Harold Isbell. London: Penguin, 1990.

———. *Heroides: Selected Epistles*. Ed. Peter E. Knox. Cambridge: Cambridge UP, 1995.

Pagès, François. *Secret History of the French Revolution, from the Convocation of the Notables in 1787 to the First of November 1796. Translated from the French of Francis Pagès*. Vol 2. London: T. N. Longman, 1797.

Pascoe, Judith. *Romantic Theatricality: Gender, Poetry, and Spectatorship*. Ithaca, NY: Cornell UP, 1997.

Perry, Gill. "'The British Sappho': Borrowed Identities and the Representation of Women Artists in Late Eighteenth-Century British Art." *Oxford Art Journal* 18 (1995): 44–57.

Peterson, Linda H. "Becoming an Author: Mary Robinson's *Memoirs* and the Origins of the Woman Artist's Autobiography." In *Re-Visioning Romanticism: British Women Writers, 1776–1837*. Ed. Carol Shiner Wilson and Joel Haefner. 36–50.

Pfau, Thomas. *Romantic Moods: Paranoia, Trauma, and Melancholy, 1790–1840*. Baltimore, MD: Johns Hopkins UP, 2005.

Pocock, J. G. A. *The Machiavellian Moment: Florentine Political Thought and the Atlantic Republican Tradition*. Princeton, NJ: Princeton UP, 1975.

Poe, Edgar Allan. "Raising the Wind; or, Diddling Considered as One of the Exact Sciences." Philadelphia *Saturday Courier* 13.655 (14 October 1843): 1.

Porter, T. *A Witty Combat: Or, the Female Victor. A Trage-Comedy.* London: Printed for Tho. Roberts, 1663.
Prins, Yopie. *Victorian Sappho.* Princeton, NJ: Princeton UP, 1999.
Quinn, Arthur Hobson. *Edgar Allan Poe: A Critical Biography.* New York: Cooper Square, 1969.
Rayner, J. L., and G. T. Crook, eds. *The Complete Newgate Calendar.* Vol. 1. London: Privately Printed for the Navarre Society, 1926.
Reese, George, ed. "The Court of Vice-Admiralty in Virginia and Some Cases of 1770–1775." *The Virginia Magazine of History and Biography* 88.3 (July 1980): 301–337.
Reiman, Donald H. "The Beauty of Buttermere as Fact and Romantic Symbol." *Romantic Texts and Contexts.* Columbia: U of Missouri P, 1987. 216–247.
Review of *He's Much to Blame. The Monthly Mirror, for March 1798.* Vol. 5. London: J. Wright, 1798. 172–173.
Review of *Knave or Not. A Comedy. The Antijacobin Review and Magazine.* Vol. I. London: J. Whittle, 1799. 51–54.
Reynolds, Frederick. *Cheap Living: A Comedy.* London: G. G. and J. Robinson, 1797.
———. *The Life and Times of Frederick Reynolds. Written by Himself.* 2 vols. London: Henry Colburn, 1826.
Reynolds, Margaret, ed. *The Sappho Companion.* New York: Palgrave, 2000.
Rich, Adrienne. *Of Woman Born: Motherhood as Experience and Institution.* New York: Bantam Books, 1976.
Richardson, Samuel. *Clarissa, Or, The History of a Young Lady.* 4 vols. London: J. M. Dent, 1962.
Robinson, Daniel. *The Poetry of Mary Robinson: Form and Fame.* New York: Palgrave Macmillan, 2011.
Robinson, Mary. *Angelina: A Novel.* Ed. Sharon M. Setzer. *The Works of Mary Robinson.* Vol. 3. London: Pickering & Chatto, 2009.
———. *The False Friend: A Domestic Story.* Ed. Julie A Shaffer. *The Works of Mary Robinson.* Vol. 6. London: Pickering & Chatto, 2010.
———. *Hubert de Sevrac, A Romance, of the Eighteenth Century.* Ed. Orianne Smith. London: Pickering & Chatto, 2009.
———. "Jasper. A Fragment." Ed. William D. Brewer and Sharon M. Setzer. *The Works of Mary Robinson.* Vol. 8. London: Pickering & Chatto, 2010. 229–272.
———. *A Letter to the Women of England.* Ed. William D. Brewer and Sharon M. Setzer. *The Works of Mary Robinson.* Vol. 8. London: Pickering & Chatto, 2010. 129–163.
———. "Letters." Ed. Hester Davenport. *The Works of Mary Robinson.* Vol. 7. London: Pickering & Chatto, 2010. 295–332.
———. "The Lucky Escape." Ed. William D. Brewer and Sharon M. Setzer. *The Works of Mary Robinson.* Vol. 8. London: Pickering & Chatto, 2010. 1–21.

———. "Memoirs of Mary Robinson." Ed. Hester Davenport. Vol. 7. London: Pickering & Chatto, 2010. 193–294.

———. *The Natural Daughter. With Portraits of the Leadenhead Family. A Novel.* Ed. Hester Davenport. Vol. 7. London: Pickering & Chatto, 2010. 1–190.

———. *Poems.* Ed. Daniel Robinson. *The Works of Mary Robinson.* Vols. 1–2. London: Pickering & Chatto, 2009.

———. *Present State of the Manners, Society, &c. &c. of the Metropolis of England.* Ed. William D. Brewer and Sharon M. Setzer. *The Works of Mary Robinson.* Vol. 8. London: Pickering & Chatto, 2010. 193–210.

———. *Selected Poems.* Ed. Judith Pascoe. Peterborough, ON: Broadview, 2000.

———. *The Sylphid.* Ed. William D. Brewer and Sharon M. Setzer. *The Works of Mary Robinson.* Vol. 8. 165–192.

———. *Walsingham; or, The Pupil of Nature.* Ed. Julie Shaffer. Peterborough, ON: Broadview, 2003.

Robinson, Terry F. "James Kenney's Comedic Genius: Early Nineteenth-century Character, Commerce, and the Arts in *Raising the Wind*, *The World!*, and *Debtor and Creditor*." *Literature Compass* 3.5 (2006): 1082–1106.

Roe, Nicholas. *John Keats and the Culture of Dissent.* Oxford: Clarendon, 1997.

Rooney, Morgan. "'Belonging to No/body': Mary Robinson, *The Natural Daughter*, and Rewriting Feminine Identity." *Eighteenth-Century Fiction* 18.3 (Spring 2006): 355–372.

Rosenblum, Joseph. "Notes on the text of *He's Much to Blame*." In *The Plays of Thomas Holcroft.* Ed. Joseph Rosenblum. Vol. 2. New York: Garland, 1980. cxxvii–cxxxii.

———. "Notes on the text of *Knave; or Not*." In *The Plays of Thomas Holcroft.* Vol. 2. cix–cxxi.

Ross, Marlon. *The Contours of Masculine Desire: Romanticism and the Rise of Woman's Poetry.* Oxford: Oxford UP, 1989.

Rousseau, Jean-Jacques. *Les Confessions.* Ed. Jacques Voisine. Paris: Éditions Garnier Frères, 1964.

———. *The Confessions.* Trans. J. M. Cohen. Harmondsworth: Penguin, 1953.

———. *Discourse of the Origin and Foundations of Inequality Among Men. Rousseau's Political Writings.* Trans. Julia Conaway Bondanella. Ed. Allan Ritter and Julia Conaway Bondanella. New York: Norton, 1988. 3–57.

———. *Emile: or On Education.* Trans. Allan Bloom. New York: Basic Books, 1979.

———. *Émile ou de l'Éducation.* Ed. François and Pierre Richard. Paris: Éditions Garnier Frères, 1961.

Russell, Gillian. *Women, Sociability and Theatre in Georgian London.* Cambridge: Cambridge UP, 2007.

Russett, Margaret. *Fictions and Fakes: Forging Romantic Authenticity, 1760–1845.* Cambridge: Cambridge UP, 2006.

Schama, Simon. *Citizens: A Chronicle of the French Revolution.* New York: Vintage Books, 1989.

Semple, James George. *The Life of Major J. G. Semple Lisle; Containing a Faithful Narrative of His Alternate Vicissitudes of Splendor and Misfortune.* London: Printed for W. Stewart, 1799.

Setzer, Sharon. "The Dying Game: Robinson's *Walsingham.*" *Nineteenth-Century Contexts* 22 (2000): 305–328.

———. "Mary Robinson's Sylphid Self: The End of Feminine Self-Fashioning." *Philological Quarterly* 75.4 (Fall 1996): 501–520.

Shaffer, Julie. "*Walsingham*: Gender, Pain, Knowledge." *Women's Writing* 9.1 (2002): 69–85.

Shelley, Mary. *The Fortunes of Perkin Warbeck: A Romance.* Ed. Doucet Devin Fischer. *The Novels and Selected Works of Mary Shelley.* Vol. 5. London: William Pickering, 1996.

———. *The Last Man.* Ed. Hugh J. Luke, Jr. Lincoln: U of Nebraska P, 1965.

Shelley, Percy Bysshe. Dedication to *Peter Bell the Third. Shelley's Poetry and Prose.* Ed. Donald H. Reiman and Neil Fraistat. New York: Norton, 2002. 339–341.

———. "An Exhortation." *The Poems of Shelley: 1819–1820.* Vol. 3. Ed. Jack Donovan, Cian Duffy, Kelvin Everest, and Michael Rossington. New York: Routledge, 2014. 259–260.

———. *The Letters of Percy Bysshe Shelley.* Ed. Frederick L. Jones. 2 vols. Oxford: Clarendon, 1964.

Smith, Adam. *An Inquiry into the Nature and Causes of the Wealth of Nations.* Ed. R. H. Campbell, A. S. Skinner, and W. B. Todd. 2 vols. Oxford: Clarendon, 1976.

Smith, Charlotte. *Ethelinde, or the Recluse of the Lake (1789).* Ed. Stuart Curran. *The Works of Charlotte Smith.* Vol. 3. London: Pickering & Chatto, 2005.

———. *The Old Manor House.* Ed. Jacqueline M. Labbe. Peterborough, ON: Broadview, 2002.

Snyder, C. R., and Howard L. Fromkin. *Uniqueness: The Human Pursuit of Difference.* New York: Plenum, 1980.

Soderholm, James. *Fantasy, Forgery, and the Byron Legend.* Lexington: UP of Kentucky, 1996.

Spear, Charles, ed. *Voices from Prison; A Selection of Poetry Written within the Cell, by Various Prisoners.* 3rd ed. Boston: Published by the Author, 1849.

Spencer, Jane. "Adapting Aphra Behn: Hannah Cowley's *A School for Greybeards* and *The Lucky Chance.*" *Women's Writing* 2.3 (1995): 221–234.

Straub, Kristina. *Domestic Affairs: Intimacy, Eroticism, and Violence between Servants and Masters in Eighteenth-Century Britain.* Baltimore, MD: Johns Hopkins UP, 2009.

Taylor, Charles. *Sources of the Self: The Making of the Modern Identity.* Cambridge: Harvard UP, 1989.

"Theatrical Intelligence." *Morning Chronicle and London Advertiser* (March 26, 1781).

Townley, James. *High Life below Stairs. A Farce of Two Acts.* London: J. Newbery, 1759.

The Trial of Henry Griffin, Alias George Hubbard, (The Pretended Duke of Ormond). Birmingham: J. Thompson, 1792.

Ty, Eleanor. *Empowering the Feminine: The Narratives of Mary Robinson, Jane West, and Amelia Opie, 1796–1812.* Toronto, ON: U of Toronto P, 1998.

Tytler, Graeme. "Lavater and Physiognomy in English Fiction 1790–1832." *Eighteenth-Century Fiction* 7.3 (April 1995): 293–310.

Wahrman, Dror. *The Making of the Modern Self: Identity and Culture in Eighteenth-Century England.* New Haven, CT: Yale UP, 2004.

Wallace, Elizabeth Kowaleski. "Theatricality and Cosmopolitanism in Hannah Cowley's *The Belle's Stratagem.*" *Comparative Drama* 35 (2001): 415–433.

Wallace, Miriam L., and A. A. Markley. Introduction. *Re-Viewing Thomas Holcroft, 1745–1809: Essays on His Works and Life.* Farnham and Burlington: Ashgate, 2012. 1–14.

Walpole, Horace. *Historic Doubts on the Life and Reign of King Richard the Third.* London: J. Dodsley, 1768.

West, Shearer. "Siddons, Celebrity and Regality: Portraiture and the Body of the Ageing Actress." *Theatre and Celebrity in Britain, 1660–2000.* Ed. Mary Luckhurst and Jane Moody. Houndmills: Palgrave Macmillan, 2005. 191–213.

Williams, Stanley T. "The English Sentimental Drama from Steele to Cumberland." *The Sewanee Review* 33.4 (October 1925): 405–426.

Wilson, Carol Shiner, and Joel Haefner, eds. *Re-Visioning Romanticism: British Women Writers, 1776–1837.* Philadelphia: U of Pennsylvania P, 1994.

Wollstonecraft, Mary. *A Vindication of the Rights of Woman.* Ed. Deirdre Shauna Lynch. 3rd ed. New York: Norton, 2009.

Wordsworth, Dorothy. *Recollections of a Tour Made in Scotland.* Introduction, notes, and photographs by Carol Kyros Walker. New Haven, CT: Yale UP, 1997.

Wordsworth, William. *William Wordsworth* (Oxford Authors). Ed. Stephen Gill. Oxford: Oxford UP, 1984.

Wroe, Ann. *The Perfect Prince: Truth and Deception in Renaissance Europe.* New York: Random House, 2003.

Yarrington, Alison. "The Female Pygmalion: Anne Seymour Damer, Allan Cunningham and the Writing of a Woman Sculptor's Life." *The Sculpture Journal* 1 (1997): 32–44.

Yearling, Elizabeth M. "Victims of Society in Three Plays by Cumberland." *The Durham University Journal* 43.1 (1981): 23–30.

Young, Edward. *Conjectures on Original Composition. In a Letter to the Author of Sir Charles Grandison.* Dublin: P. Wilson, 1759.

Index

CPSIA information can be obtained at www.ICGtesting.com
Printed in the USA
LVOW04*0055160515
438697LV00007B/245/P